P9-CQM-741

Disability Management

Disability Management

A Complete System to Reduce Costs, Increase Productivity, Meet Employee Needs, and Ensure Legal Compliance

Sheila H. Akabas
Lauren B. Gates
Donald E. Galvin

amacom
American Management Association

This book is available at a special discount when ordered in bulk quantities. For information, contact Special Sales Department, AMACOM, a division of American Management Association, 135 West 50th Street, New York, NY 10020.

Library of Congress Cataloging-in-Publication Data

Akabas, Sheila H., 1931–
Disability management : a complete system to reduce costs. increase productivity, meet employee needs, and ensure legal compliance / Sheila H. Akabas, Lauren B. Gates, Donald E. Galvin.
p. cm.
Includes bibliographical references and index.
ISBN 0-8144-5027-X
1. Insurance, Disability—United States. I. Gates, Lauren B. II. Galvin, Donald E. III. Title.
HD7105.25.U6A43 1992 *91-45130*
658.3'254—dc20 *CIP*

Printing number

10 9 8 7 6 5 4 3 2 1

To our
support systems
Aaron, Stephen, and **Janet**

Contents

Foreword
by Senator Bob Dole

Politicians are usually not known for their speed, but when asked to write the Foreword to this book, I accepted in record time—for two reasons.

First, I am tremendously impressed by the dedication and commitment of Dr. Akabas, Dr. Gates, and Dr. Galvin. Each is an expert in the field of disability management, and the three have combined to write a book which will greatly assist businesses in hiring and managing workers with disabilities.

And second, as America prepares to face the economic challenges of our increasingly complex global marketplace, there is no more important mission than ensuring that our workforce is utilized to its full potential.

Unfortunately, the unemployment rate for persons with disabilities is the highest in the nation. All too often, misconceptions about persons with disabilities deny many the opportunity to work. These misconceptions lead to a waste of human resources as completely capable workers are kept dependent on federal financial assistance.

We took an important step in breaking this cycle of dependence on July 26, 1990, when President Bush signed into law the Americans with Disabilities Act. The ADA prohibits discrimination against persons with disabilities in all areas of American life, including employment, public accommodations, transportation, and telecommunications.

Perhaps the most important aim of the ADA, however, is to remove both physical and psychological barriers which have kept qualified individuals with disabilities out of America's workplaces.

Through its provisions—which include comprehensive technical assistance programs, and tax credits to help defray the costs of accommodations—the doors of employers will be open wide to persons with disabilities.

What the authors have provided in this book is a prescriptive strategy for achieving continued employment for those who are already employed, but whose employment may be at risk because of the onset of disability or its worsening. In short, they show how we can hold on to those who are already making a major contribution to American workplaces. That is an obligation that employers will have under the ADA, and a goal which will help keep American industry strong, productive, and competitive.

We are not only concerned, however, with maintaining at work those who are already a part of the employed workforce. It is our hope that by retaining those workers who are newly disabled, industry will become more aware of the great potential contribution of all Americans, regardless of disability.

I will always remember a meeting I had with the Kansas Bankers Association in Dodge City, early in 1983. Waiting for me outside the room were two severely disabled young people with their parents. Tim was in a special wheelchair, unable to move anything except his eyes. Carla was only slightly more mobile. Both wanted to talk to me about help in gaining greater access to a more integrated and independent lifestyle.

On my way back to Washington that evening, I kept thinking about Tim and Carla, their courage, and the challenges they faced. That evening, I shared with Elizabeth how deeply moved I had been by this encounter. "I've been meaning for years to start a foundation for disabled persons," I said, "and I haven't done it. This is the time."

The Dole Foundation is one piece of my answer to moving people with disabilities into the employment mainstream. The Foundation's mission has been to increase the opportunities for employment for Americans, regardless of their disabilities, and to increase our understanding of how that may be achieved. Since 1983, the Dole Foundation has awarded over 3.5 million dollars to innovative employment and training programs for persons with disabilities. It is another piece of the total effort to which this book makes a pioneering contribution.

The remarkable Helen Keller once said, "One can never consent to creep, when one feels an impulse to soar." The mission of the Dole Foundation is to provide those opportunities which allow persons with disabilities to soar as high as their skills and determination will carry them. It is my hope that readers of this book will find new methods in which to share in this mission.

Preface

Change is occurring so quickly in contemporary society that one does not have to be Rip Van Winkle to wake up startled by the state of affairs in some particular arena of activity. Disability in the workplace is one such arena. A relatively short time ago attention to this issue, if any, was focused on how to help a person with a disability achieve an acceptable income level following early retirement. Because that outcome became too costly for business and too unfulfilling for people with disabilities, pressure for other solutions developed. This book offers a comprehensive disability management program as one alternative.

In considering the management of disability in the workplace, we start with the assumption that the knowledge and skill of an experienced worker is valuable to an organization and that to pay such a person to stay home because of the onset or worsening of a disability is contrary to effective and profitable practice. The challenge facing a workplace, then, is how to organize itself to deal systematically, equitably, and responsively with the needs of the person with a disability so that the value of his or her contribution can be optimized in relation to the cost of achieving it. What we have attempted to provide in this book is a step-by-step consultation to the various organizational parties in working toward that goal.

Although the system may seem complex in its entirety, we have tried to present it so that it can be implemented in successive stages. We consider its goals and application to be relevant to the public as well as the private sector, to small businesses as well as international corporations. Our expectation is that managing disability will increase the efficiency and therefore the profitability of any work organization. We believe that the beneficiaries of disability management include all persons, since disability can happen to anyone at any time.

We contend that American employers and unions spend many dollars on the aftereffects of disability in the workplace and receive very little in exchange for that expenditure. In most work settings, large and small, the response to disability is scattered, disorganized, and unfocused. This nondirective approach is the result of a situation in which data are unexamined and feelings, while undefined, incorporate guilt, anger, despair, and uncertainty. In no other arena of managerial decision-making do the parties tolerate such indecision concerning goals and objectives. Nor need they accept lack of control in the arena of disability. The disability management system set forth in this volume is a soup-to-nuts menu for achieving cost containment and successful readjustment to work for employees who are confronted by the onset or worsening of disability. It also offers guidelines to an organization that seeks to incorporate, as new employees, persons with pre-existing disabilities.

Economic and humanitarian considerations that might cause employers to review their policies and procedures in relation to disability among their employees constitute only one aspect of the pressure for a rational disability management policy. The Americans with Disabilities Act *requires* that employers acknowledge and implement their role in achieving the goal of equitable employment opportunities for the many millions of adults who seek to maintain or secure employment regardless of their existing disabilities. A significant body of research supports such goals by finding that workers with disabilities are just as productive as their nondisabled counterparts, and that accommodating them does not increase the cost of their employment.

The research also indicates that the economic gains that accompany early identification and intervention into the experience of workers with disabilities are most likely to occur when organizations have explicit policies that ensure a responsive workplace. Such a policy carries a message that the worker is valued and his or her optimum return to work is an ongoing commitment of the employer. Along with this type of policy, the recommended systems approach includes other ingredients, which are detailed in this book. These measures have been identified and tested through a program of research and demonstration supported, in major part, by the National Institute of Disability and Rehabilitation Research of the United States Department of Education. Without that support old myths might have remained undebunked and new methodology put forth in this volume might have remained undiscovered.

The authors are indebted to the National Institute of Disability and Rehabilitation Research for its support. Particularly valuable has been the Institute's long-term commitment, which has allowed the findings of one effort to be pursued further in additional research and within a variety of industries and work settings. Such support increases the credibility of the results and the sense of certainty with which we can prescribe remedial systems. Our indebtedness extends to the many sites that provided us with access during the research process and to the many individuals who shared their experience so that we might generalize to a larger arena.

This book reflects the work and ideas of our colleagues at The

Workplace Center of Columbia University and at the Washington Business Group on Health. They have been consistently inquisitive and helpful. We are particularly appreciative of the effort of Landra Haber, who dealt with the production of this document through its many stages with competence and patience.

No list of acknowledgments would be complete without our expression of sincere gratitude to Adrienne Hickey, Senior Acquisitions and Planning Editor at AMACOM. Her advice has been unfailingly helpful, and her encouragement and understanding have made it possible for us to see this project to fruition. We are equally grateful to Barbara Horowitz, Associate Editor at AMACOM, who has watched over the publishing process with consideration, timeliness, and a pursuit of standards that has ensured that the quality of this volume would meet our fondest hopes.

S.H.A.
L.B.G.
D.E.G.

Disability Management

Chapter 1
An Overview of Disability Management

Disability is an everyday event waiting to happen to any employee. At one moment an employee is a valued member of a work team and then he has a motorcycle accident and sustains a traumatic brain injury, or she slips in the bathroom and breaks her arm, or he sprains his back helping load a truck, or she does so helping lift a patient. Suddenly a formerly productive employee who knows the organization and has vital skills and knowledge of its operations is paid to stay home—that is, he or she is placed on disability benefits, either temporarily or permanently, as a disabled individual.

Little more than a decade ago, it was a widespread business practice, and applauded as humane and reasonable rehabilitation policy, to encourage someone with a disability to exit the work force. The belief was that a loyal employee who experienced a serious disability had earned the right to be supported. In that view, workers with disabilities became candidates for early retirement—persons appropriate to join the ranks of the permanently, totally disabled.

But that is hardly the scenario to make American industry competitive in a world market. As the vice-president of human resources of a major bank remarked, "Every time we allowed someone like that to retire, twenty years or more of experience walked out the door. Were that person not disabled, we would have done almost anything to retain him or her. We finally realized that the fact that the person had developed a disability did not make our investment in that person any less."

Furthermore, recent explosive increases in costs of both disability payments and medical care have caused serious questions to be raised concerning the economic viability of retirement for workers who become disabled. At the same time, civil rights advocates have decried the waste involved in writing off, just because they are disabled, persons who can contribute to the productivity of America.

Persons with disabilities, moreover, have demanded job opportunities for themselves, demands which culminated in the passage in July 1990 of the Americans with Disabilities Act (ADA). That Act and its accompanying regulations, under certain circumstances, make it illegal for an employer to require early retirement on the basis of disability. The employer is expected to make a concerted effort to accommodate an employee with a disability, provided such accommodation does not constitute "undue hardship." (Full discussion of this issue appears in Chapter 2.)

Given that persons with disabilities are America's largest minority, and in response to the many pressures just described, employers and unions have begun to pay more attention to disability issues. This book is about disability management, a state-of-the-art response to disability in the workplace. It provides human resources managers and other key corporate professionals and trade unionists interested in manpower planning and benefits management with practical information focused on decision-making criteria and examines strategies for implementing disability management.

Disability management is a workplace prevention and remediation strategy that seeks to prevent disability from occurring or, lacking that, to intervene early following the onset of disability, using coordinated, cost-conscious, quality rehabilitation service that reflects an organizational commitment to continued employment of those experiencing functional work limitations. The remediation goal of disability management is successful job maintenance, or optimum timing for return to work, for persons with disability. A similar description was elaborated by Schwartz and colleagues (1989):

> Disability management means using services, people, and materials to (a) minimize the impact and cost of disability to employers and employees; and (b) encourage return to work for employees with disabilities. A good program utilizes a company's financial and human resources in the most efficient manner and helps employees with disabilities perform at their greatest potential and satisfaction. Disability management, therefore, complements corporate values in both human resources and fiscal performance. Simply put, a disability management program encourages a healthy workforce while ensuring the company's long-term profitability.

Major goals of disability management, and, therefore, this book, include the following:

- To improve the competitive condition of the company in a global economy

- To achieve a healthier, more productive work force by reducing the occurrence and impact of disability among the labor force
- To reduce the cost of medical care and disability benefits
- To shorten the time of absence and workplace disruption caused by the onset of disability among employees
- To reduce the personal cost of disability to employees
- To enhance morale by valuing diversity
- To achieve compliance with the ADA and other legislation

In this chapter we further define the term *disability,* provide some dimensions of the issue as it affects the workplace, lay out the reasons for a program of disability management, and introduce the components of such a program.

What Is Disability?

As soon as we start to talk about *disability,* we encounter serious problems with the word. There are legal definitions and social experiences, legislative specifics and international agreements, corporate protocols and union trust fund provisions; for each there is likely to be a different definition.

For purposes of this book we will consider disability to constitute *any condition which results in functional limitations that interfere with an individual's ability to perform his or her customary work.* Such a disability may result from many causes. People may be born with a limitation, that is, have a congenital disability, that prevents their doing the kind of work they would like to (for example, a blind person who would like to be a taxi driver). Other people may have an accident or contract an illness that limits the job functions they can perform. Such accidents or illnesses may be work related (that is, arising out of and in the course of employment, as, for example, when someone slips on a wet spot at work and sustains a concussion). The employee is entitled to workers compensation, but her injury and its work implications are no different from those of an employee who has a similar accident at a hotel while on vacation. If the outcome is seizures (epilepsy) in both cases, the impact on the individual, the work group, and the workplace is likely to be similar, given similarity of job position and functions. Whether an employee is said to have a work disability depends largely on her and her employer's attitudes and behavior toward the medical condition. It is interesting to note that the diagnosis of an illness is not as significant as how the diagnosis is perceived and treated by the employer and the employee and her co-workers.

Finally, a person may become work disabled because his or her condition deteriorates, or a change of assignment makes a previously existing condition now constitute a work disability. Consider a sewing machine operator who has osteoarthritis. As the condition progresses there may come a time when she can no longer press the fabric through the needle position. She would then have become functionally disabled for her customary work because of the worsening of her condition.

On the other hand, many people with medical conditions function quite effectively until their jobs disappear. Then, as they join the labor market seeking new jobs, they may be perceived as disabled and find it difficult to achieve alternative employment. This has been the case when companies have closed down a facility. Among the displaced workers, all of whom had been functioning productively prior to closing, approximately 20 percent are classified as disabled when they enter the labor market for alternative employment.

There are, of course, other ways of classifying persons with disabilities. They may be viewed as having either a stable or progressive condition, as being permanently or temporarily disabled, or as being physically or emotionally disabled. Disability may be singular in cause and impact (for example, a broken arm) or multiple (for instance, hypertension and osteoarthritis afflicting an older person). The combinations are numerous, as might be expected of a complex phenomenon such as disability.

The Labor Market and People With Disabilities

It should come as no surprise, given the many definitions of disability, the varied work available in our society, and the diversity among the population, that it is difficult to find concurring estimates of the number of persons with disabilities. It is relatively easy to identify how many persons have a serious hearing loss, but more difficult to identify for whom the loss constitutes a disability. If the person with the hearing loss lip-reads well, has minimum need to communicate with others on the job, or is in a work environment where most people sign, the hearing loss may have no impact at all on the functional capacity of the individual to perform the job. Such a person would not be work disabled. On the other hand, lacking any or all of those conditions, a serious hearing loss may constitute a severe work disability. The degree to which the individual adapts to and the workplace is accommodated to the condition is a major determinant of disability in the work force.

But estimates of the prevalence of work disability do not differ only because of the differential impact of a condition on functional performance. They differ also because of differences in age groups studied, methodology, and sampling error in the various surveys.

People with disabilities, whether they number 17 million or 43 million, are America's largest minority, and the cost of dealing with the problem has been estimated, as long ago as 1982, as $122 billion, or 4.7 percent of personal income a year. U.S. employers are paying up to 3 percent of their payroll costs in workers compensation expenses alone, according to Shrey (1990). Galvin (1990) reports that the probability of becoming disabled between the ages of 20 and 60 is almost one in five for males and more than one in seven for women. American business cannot afford to lose almost a fifth of its active work force during their prime working years.

In an address at Yale many years ago, John F. Kennedy pointed out that it is not lies, purposefully promulgated, but myths, insidious and irrefutable, that stand in the way of social progress. The idea that persons with disabilities do not wish to work, and the companion notion that workers are happy when they develop compensable illnesses or injuries that allow them to cease work, are myths that have been ascribed to for too long. The Institute of Social Research at the University of Michigan has conducted studies over many decades in which it asks Americans what they would do if they suddenly had sufficient funds to live comfortably for the rest of their lives without ever working. Kahn (1981) summarized those data as indicating that between 75 and 90 percent of all Americans (depending on age, sex, and ethnic group) answer that they would continue to work. The same finding, interestingly, has been confirmed across industrialized countries, whether socialist or capitalist, by an international study on the meaning of work, according to the Meaning of Work International Research Team.

This is not so surprising when we consider that work supplies not only our source of financial support but also our sense of status and achievement, provides a basis for our social interactions, and serves as an organizing theme for our daily lives. For the retiree, the loss of work is often cause for emotional and physical breakdown. And all too often we hear the hard-working housewife respond to a question about what she does by saying, "I am only a housewife"—apologetically rather than proudly, because to be outside the paid labor market is to be apart from the mainstream of approved activity.

In short, the work ethic is alive and well in American society and around the world, and work is as valued by people with disabilities as by all others. The 1986 Harris poll of people with disabilities confirmed that two thirds of all disabled adults are unemployed, but found that two thirds of the disabled unemployed say they would prefer to work. Logic suggests that this must be even more true for individuals who have been employed in the immediate past and have just experienced the onset, or worsening, of a medical condition resulting in functional limitations that can constitute a work disability.

Concepts of Disability Management

A disability management effort is built on two underlying concepts: a bio-psycho-social assessment of disability and a systems approach to organizational understanding. These concepts are interrelated. They recognize that both human problems and organizational issues are usually a complex interplay of many factors. In the case of individuals, the bio-psycho-social model recognizes that it is necessary to view the person in the context of the situation. Just as a work disability is a function of potential for performance of a specific set of tasks and requirements rather than a question of diagnosis, so, too, understanding a particular individual with a disability is a matter of considering the whole person in light of his or her biological, psychological, and social situation rather than looking at only one aspect of the person.

In assessing the whole person, one must consider the answers to relevant questions. For example, if the problem to be resolved is how to meet the needs of a clerical worker with a severe hearing loss, we would need biological information on the nature of the hearing problem and its expected course. It would not necessarily be relevant to know the biological data that the employee had recently had a hysterectomy unless there were heavy lifting involved in the job. As well, psychological data that an individual is well regarded by co-workers would be more important than his or her sibling order in tailoring a work assignment to the person's strengths and limitations.

Thus, the bio-psycho-social model stresses the importance of asking appropriate questions to understand the whole person in the specific situation. In addition to diagnosing the medical condition, the model calls for examining the individual's sense of the adequacy of, and satisfaction with, the medical care provided, the psychological state of the person and his or her family, and the nature of the social environment—specifically the tasks, routines, and relationships at the workplace in relation to the employee's specific job and general well-being.

Just as the bio-psycho-social assessment of disability seeks to identify relevant questions and interrelationships to understand the whole person, so too does the systems approach to understanding organizations seek to identify relevant units and their interplay in attempting to resolve disability issues. Many dimensions of an organization come into play and need to be involved in resolving the problems of disability in the workplace. There are also numerous external organizations, such as community agencies, that might help solve a particular problem. The systems approach requires identifying all these units and their roles and potential in finding a solution. In sum, both these concepts suggest that the whole is greater, and more informative, than its parts.

Why Have a Disability Management Program?

At first thought, no one would quarrel with the goal of a healthier, more productive labor force. What worker would not want to be healthier and live well and longer? What doctor would not like to achieve extended and healthy life for her patients? What employer or union president would not like to lead a healthier, more productive group of employees or members?

But how do we achieve this goal? Will workers practice the safety lessons they learn or will they continue habitual behavior that shortcuts the safeguards but speeds up the task? Will workers give up that second piece of chocolate cake in favor of carrot sticks and exercise? Will they do so without a guarantee that their lives will actually be extended? Can doctors surrender their lucrative custom of treating a host of minor ailments among their patients and encourage a life-style change that might prevent illness? Will employers invest in long-term productivity gains if it means spending more money in the short run for disability management and health and safety provisions? Can union leaders risk support for a program that abrogates their expected adversarial and litigious role and places them in a position of demanding responsible and independent behavior on the part of members? Will the price for such support be vulnerability at the next union election?

These are some of the real-life issues we face as we consider embracing a program of proactive and aggressive disability management and health promotion. What we need to ask ourselves is whether we are ready for such a commitment and then, if so, how we go about achieving it. It would seem on thoughtful consideration that we have little choice. The circumstances that industry, labor, and individual workers face today make it essential that we move quickly and effectively toward this goal—a partnership of all parties for a healthier, more productive, more competitive work force.

We could think about the circumstances of employers today by paraphrasing Charles Dickens in his writing about the French revolutionary period: It is the best of times, it is the worst of times. It is the worst of times because our economy is faced with many difficult problems, including global competition, an aging work force, increasing stress in all aspects of workers' lives, increasingly adversarial workers compensation litigation, and the high cost of disability. You may ask, "What do these issues have to do with disability management and health promotion?" Well, the following facts will not come as news to any reader:

• *The United States is experiencing global competition, making it vital that we achieve a highly productive labor force.* Competition can lead to a search for immediate cost savings without attention to long-run consequences. At such times, in a Darwinian game of survival of the fittest, management can be tempted to get rid of any worker who does not seem to be carrying his or her weight. We know, however, that the quality and commitment of its labor force is America's secret weapon in the global competitive struggle. Peters and Waterman, in their book, *In Search of Excellence,* reported that "excellent" companies, measured by criteria such as increase in sales volume, share of the market, and percentage of profits, were invariably those companies that demonstrated concern for employees as a fundamental element in their corporate culture. A demanding, unsupportive environment is unlikely to realize the potential of the work force, creating a hidden but costly drain on productivity.

• *Our population is aging.* By the year 2020, one out of every three Americans will be over fifty. The Hudson Institute's publication *Workforce 2000* (Johnston, 1987) has called attention to the reality: As the aging process progresses, the work force is bound to develop disabilities. We also know that although workers are more likely to be injured in their first year of employment than ever after, aging workers develop more serious injuries than their younger colleagues. The cumulative impact of successive injuries over a work life becomes more disabling the older we get. Hence, as we age, disability is likely to be an increasing and, if left unattended, an increasingly expensive fact of life among the work force.

• *Work, and all other aspects of life as well, is increasingly stressful for most people.* The tempo of competition and the frequency of change have increased geometrically, and the ensuing illnesses, accidents, and long-term disability have resulted in a whole new class of claims for stress-induced problems that have proved ambiguous in their cost and remediation and difficult to treat in customary ways.

So, to answer the question "What do these issues have to do with disability management and health promotion?" we need simply look at some of the results of these changes in the work force:

• *Escalating adversarial claims and high-cost litigation have accompanied these developments.* Litigation carries its own burden. When the parties become invested in the claim, they find it difficult to focus on working together to restore physical and mental abilities.

• *There is a high cost to disability accompanied by lost time.* The work of previously productive employees is lost while they are paid to stay at home (or in a health care facility); often alternative workers must perform and be paid for that work; the work group is disrupted; and medical care costs escalate as an employee remains on disability. Studies show that medical care costs correlate not with severity of diagnosis, as might be predicted, but with the length of time workers remain out of work on disability.

• *It also costs to investigate a disability or accident and to administer benefits,* to say nothing of the indirect and unmeasured costs of undermined morale, guilt, and hostility that often result from the onset of disability. Just one day of lost time for disability sets in motion a cost of $13,000 per employee experiencing the disability, according to a Du Pont study reported by McDonald (1990). The national costs of disability will reach an estimated $200 billion a year by the year 2000 according to a projection of Northwestern National Life Insurance Company. Every employee not rehabilitated costs $154,000 to age 65 according to the same study.

But, to complete the analogy, this is also the best of times—we have identified the cost drains; the shifts that have been taking place in the nature of work have reduced the likelihood of accidents; methodology exists for health promotion and disability management; and we know that rehabilitation and early return to work are cost-effective. As just one example of why this is also the best of times, research indicates that back injuries, which comprise the single most frequent disability, are largely preventable. Consider what else makes this the best of times:

• *We have identified the major cost drains, providing a motivation to do something about them.* Disability has been a hidden cost of doing business for a very long time, for two reasons. First, it is dispersed among many different programs within a company: For example, workers compensation is often handled by risk management, whereas sickness and accident claims come under benefits administration; employment of persons with disabilities is the responsibility of the equal employment opportunity (EEO) office; and handling the onset of disability, especially when it involves mental health, alcohol, or substance abuse, resides with the employee assistance program (EAP). Second, retiring someone on disability seems like the kindly, humane action to take, and therefore not one to be studied in relation to cost, until we begin to realize that it is not only financially costly to the company, but also highly damaging to the individual.

• *The nature of work, as we all know, has changed for the most part from agricultural to manufacturing to service jobs over the last century.* Of the three, service work is the safest kind of work. Further, accidents in even those industries that traditionally accounted for a majority of injuries have declined steadily—the incidence rate for occupational injury and illness per 100 full-time workers in the private sector has dropped from 11 in 1973 to 7.6 in 1983 (Victor 1985).

• *We have developed a methodology and technology for promoting health and managing disability in the workplace.* There are at least three aspects to this achievement. First, we have come to understand the importance of a focus on life-style and prevention. Good nutrition, adequate exercise, and abstention from smoking, drinking, and drug abuse constitute healthful activities that can strengthen the worker against the occurrence of disability or limit the impact of an accident or illness. At the same time, ergonomics and other occupational health and safety initiatives, such as practices that protect knees and backs, have shown the way to improving the workplace environment so that the causes of disability are minimized. Third, these prevention components are reinforced by the development of computer tracking, which can increase our knowledge of the actions that are related to disability and thus direct our prevention strategy. For example, employers can find out whether back problems are the prime disabler in a particular type of workplace (as the National Workers Compensation Research Center did) and then develop a back program (as Mississippi Power did, saving over $25,000 by training people how to use their backs safely). The year before Mississippi Power instituted their program, back injuries cost $26,000. One year after training employees how to use their backs effectively, for example, how to lift to avoid injury, how to strengthen muscles so that chances of injury are reduced and disability following injuries is limited, back injuries cost only $800.

• *Rehabilitation and early return to work are readily achievable and limit individual and organizational costs.* All studies show that workers recover faster, with fewer residual disabilities, and litigation costs are lower when an employer has a policy and program that provide good case management and early return to work, modified as necessary. Not only Mississippi Power, but a host of other firms report significant savings. For example, Chrysler brought disability costs down almost $100 per employee in a two-year period, and Weyerhaeuser reduced workers compensation claims by almost 30 percent within six years after establishing a disability management effort. Before 1983, Weyerhaeuser faced 9,948 compensable claims a year. By 1989, after a disability management program was established (described more fully in Chapter 8), claims were down to 7,042 for the year *with a 5,000-person increase in the firm's total employment.* Similarly, in 1986, disability costs before return to work were $625 per Chrysler employee. Just two years later, in 1988, with a disability management program in place, these costs were $537 per employee. These reductions in costs or claims are occurring while all other costs (for example, medical care) are increasing.

In sum, a review of the situation suggests that the problems we face are escalating (it is the worst of times); yet the potential solutions are known, documented, and available (it is the best of times).

Disability Management: Two Scenarios

As we've noted, disability management is a coordinated, cost-effective prevention and early intervention effort, the purpose of which is to eliminate as many situations that cause disability as possible and to assist a newly disabled worker in successful job maintenance or return to work. We know that if we do not assist workers in early return, but rather allow time to take its course, the outcomes are disastrous for individuals. As Berkowitz (1987) notes, "The slower and less coordinated an employer's intervention after an accident or illness, the more likely an employee will progress from illness to disability." Studies show that of the 500,000 newly disabled workers each year who remain out on disability five months or more, only one in two will ever return to work.

Shocking as that figure may be, it is easy to understand why so many disabled workers fail to return to their jobs. Imagine that you are experiencing the onset of disability. One day you are working, a fully functional human being. You leave your office to visit a customer, and have a serious automobile accident. If you're like most Americans, you were not wearing your seat belt, are a little fat, and have not been exercising, and so your injuries are more serious than they needed to be, and clearly disabling. You lie abed, contemplating your financial and health problems, with lots of time, particularly since not too many calls come from your workplace supervisors and managers. You wonder if you will ever be able to return to your former job; then, a week or so into your disability, a check arrives from the workers compensation insurer. It's not as much as your usual earnings, but it's some help with the bills that are beginning to pile up, and all your medical costs are covered as well. Then, two weeks later another compensation check arrives. The doctor keeps telling you to be patient, that your body will heal after a while, but you know how much you are hurting, how little you can do. You feel sure that you cannot perform all the tasks of your usual work and suspect that you may never be able to do so. With no word from the workplace, you begin to believe that there is no interest in your return.

The message from the workplace is, "Stay away and we'll pay you." This is one instance where the old shibboleth "When in doubt, send money" is poor advice. The money itself becomes the problem. The checks keep coming and pretty soon you begin to regard those checks as the only ticket to security for yourself and those who depend on you. You have become a permanently disabled person, seeking permanent payments, either from Social Security Disability Insurance (SSDI) or as a workers compensation claimant—not a fraud, or an abuser of benefits—but surely a frightened person. No wonder Berkowitz and Hill (1986) observed that "disability cannot be explained by examining a person's medical condition alone."

A different scenario would exist with a disability management program in place. Within a day of your call informing your workplace of your accident, you would receive a call from your supervisor as provided for in the company's disability management procedures. He or she would reassure you that there is a place to which you can return. Then, you might be called by a case manager who would check on your medical care and other concerns, refer you to services and for care that would fill any gap in the system you have activated, and begin to talk with you and your attending physician about the possibilities of accommodated work, or a transitional assignment. If disability is the loss of ability to perform socially accepted or prescribed tasks and roles, a company representative's discussion about assignment would keep you from feeling that loss as deeply and help you keep your thoughts at the workplace and your focus on early return to work. You would not view yourself as a disabled person.

Getting Started in Disability Management

The preceding scenario suggests the components of a disability management initiative. These are discussed in detail in Chapter 3. The components are as follows:

- Evaluate the present situation (needs assessment).
- Convene a coordinating committee.
- Establish policy and procedures.
- Provide a mechanism for case finding and early intervention.
- Appoint a case manager and develop ties with community agencies.
- Offer flexible employment options.
- Provide training to key participants.

- Set up a data collection and evaluation scheme.
- Invest in prevention.

The process is outlined in Figure 1-1.

Lest you become fearful that the complexity of the plan makes it an unlikely undertaking at your own place of work, note that an ideal program can be a goal and its details can serve as your long-range planning document. We all know Aesop's adage "A journey of a thousand miles must begin with a single step." It is possible to establish a disability management program in increments. But first you have to make a commitment to that goal. And whether business, union, health and welfare agency, or legal or medical player, each has something to gain, while collectively, we all have a great deal to gain in making the workplaces and work forces of our country healthier and more productive.

To develop a disability management game plan, an organization needs to specify a policy and procedure. It should include provisions for incentives for both the employee with the disability and the supervisor, to ensure appropriate commitment. What is required is some assurance that the income of the person facing disability will be maintained, and that that cost will not be absorbed by a general company fund, but rather will be charged to the supervisor's unit, thereby providing a significant incentive for supervisors to accommodate disabled persons at work, since the unit budget is being charged in any event.

A main thrust of disability management is to provide early identification and referral and humane, responsive attention to the needs of the person with the disability. The system requires specific transitional employment opportunities, flexible work schedules, the potential to receive time off for medical care, and other accommodations to help keep the job or speed return to work. A coordinating committee of all those with an interest in the program (for example, persons in medical care, benefits payments, EEO and EAP, the work supervisor, and the union representative) should be convened to work out arrangements, create opportunities, and ensure their uniform application. A case manager with good ties to the community's social and medical agency network, and skill in advocating for services for clients, should be responsible for making the program responsive to individual needs.

Ensuring continuity and effectiveness of disability management requires training key players (supervisors, union representatives, managers) and communicating information to all levels of personnel. It also needs a good data-gathering capability that will permit evaluation of program operation, identify unsafe practices causing accidents and illnesses, and provide feedback to establish a means of process refinement. Finally, and perhaps most important, are two other strategies: (1) prevention and (2)

Figure 1-1. Disability management process.

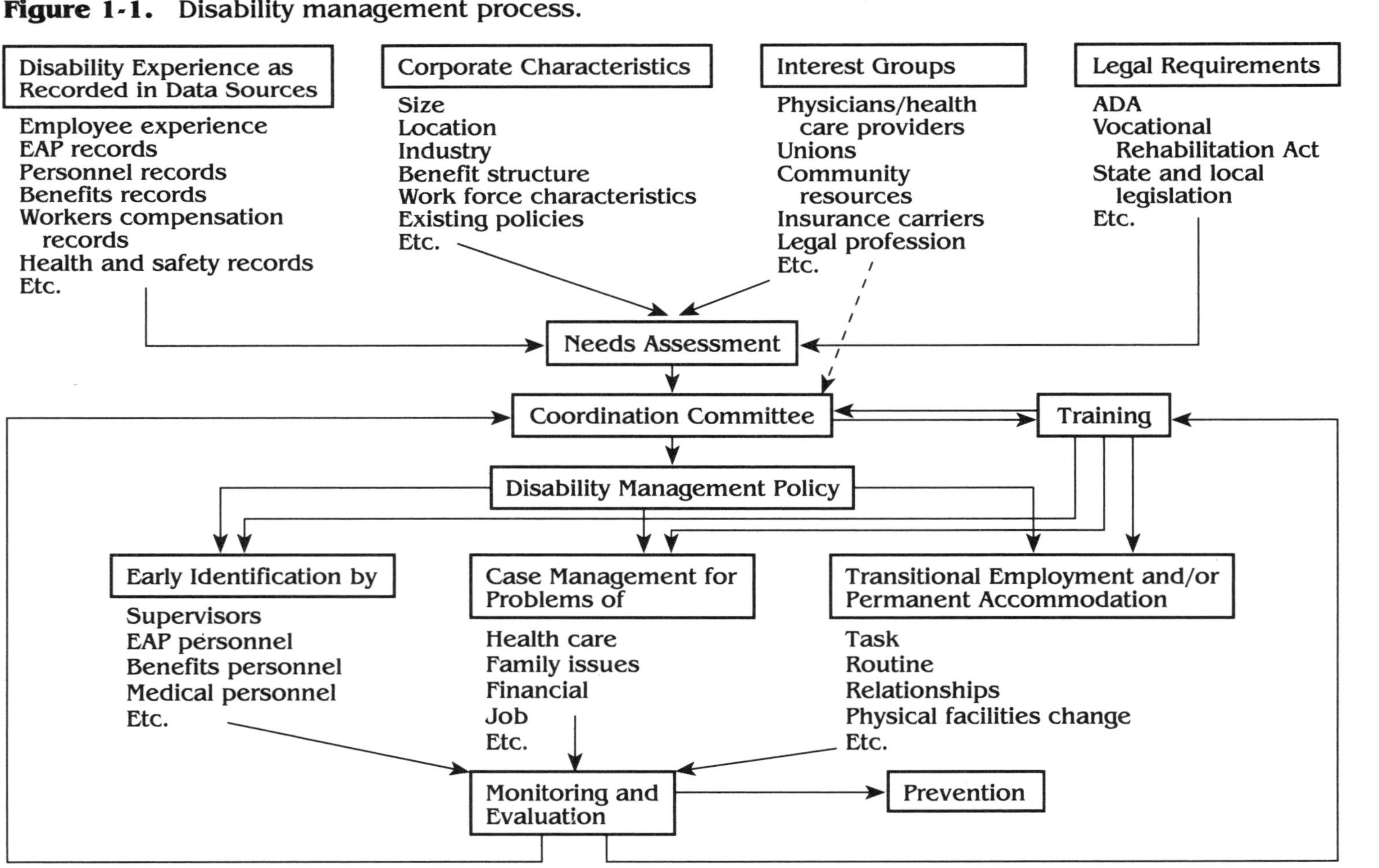

health promotion. A disability management program needs prevention measures—means of identifying existing disability patterns and addressing them through occupational safety and health initiatives. A disability management program must also aim to achieve a healthy work force through health promotion programs that provide risk evaluation and encourage healthy life-style behavior, including good nutrition, weight reduction, smoking cessation, stress management, personal safety training, and regular health screenings for control of cholesterol, hypertension, and breast cancer.

Again, you do not have to accomplish the whole program in a day, but you should pick a place to start. And if you are a small company (or even a few persons in a professional practice or service business), you can enter into the disability management–wellness mode by doing something—buying the idea and assigning yourself the roles that need primary attention.

Barriers and Obstacles

Given that a healthy and productive work force is a goal with which no one would quarrel, it is still an elusive goal. We know about the path to it, and some have begun to travel that path, but the walkers are all too few, so we must ask ourselves why—what stands in the way?

Health promotion and disability management is a case of buying in to delayed gratification instead of instant satisfaction. It requires a leap of faith (and acceptance of the risk that your faith may be unjustified, even if only in the short run) *and* a commitment to compliance—both difficult ends to secure. Although we all know people who jog, one only has to pass the pained-looking, sweaty figure of the runner to be convinced that it is more fun to sit watching a good TV program. And even if we start to exercise, it's hard to keep it up on a busy schedule. Unless one really enjoys the particular activity, adhering to an exercise regime requires the leap of faith that it will pay dividends in the long run by achieving a healthier or longer life. Psychologically, we all know that rewards, not hope, sustain commitment and the action that accompanies commitment. Therefore, managers must help employees focus on long-term goals and provide continuous support for their efforts to make a commitment to health promotion and prevention.

Management must stimulate supervisors, as well, if it expects supervisors to foster disability management outcomes. What supervisor wants to encourage a partially functioning person to come back to the workplace when work has to get out, knowing that when the figures are in probably no one will remember that two employees with disabilities were in a transitional work arrangement in the unit? What union leader wants to face down the angry member who, having sustained a disabling accident, wants to parlay it into an extended vacation? How does the union official answer the threat that election support will be removed unless advocacy for continuing disability is forthcoming? And what employer wants to spend good dollars to accommodate the workstation to the worker with a disability? Even the survey finding reported by McDonald (1990) for companies that have made efforts to hire the handicapped—"Rarely did accommodation involve much cost: 51 percent of all accommodations cost nothing"—may not offer sufficient reassurance to the uninitiated.

Here is a perfect example of how, once an employer becomes interested in disability management, solutions to problems can be developed. There is a national Job Accommodation Network (JAN) that provides assistance in making accommodations. (For more information on JAN, see Chapter 2.) JAN has devised and recorded many thousands of accommodations designed to improve the functional performance of persons with a great range of disabilities who were asked to undertake an equally great range of tasks. Accommodating an employee may produce benefits beyond the gain to the particular individual. Many technically oriented employers may find, as IBM has, that there is a broader consumer market for accommodations that were devised initially for a particular employee with a disability.

"Buying In" to Disability Management

But let us return to those more difficult questions—of the "what's in it for me?" variety. The research evidence on the benefits of a healthy life-style and early return to work is pretty clear. The death rate in the United States has declined precipitously in recent years, accounted for in large part by the reduction in coronary deaths. The connection between good nutrition, lowered cholesterol, hypertension control, exercise, and not smoking and the decline in heart disease is well established. Organizations and trade unions that do not take advantage of promoting health will pay more for medical care, lose more productivity, and have more employees who die earlier than those that establish effective health promotion schemes.

So much for health promotion. The case for disability management is equally compelling. Research evidence confirms that those who participate in an effective early intervention program return to work faster and are less disabled, with fewer dollars having been spent on their care. Participating in health promotion and disability management should be routine for adult workers. Structures of self-help and more formal incentive systems must be developed to ensure compliance of disabled workers.

For those who choose not to comply, a reasonable time limit should be established for participation in rehabilitation or a return to work, and then their jobs and benefits should no longer be guaranteed. This successive carrot-and-stick strategy may precipitate a major change in the organizational culture if workers are accustomed to easily extended disability leaves. In organized settings, such a cultural change may require labor-management negotiations as well. It is essential, however, that the message of a disability management program be loud and clear: "We will offer every help possible to facilitate the continued functional work performance of our employees with disabilities. Despite these efforts, for some it may be necessary to support long leaves, or early retirement. These latter options are available, however, only to those who participate in an organized rehabilitation effort."

When an injury occurs at the workplace, there is a mix of guilt and anger. Workers are angry that the work was "dangerous to their health," yet they feel guilty for whatever they may have contributed to the accident. The employer has the reverse syndrome: anger at the worker for causing the accident, but feelings of guilt for any contributory circumstance of the workplace. Let us identify these feelings honestly and then set them aside—in short, not cry over spilled milk, because it costs too much.

Leadership from the business community is essential in reducing disability costs. Complaints about the high cost of workers compensation are rampant among employers. But they have the means to reduce those costs. Some employers, such as Weirton Steel in West Virginia, have established on-site, cutting-edge rehabilitation facilities where disabled employees can receive the best rehabilitation care on the most up-to-date equipment available. When the worksite provides the care, workers and their union leaders have to overcome initial suspicion about using an employer's facilities rather than opting, under free choice of medical care, for some private provider or community resource. An employer can help accomplish this by using rehabilitation as a reward for service rather than as harassment designed to return employees to work regardless of their condition. But once trust is established, there is great enthusiasm among workers at such sites about the opportunity to receive this treatment and the quality of the treatment offered. The group spirit that develops among those using a well-run facility sponsored by the employer is instrumental in shortening the recovery period for many workers. Clearly, few employers can be expected to develop such a facility. But we can each do a great deal toward achieving comparable results.

An employer who provides a safe work environment and offers health risk assessment and wellness programs will benefit by cutting costs for health care, workers compensation, and sickness and accident benefits. Savings will also accrue because work teams will function more efficiently when not disrupted by missing co-workers and there will be less need to recruit new workers to replace those absent or permanently separated from the work force. The old myth of abuse of disability leave will be exploded because fraudulent behavior on the part of satisfied workers is rare and will be unsupported by a culture at the workplace that views the employer as fair, consistent, and within the law. It is appropriate to give workers that to which they are entitled, and to send a clear message that fraudulent behavior will not be rewarded but fought. The expenses of doing so will decline as the message becomes firmer and clearer.

Unions lose considerable credibility when they advocate for bad clients. Said another way, the union should be concerned that members receive their entitlements, but should be equally concerned that the few do not abuse those entitlements at the expense of the many. In their legitimate desire to protect members who are disabled, union leaders sometimes bend to the pressure of vocal but uncooperative members who have a way of harnessing discontent—a constant in the ranks of any membership organization. It takes considerable courage to separate legitimate issues from loud talk, but such action is necessary by union leaders if disability management is to become a cost-effective intervention. It is appropriate for workers to be well cared for, but it is also appropriate for them to cooperate with a rehabilitation regime. Being on the right side of that very thin line requires union leadership that has confidence in itself, and enjoys the confidence of a majority of the members. The savings that accrue when efficient disability management and return-to-work programs are in place can be used for support of alternative benefits. Such trade-offs are the appropriate agenda for labor-management negotiations.

When a new disability management program goes into effect, however, past patterns and expectations are disrupted. The complaints of union members who find that a disability is no longer a ticket to a long rest, or outright malingering, can be bitter. Furthermore, such complaints are likely to occur sooner than the increased benefits, and union leaders need to be sufficiently committed to the goals of disability management and health promotion to take the initial heat as the existing system is brought under tighter control. This should be less difficult for union leaders to accept if they understand that all research evidence confirms the long-run advantages of disability management to their members. It is also less difficult for union leaders when management understands the pressure they face.

There are other actors, too. Doctors, lawyers, and community agencies all influence program outcome. They need to provide more positive reinforcement for return to work. As one study, reported by Debusk, Dennis, and Sidney (1988), stated in discussing back-to-work advice for cardiac patients:

> Because of their unfamiliarity with the physical and psychological demands of their patients' occupational tasks, physicians often are reluctant to provide explicit guidelines to patients regarding the resumption of occupational work. . . . They generally ascribe a higher risk [than correct] to occupational activities.

Lawyers should recognize that building a case for a claimant that depends on keeping someone out of work, and using excessive medical care, is irresponsible behavior that is hurtful to the long-run interests of clients. Most workers want to work, not just for the financial compensation but also for social contacts, the sense of accomplishment, the value work serves as an organizer of daily activity, and the sense of self-worth it provides. Prompt settlements may serve clients best.

Community agencies can help by expanding their rehabilitation and health promotion offerings. Positive outcomes require working partnerships of all parties, and willingness on the part of each to defer gratification and work toward long-run gains for which the only credit is the well-being and productivity of individuals and the efficiency and effectiveness of the work enterprise.

Again, the arena of disability management and its related prevention and health promotion opportunities present a fertile field that can yield many positive outcomes, including the following. We need only have the patience and commitment to wait for them.

- Healthy, committed employees/members
- Increased productivity
- Reduced health and disability costs
- Fair and predictable treatment for workers
- Compliance with the letter of the law
- Safer workplaces

Who could quarrel with such results? The remainder of this book offers a blueprint for such an endeavor and shows how to apply the model to any particular individual employer or trade union.

We hope that by the end you are as convinced as we are that disability management is a strategy of great promise, meeting the needs of all the interested parties in a work setting.

Endnote

Under the Social Security Act, a person may draw disability benefits only if he or she proves an inability to engage in substantial gainful activity by reason of any medically determinable physical or mental impairment. Such an individual must be unable to engage not only in his or her own customary work but any other kind of gainful work considering his or her age, education, and work experience and the work available in the labor market. Clearly this delineation includes medical, social, and economic criteria. Similar criteria are also reflected in the definition of disability provided in the Americans with Disabilities Act (ADA) of 1990. ADA defines a person protected under the legislation as someone who has a physical or mental impairment that substantially limits one or more of the major life activites of the person, is regarded as having such an impairment, or has a record of such an impairment, making disability, here, as often as not a socially determined phenomenon. Although legislative definitions will be discussed more extensively in the next chapter, two major points are worth noting here. Anyone who becomes disabled while employed, whether the disability is compensable because it arises "out of and in the course of employment" or merely in parallel with employment connection, is covered by ADA's protection. Second, this includes substance abusers except for the legislatively expressed exemption from protection of *current* abusers only.

The diversity of definition is equally apparent in the terminology among scholarly observers as well, reflecting their varied vantages. Monroe Berkowitz and M. Anne Hill, two economists, have defined disability as ". . . the loss of the ability to perform socially accepted or prescribed tasks and roles due to a medically definable condition" (1986: 4). Edward Berkowitz, a historian, comments, ". . . disability resists precise definition and measurement . . . represents a social judgment and, in some cases, a personal choice" (1987: 3). A disability rights activist, Harlan Hahn, views disability as "a product of the interaction between the individual and the environment" (1984: 10). Such a definition suggests that disability might not exist were it not for society's norms. This has implications for how we view disability of workers. The United States Household National Health Interview Survey uses the term *work disability* to refer to "limitation in the amount or kind of work or inability to work" (La Plante 1988: 7). A 1986 Harris poll of people with disabilities defined someone as disabled if the person met one of the following requirements:

- Had a disability or health problem that prevented full participation in work.
- Said that he or she had a physical disability; a seeing, hearing, or speech impairment; an emotional or mental disability; or a learning disability.
- Considered himself or herself disabled or said that others would consider him or her disabled.

Estimates of the extent of disability in the work force vary considerably. Consider the 1988 publication by the National Institute of Disability and Rehabilitation Research, based largely on data from household surveys. It contains an estimate that 11.5 percent (17.4 million) of persons between the ages of 18 and 69 report some degree of limitation in working at a job or business due to chronic health conditions (La Plante 1988: 11). The highest rate of work disability was reported by a 1978 survey of the Social Security Administration, which found a 17.2 percent level among persons ages 18 to 64 (La Plante 1988: 13). The Harris poll, using the definition detailed earlier, reported the prevalence of disability to be 15 percent among Americans over age 16, or 27 million Americans. In all the surveys, however, a significant number of persons report serious limitations. Among them, clearly, are many working Americans, and even more Americans of working age.

Chapter 2

Legislation Affecting Disability Management Practices

This chapter describes the major legislation that affects employment of people with disabilities. Three types of legislation are covered: (1) the federal and state legislation that mandates employers to eliminate policies and practices that have excluded people with disabilities from, or limited their equal opportunity in, employment; (2) the laws entitling people with disabilities to rehabilitation services intended to permit them to seek or maintain employment; and (3) the legislation guaranteeing wage replacement for people with disabilities who are unable to work, whether for a fixed period after onset of disability or permanently. While disability management is usually concerned primarily with retention of employees who acquire a disability rather than hiring of new employees who already have a disability, virtually all legislation applies to both situations.

Equal Opportunity in Employment

All state and federal laws that have been enacted to promote equal opportunity in employment have one basic principle in common: to foster decisions about an individual applicant or worker based upon that person's capacity to perform the duties of a particular job the employer needs done. Stripped of rhetoric and technical language, their purpose is to promote merit and fairness as the basis for making employment decisions. The laws are premised on the belief that employers want and deserve the

This chapter was prepared by Adrienne Asch, an expert on legal rights of people with disabilities and a senior human rights specialist on leave from the New York State Division of Human Rights, and by Sara Watson, Manager of Public Policy for the Washington Business Group on Health and Associate Director of WBGH's Institute for Rehabilitation and Disability Management.

most competent work force they can find and that employees want and deserve work that suits their overall physical and mental capacities and interests. Equal opportunity laws are designed to rid the workplace of any arrangements or habits of doing things that intentionally or unintentionally undermine such goals. For a long time employers have had to evaluate their hiring, promotion, compensation, termination, training, and benefits policies to remove differentiations of individuals based on race, ethnicity, religion, or gender. Equal opportunity laws for people with disabilities are designed to eliminate those practices and assumptions of employers that have unnecessarily limited participation of people with disabilities in the labor force. Whether we are speaking of a state antidiscrimination law, Title V of the Rehabilitation Act of 1973, or the Americans with Disabilities Act, their purpose, like affirmative action, equal opportunity, and anti-discrimination legislation, is to promote the evaluation of each individual, in this case those with a disability, in terms of his or her capacity to perform the duties of a particular job.

The Americans with Disabilities Act of 1990

The recent passage of the Americans with Disabilities Act of 1990 (ADA) has brought renewed attention to both federal and state legislation affecting employment practices for people with disabilities. The ADA and its regulations were written to augment, not conflict with or diminish, the protections of existing employment statutes. Many employers and unions are subject to Sections 503 or 504 of the Rehabilitation Act of 1973, or to state antidiscrimination laws protecting people with disabilities. The ADA does not supersede any federal or state law that is stricter in its provisions; for this reason, among others, employers must familiarize themselves with all other applicable state and federal laws.

Signed into law on July 26, 1990, the ADA (Public Law 101-336) is much broader than previous federal equal opportunity legislation covering people with disabilities. On July 26, 1992, the law takes effect for all employers with twenty-five or more employees; two years later, all employers with fifteen or more employees will be subject to its requirements.

The ADA prohibits discrimination on the basis of disability in the areas of employment, transportation, use of public facilities, and communications. Its breadth means that some societal factors external to an employer's practices will change to ease the way for disabled people to seek or resume work. As transportation systems become more accessible to people with impaired mobility, and as communication becomes easier for people with speech and hearing impairments, fewer obstacles apart from particular employment practices will prevent them from working. Thus, although equal opportunity provisions of the ADA and other civil rights laws are the main focus of discussion here, they must be understood in a context of larger social changes that will affect businesses. Companies will be required by Titles III and IV of the ADA to serve people with disabilities as customers; these changes will also ease the way for the same companies to employ disabled people.

Who Is Covered?

Disability under the ADA is defined in the same manner as in the Rehabilitation Act of 1973:

- A physical or mental impairment that substantially limits one or more of the major life activities of an individual
- A record of such an impairment
- Being regarded as having such an impairment

This definition is used to cover not only people who currently have a physical or mental condition that affects a life activity, but also people who may be treated as having such a condition. For instance, people with visible birthmarks or scars, those of short stature, or those with misshapen arms or legs may be able to perform all of what are termed "major life activities," but they may be treated as though they were not. Regarded as having a disability, they may be targets of discrimination. Someone who had cancer but is now in remission may similarly not be impaired, but may be treated in a discriminatory manner by people who know about the cancer history. Other applicants may not be disabled at the time they apply for work, but may have conditions discoverable through a pre-employment medical history or medical examination (such as lower-back pain, a recurring disease, or a family history of diabetes) that suggest they may become disabled in the future. The ADA also covers people who themselves are not disabled but have relationships with people who are (for example, friends of people with AIDS, or spouses of people with heart disease or cancer). This law protects all those individuals from being treated differently from people without such characteristics.

Discriminatory Practices

Discriminatory actions under the ADA are analogous to those actions considered discriminatory under Title VII of the Civil Rights Act of 1964 when they occur to members of racial, ethnic, or religious minorities, or to women. The Equal Employment Opportunity Commission (EEOC), which now enforces Title VII, has been assigned responsibility for enforcement of the employment aspects of the ADA. The discrimination prohibited by the ADA is also analogous to that prohibited against people with disabilities under Sections 503 and 504 of the Rehabilitation Act of 1973. Thus, for many employers who are experienced in examining their practices to eliminate barriers to women, racial minorities, or people with disabilities under these other laws, the ADA may not require noticeable alterations in their operations. For many private-sector employers without government contracts, located in states whose antidiscrimination laws do not cover people with all disabilities, the ADA constitutes new coverage that may cause an employer to reevaluate and change certain long-established patterns.

Important differences exist between the ADA and Title VII of the Civil Rights Act of 1964, with which most employers are more familiar, yet the central concept is the same: eliminating treatment of individuals based on beliefs about a disabling characteristic, rather than on a demonstrable relationship between an individual's capacities and the duties of a job. Prohibited practices include those affecting the hiring process, promotion, work assignments, transfers, job training, compensation, discharge, or any other aspect of the employment relationship. If, for example, an employer's beliefs about reactions of others to people with disabilities caused him to assign all visibly disabled clerks to telephone work rather than to work that would have them meet the public, such a practice would be an instance of different and discriminatory treatment. Similarly, if an employer's medical examination screened out all people with diabetes or epilepsy from a class of jobs, without regard to the capacity of an individual to perform the duties of the job, that practice would be prohibited.

Like all other civil rights laws, the ADA is not intended to require the hiring or retention of workers unqualified for the jobs they are expected to perform. Like the Rehabilitation Act of 1973, on which it is patterned, the ADA includes provisions designed to promote the hiring and retention only of people who can perform work of the quality and quantity expected of nondisabled people in the same job category. It is not discriminatory to refuse to hire a person whose uncontrollable seizures make it dangerous for him to operate moving machinery, or to reassign a person whose arthritis makes it impossible to manipulate tools necessary in a construction task.

Consonant with the philosophy of disability management expressed throughout this book, but different from the traditions of some employers in the past, the ADA obliges an employer to *attempt reassignment* rather than immediately discharge an employee experiencing the onset of disability. Take, for example, a carpenter with arthritis who can no longer handle the construction task. If there is no job in the company that the craftsman is capable of performing at the level of others doing that same job, and if, even with special tools or accommodations, there is no way the carpenter can do the original job, the employer would not be expected to retain the employee. This example introduces concepts key to understanding how the ADA promotes both the inclusion of people with disabilities in the work force and the maintenance of a company's smoothly running, high-quality operation. Understanding the implications of the ADA for a company's employment decisions requires comprehending the concepts "essential functions" of a job, "reasonable accommodation" to a person's disability, and "undue hardship" on an employer.

Essential Functions of a Job

To determine whether a person who develops, say, emphysema can resume his machinist job, the employer must know what the key duties of the job are in that particular establishment. How much moving does the machinist have to do, and how quickly? What is the physical environment in which the work is performed? How much work is expected in a day? The employer should develop a written job description, specifying as clearly as possible the tasks to be performed, the percentage of total time each task is likely to take, and the amount of work expected in a given time period. After going through this process, the employer should ascertain duties expected of machinists that are less frequent or important, and perhaps more marginal to the satisfactory execution of the overall job.

Determining what is "essential" is based on several factors: the amount of work time taken up with a particular task; the proportion of the total job function taken up by the particular task (examining written documents for errors might be the total function of a proofreader but only an hour-a-day task for an executive secretary); whether all employees with the same job title must perform a particular component of the job; the consequence to the total operation of having some people performing only some of the tasks customarily thought to be part of a certain job; and so forth.

In our machinist example, if the work is done in an environment that aggravates the emphysema and makes the worker's health deteriorate, but the work cannot be done elsewhere, working in a particular environment is an *essential* function of that job. It may not be essential to another machinist job at another site, or to another machinist job of another employer, but it may genuinely be indispensable for the job of the employer in question. In such a circumstance, the worker may be unable to perform the essential job, and it would not be discriminatory to prevent him from working at it.

On the other hand, if the majority of a machinist's time is spent in a work setting that does not exacerbate the health condition, and if the employer refuses to hire an individual or allow resumption of work because the employee cannot do 10 percent of the work, the employer may be discriminating. The worker may actually be performing the essential functions of the job but be unable to perform only peripheral or occasional parts of it. If an employer has determined that employees must perform a certain quantity of work in a certain time (such as a service worker cleaning sixteen rooms in a day), and if an employer can demonstrate that people who do not meet this standard are disciplined or terminated, an employer would not be discriminating if a job were denied to someone whose energy permitted cleaning only twelve rooms a day.

Reasonable Accommodation

Even employers who have never hired workers known to have disabilities might already have valuable experience in having them in their work force. For instance, they may have retained people who had back injuries or heart attacks. Perhaps the workers resumed their assignments without any changes after their absence. Perhaps, especially in a small company where people knew one another well, the employer and co-workers made small but useful accommodations to a worker's changed health condition by giving the employee relief from heavy lifting, or by rearranging a work schedule to fit in physical therapy appointments or necessary rest periods. These are examples of the type of "reasonable accommodation" to the disability of a worker that will be incumbent upon all employers by mid-1994.

If an employer transfers a woman who develops hypertension to a different job because of the employer's belief about hypertension, the transfer may be considered a discriminatory act. If, however, the transfer is, in fact, based on accurate information about the particular person's job assignment and physical condition, the transfer is probably an instance of reasonably accommodating a worker's disability.

Under the ADA an employer is required to make "reasonable accommodation" to the known disability of an applicant or employee unless doing so would impose a substantial burden ("undue hardship") on the organization. Such accommodations include providing tools or equipment that permit someone with a mobility impairment to manipulate objects; arranging for an assistant to read to a customer service representative with dyslexia; restructuring a job to eliminate peripheral functions (having someone other than the receptionist serve food if she has poor coordination due to multiple sclerosis); and arranging a work schedule to permit an employee to attend medical or therapy appointments.

Reassigning a worker with a back injury to a job in which alternate sitting, walking, and bending is possible may also be a form of reasonable accommodation. In general, though, reassignment should not be contemplated unless it is difficult to accommodate a newly disabled worker in the current position. And reassignment should not be done in a way that segregates people with disabilities into undesirable, low-status, less remunerative positions, or to particular physical facilities in which nondisabled people do not work.

Identifying what types of accommodations are appropriate in a particular situation entails a process in which the employer and employee examine the tasks essential to the position in question and the specific limitations imposed by the disability. Together, they should explore the methods that might be used to facilitate performance of the essential tasks. Employers should keep in mind some basic principles as they consider the question of accommodation to a worker's disability:

- *Talk to the person who needs the accommodation.* If the person has lived with the disability for some time, he or she may be the best resource about what arrangements are necessary, how to make them, and what help both worker and employer can obtain to make them. Even if the disability is relatively new or has changed, it is the worker who must live with the accommodation. Not all people with the same disabling characteristic will need exactly the same adaptation. Some people with hearing impairments will benefit from an amplifier on a telephone, whereas others will not.

- *Accommodation does not have to be complicated and costly.* Reassigning a task to another worker, providing a parking space near the facility, adapting a tool, or arranging a work schedule to include breaks for prescribed exercise, medication, or rest may be all that stands between keeping and losing a worker. Sometimes even physical changes may be accomplished simply. A company can provide drinking water for its workers by lowering a water fountain to be reached from a wheelchair, or by providing a cup dispenser. Simple solutions may be as effective as expensive ones.

- *Before assuming that something can't be done, ask others who may know.* The best source may be the employees or applicants who need the accommodation. If they are uncertain, the state vocational rehabilitation agency, independent living centers, organizations serving people with disabilities, or other agencies with similar jobs may have the needed information. Employers can contact the Job Accommodation Network through a toll-free number (800-JAN-7234). JAN provides advice over the telephone on making specific modifications to fit individual needs.

Employing those with disabilities does not have to involve making any accommodation to their disabilities. According to studies cited by the EEOC in its discussion of the ADA, it has been estimated that only one half of those with disabilities require any type of accommodation in order to maintain employment. For those who would need some sort of accommodation, the expected cost to an employer has been estimated to be very low: More than 80 percent of accommodations cost an employer less than $500. (U.S. Equal Employment Opportunity Commission 1991: 25–27).

To comply with the provisions of the ADA, an employer cannot fail to make reasonable accommodation to the known disability of an applicant or employee if making such an accommodation would not pose substantial burdens to the employer. The obligation to make such reasonable accommodation is, in fact, considered a form of nondiscrimination; the failure to make it when it can be made is considered a discriminatory practice prohibited by the Act. Hiring an applicant who will not require such accommodation, in preference to an equally qualified person who will, is also considered a discriminatory practice. The law has been written to remove the matter of need for accommodation from the hiring, retention, promotion, or transfer decision. If the applicant or worker, with or without an accommodation that would not substantially burden the employer, can perform the specific job, the person with a disability should have the same chance at that job as a worker without one.

Undue Hardship

An employer is not required to provide an accommodation to an individual with a disability that will impose substantial difficulty for the conduct of the overall operation of the business. The employer could show that accommodating a worker with a disability would pose an "undue hardship" if doing so would be "unduly costly, extensive, substantial, or disruptive" or would "fundamentally alter the nature or operation of the business."

If a particular accommodation would pose such a hardship, but another method of accommodating a worker would not, the employer would be required to make the latter accommodation. For example, a maintenance worker who incurred a back injury and could no longer bend for long periods to do some of the work asks to have the tasks eliminated from the job description. The employer may be able to show that removing the tasks would be an undue hardship, because no other employee could perform them. However, suppose the employer learned that using different tools would permit the worker to perform the tasks without bending. The employer would be required to provide the worker with the requisite tools to do the job.

If an employer can show that the cost of the accommodation (for example, purchasing modified computer equipment for a person with multiple sclerosis who can use only one hand) would be inordinately expensive, the employer may be freed from the obligation to provide it. If the employee is willing to invest in the special computer, or if a rehabilitation agency will pay for the device, the employer would no longer be able to evade retaining the employee because of the need for this accommodation. If the cost to the employer is the only claim that an accommodation is an "undue hardship," and the cost is borne by someone other than the employer, the hardship has been removed. Failing to make the accommodation and retain the worker would then constitute a discriminatory practice.

In the past, employers may have been more willing to make accommodations for long-time workers with exceptional skills, but not for mediocre employees or those in less skilled positions. A newspaper editor who could no longer type because of a car accident might have been provided with extra secretarial assistance because of proved value to the paper in several years of excellent work. Suppose an employer refused to provide similar accommodation to a reporter with the same injury who needed the same type of assistance but had worked for the paper for only a year and whose performance had been rated only as satisfactory. Failing to make the accommodation in this latter situation might be considered a discriminatory practice, since decisions about accommodation may not be based upon a worker's past performance or length of service, as long as that performance has been at least satisfactory.

Performance Standards and Medical Examinations

The ADA facilitates employment of disabled people by eliminating barriers that may face them in the application or reassignment process, but not in doing the job itself. Sometimes employers use personality, intelligence, aptitude, or other tests that may screen out a person with impaired capacities in hearing, speaking, reading, or writing that pose more problems in taking the test than in doing the job. Employers must now ensure that their tests truly measure the skills needed for the job, and not simply the ability to manipulate a pencil, which may not be needed in doing the job. If the test is necessary, it must be provided in a manner that accommodates the disability of an applicant: with a sign interpreter for someone who is deaf; with a reader or taped, large print, or braille format for someone who is blind or has a learning disability; with an assistant who can record answers for someone who cannot write; or in an accessible physical location for someone with locomotion limitations.

Of even more consequence for the employment and reemployment of people with disabilities is the change in the procedure of using general medical examinations and medical standards. Rather than posing such questions to an applicant as: "Have you ever had (list of disabilities), an employer may only ask on an application or in a personal interview about the capacity to perform a function—moving, lifting, or the like—that is related to handling an essential job task. Medical examinations may be given, but only under the conditions that they are administered *after an offer* of employment has been made; that they are administered uniformly to all people considering a particular assignment or job; and that the material obtained in them is kept confidential and separate from employment personnel files and other employee records.

Although a postoffer medical examination may ask about medical history or physical conditions that are not strictly related to performing the tasks of a particular position, the information obtained about non-job-related functions may not lawfully be used in making an employment decision. If, for example, a worker's hypertension is revealed during a medical exam, and if such hypertension may predispose the individual to a heart attack or stroke, the employer cannot withdraw an offer of a job, promotion, or assignment because of concern the company will someday have to pay disability benefits to the worker.

Direct Threat

An employer does not have to reinstate, promote, or hire someone for a position if there is evidence that the individual's disability will cause a substantial, direct threat to the health or safety of others, or to the person's own health or safety. An employer may not contend, however, that hypertension prevents a nurse from caring for a patient or a driver from operating a bus simply because of a myth, belief, or suspicion about hypertension. The direct threat must be based on knowledge of the duties of the job and the condition of the particular individual, not on ideas about people with disabilities in general or about people with a particular diagnosis. If the threat to health and safety can be removed by making a modification or a reasonable accommodation, the employer needs to make the accommodation if the person is capable of handling the job with that accommodation. Slightly increased risk to health or safety from employing in a particular position a worker with a disability does not constitute sufficient reason to refuse employment to such a person. For a threat to be a "direct threat," there must be objective, factual evidence to show that employing a particular person to perform a particular task poses a substantial risk of harm to self or others; that the harm is likely to occur; that the harm, should it occur, will be significant; and that no accommodation will ameliorate the problem. All these determinations—about a particular job, a particular employee, and a particular risk to the individual's or to others' health or safety—must be based on valid medical evidence and an individualized case-by-case determination, not on prevalent beliefs about conditions such as heart disease, cancer, diabetes, or deafness. The possiblity that strenuous work will exacerbate a back problem or that stress will cause a heart attack constitute speculation, not the sort of objective evidence intended by this exception. The exception of "direct threat" is designed, in fact, to indicate that some situations exist in which a person with particular skills is actually incapable of safely performing a task, and thus, in the broad sense, unqualified for it.

Employee Benefits

The benefits associated with employment must also be provided in a nondiscriminatory manner. The term *benefits* here refers not only to insurance, pension, and so forth, but also to such matters as leave policy or the use of the cafeteria, lounge, or health club provided for other workers. If an employer's attendance policy or insurance plan, however, adversely affects an individual with a disability, that employer may not be required to change it to accommodate the worker. Although such a change may be a reasonable accommodation, the employer may be able to show that making such a change would be an undue hardship. If an employer's proposed new insurance plan with exclusions for pre-existing conditions would exclude a worker from coverage for a pre-existing heart condition, the employer's insurance plan may refuse to provide the worker with coverage for the existing condition, but not for other conditions.

Drug Addiction and Alcoholism

The obligations of the Americans with Disabilities Act do not extend to the employment or reinstatement of people known to be using illegal drugs, or require the employment or retention of workers whose performance is impeded by alcoholism. If, however, an individual is completing or has completed a rehabilitation program designed to permit the person to function without drugs or alcohol, the Act's employment obligations extend to such an individual. The person, while perhaps no longer disabled, has a record of disability, or may be regarded as having a disability. If she or he can perform the job satisfactorily and safely, that history of previous addiction cannot be a bar to reinstatement or to new employment.

Employment Provisions of Other Laws

By 1994, all but the smallest employers in the nation will be subject to the obligations that have been discussed. Many large and small employers are already subject to equal opportunity laws covering people with disabilities. Requirements are substantially similar across laws. The Rehabilitation Act of 1973 requires contractors with federal government agencies to take affirmative action to employ and to advance in employment those with disabilities. Such contractors have been obliged to comply with various requirements of affirmative action plans, which will not affect those companies that comply with ADA but do not do business with the federal government. Section 504 of the Rehabilitation Act requires recipients of grants from the government to remove discriminatory barriers to the employment of people with disabilities and to make reasonable accommodations to such workers that closely resemble those of the Americans with Disabilities Act.

More than half the states in the nation have equal opportunity laws that cover people with some or all disabilities in some or all sectors of employment. Although not all these laws require employers to expend money to accommodate disabled workers, some do. Others, while not requiring such employer investment, require that a person who is qualified to perform the job in a reasonable manner, even with somewhat different techniques that do not cost an employer any money, may have to be hired or reinstated. Some provisions of state laws (for example, in New York) may contain more stringent obligations on employers than does the Americans with Disabilities Act, particularly with regard to employment medical exams and insurance benefits. The ADA explicitly indicates that employers governed by a law giving greater protection to the person with a disability than given by the ADA must abide by the stricter standard.

Legislation Providing Services to Employer and Employee

Numerous government programs, provided as a result of legislation, offer services to people with disabilities. Many of them are appropriate resources for both employers and employees to utilize in a disability management effort.

The Rehabilitation Act of 1973

One section of the Rehabilitation Act of 1973 addresses the provision of vocational rehabilitation services by public agencies. Every state has a public vocational rehabilitation program that provides services to disabled individuals, whether they incurred their disabilities on or off the job. Since 1920, a system of state vocational rehabilitation agencies has existed to provide such services. The most comprehensive provisions are contained in Title I of the Rehabilitation Act of 1973. The agencies can provide counseling, guidance, referral and placement services; vocational and training services; physical and mental restoration services; an income stipend during the rehabilitation program; interpreter and reader services; transportation to rehabilitation facilities; and assistive aids and devices. Generally, people with disabilities who wish to obtain these services are assigned to a vocational rehabilitation counselor who coordinates access to them.

In the past, neither people with disabilities nor employers have given uniformly high marks to the vocational rehabilitation system. Access to services has been slow and cumbersome and all-too-dependent upon the views and inclinations of overworked counselors. Often problems in the receipt of rehabilitation services arise because there is little or no coordination between a worker's predisability employer and the rehabilitation counselor.

Key to effective disability management is linkage by the employer with the public, nonprofit, and private rehabilitation facilities available to its workers. All those units of a company that might be involved in employing or terminating a disabled worker—whether the EEO officer, benefits manager, human resources department, or EAP—should establish a working relationship with such agencies and know the name of someone who can be called on for advice as soon as the company foresees a problem relating to a worker's disability.

In fact, the employer can offer to assist a newly disabled worker with his or her initial contact with the agency. If the employer advises the rehabilitation agency that it is interested in retaining a newly disabled worker, the process of rehabilitation is immeasurably eased. The worker knows that there will be a place to which to return when rehabilitation is completed, or perhaps even while rehabilitation is going on. Employer, employee, and agency staff should meet as soon as a worker is well enough to discuss the future. The company can offer to have the counselor visit the worker's jobsite to see whether the assignment can be resumed, with or without modifications or accommodation. If not, the counselor can work with the employer and employee to fashion a satisfactory set of accommodations or new assignments. Perhaps the employer can arrange to have a worker use accrued sick leave, disability leave, or other time in order to get any necessary specialized training from a rehabilitation facility that will enable a return to employment.

Past frustrations with the public system have caused some employers to look to the for-profit provider of rehabilitation services for its disabled employees. In some instances, the for-profit provider may have more flexibility than a state program or may be more skilled in dealing with a specific type of work assignment. This is discussed further in Chapters 5 and 6. However, the Rehabilitation Act provisions, the public agencies it establishes, and a creative partnership between employer and agency all can provide a network of effective and free services to people who might otherwise remain unemployed.

Other Assistance for Employers and Workers

In addition to the comprehensive rehabilitation services for people with disabilities authorized by federal legislation, workers and their employers can take advantage of technological support and financial incentives created by recent federal and state legislation seeking to increase the productivity of the nation's disabled citizens.

Technology-Related Assistance for Individuals with Disabilities Act

Recent legislation is providing a means for states to establish programs to develop, provide, and promote technological devices that help people with disabilities perform everyday tasks. Although the program established by the Technology-Related Assistance for Individuals with Disabilities Act of 1988 is still small, it is an important potential source of aids and devices that would allow a worker with a disability to live more independently, perform a wider range of jobs, or return to work more quickly.

Public Law 100-407 has two parts. Title I establishes a series of grants to states to set up programs to encourage the use of assistive technology. Title II sets up several national programs, including studies to investigate financing of technology, the development of an information and referral network, and a public education campaign. Employers and employees in states with such technology programs (which eventually will be the entire nation) can call the local organization sponsoring the project and ask for help in devising a technological accommodation for an employee. A list of the state organizations is found in Appendix 2-3.

Americans with Disabilities Act

Until the ADA, all organizations that received federal contracts were required to meet certain accessibility standards. The ADA moves the accessibility requirement into the private sector. Title III requires that public places be made accessible to people with disabilities. Examples of public places include hotels, restaurants, stores, service establishments, museums, libraries, public transit stations, schools, parks, and recreation facilities. Virtually every employing establishment must alter its facilities or practices to better serve customers with disabling conditions. Not only must the places be physically accessible, but the services offered must also be offered in the most integrated setting possible. "Reasonable modifications" must be made unless they would "fundamentally alter" the nature of the service or pose an "undue burden." Structural barriers must be removed if such changes are "readily achievable," which is defined as "easily accomplishable and able to be carried out without much difficulty or expense." These changes will not happen quickly or easily, but they remove some of the non-worksite barriers to employment of people with disabilities.

The ADA also requires that virtually all public (subways, buses) and some private (intercity bus companies, trains) transportation systems become at least somewhat accessible to people with disabilities. The lead time for some modifications is as long as twenty years, and there are significant limits on the extent of the requirements. To the extent that transportation becomes accessible, it will become much easier for employees with disabilities to get to and from work. It will also be much easier for them to travel in the course of their work. Discrimination in air travel is prohibited by another law, the Air Carrier Access Act.

Work duties will also be facilitated by Title IV, which requires that public communications be accessible to people with hearing and speech impairments. All organizations that are reachable to the public or to other places of business by telephone will be required to cooperate in relay systems that make their telephone service available to people with speech and hearing disabilities. This will enable a deaf secretary to conduct work requiring communicating with people outside the company through such relay systems.

Financial Incentives for Employers and Employees

Various state and federal laws permit an employer who makes extensive physical modifications to a place of work in order to accommodate someone with a disability to obtain some tax credit for this activity. It is not clear whether the Title III or IV requirements of the ADA will affect such tax laws, but employers should learn whether any of their expenses entailed in employing or reemploying people with disabilities can ease their tax burden.

In contemplating the return to work, the person with a disability has faced financial disincentives as well. If the person was receiving a benefit from Social Security Disability Insurance (SSDI) that entitled him or her to a monthly income and to reimbursement for medical expenses through Medicare, he or she might have feared that an unsuccessful try at work would deprive self and family of the sole source of financial security. Changes in the Social Security program aid both the worker and the employer in attempting to arrange work after onset of disability.

Wage Replacement: Last Resort

Three types of laws provide wage replacement to people who, temporarily or permanently, cannot return to their former job or to any other available work. Workers compensation benefits and short- and long-term disability benefits are part of what an employer will contribute to a person's livelihood if that person cannot be reemployed. Such benefits payments are already a substantial portion of every employer's costs; any costs of modifying facilities and accommodating workers with disabilities can be considered as potentially reducing the costs of paying people to stay out of the work force.

Workers Compensation Laws

Workers compensation laws vary by state. All of them presume that the employer must contribute some portion of a worker's former salary to his or her support if an incapacitating or partially incapacitating injury or illness can be attributed to the work environment or was somehow sustained in the course of performing the job. One major difference in the compensation laws that seems to affect employees' return to work is the wage replacement ratio (the percentage of the employee's original wage paid by the workers compensation program). This ratio ranges from 50 to 80 percent and is most commonly two thirds of the employee's salary, but it is subject to minimum and maximum provisions.

Numerous studies (see Chapter 9 for a fuller discussion of these issues) have shown that the higher the wage replacement ratio, the more difficult it is to bring employees back to work. If a worker is relatively highly paid, the maximum provisions will cap his or her benefits at a level far below the ratio, prompting return to work. The higher-salaried worker may also feel most connected to the workplace as a source of self-definition and social relationship. Or, perhaps, high-salaried employees are more valued by their companies, and the companies have in the past made greater efforts to take them back.

The ADA provisions may increase a company's and a worker's conviction that reemployment and not compensation is appropriate and desirable. Rehabilitation benefits are part of the workers compensation benefits package. Different states have mandates as to the extent of the employer's obligation to pay for rehabilitation services. Many state laws require that the employee cooperate in rehabilitation or forfeit cash benefits.

Mandatory Employer Disability Programs

The workers compensation laws apply only to an employer's obligation to someone whose disability is linked to the workplace. Obviously, off-the-job accidents or illnesses contribute substantially to the total disability that affects one sixth of Americans of working age. Five states and one territory (California, Hawaii, New Jersey, New York, Rhode Island, and Puerto Rico) have mandatory, state-sponsored short-term disability programs. The programs provide wage replacement benefits for employees disabled off the job for twenty-six weeks (California has fifty-two weeks and Rhode Island thirty). There is generally a waiting period of seven days before benefits begin. The different jurisdictions have different maximum benefits levels. Benefits are offset by other sources of income.

Many categories of employers in most states provide some amount of long-term disability coverage for people who can no longer work, regardless of the reason for their incapacity. Benefits levels, employers covered, amounts of work done by an eligible employee, and length of coverage all vary and are not explored here. (Any employer of any size is already familiar with such obligations.) Many employers' and insurers' long-term disability (LTD) programs have provisions that reduce LTD benefits by the amount of the SSDI payments if the employee qualifies for the SSDI program.

Social Security Disability Insurance

Two aspects of the Social Security program are of critical importance to employers: the use of Social Security Disability Insurance (SSDI) benefits to offset long-term disability claims, and the availability of work incentives to encourage current SSDI recipients to enter the work force. To qualify for the SSDI program, applicants must have paid Social Security taxes for a certain number of quarters, which varies by the age of the applicant (maximum requirement is ten years). Entry into the SSDI program also qualifies people for Medicare two years after SSDI eligibility. In order to make use of the provision that offsets an employer's disability payments with SSDI benefits, many plan policies require employees entering LTD to apply for SSDI benefits at the same time. Obtaining SSDI benefits is not automatic by any means, and sometimes employees must appeal initial benefits denials. Some companies have found it cost-effective to provide employees with legal counsel and even legal representation at appeal hearings in order to maximize the chances for a positive decision since SSDI benefits reduce the employer's liability under most LTD insurance plans.

To qualify for benefits, the employee must prove that he or she is "disabled." The Social Security Administration definition of disability differs from that used by the Rehabilitation Act of 1973 and the Americans with Disabilities Act of 1990. It consists of two parts:

1. The inability to engage in any substantial gainful activity (SGA) by reason of any medically determinable physical or mental impairment that can be expected to result in death or has lasted or can be expected to last for a continuous period of not less than twelve months.

2. The level of substantial gainful activity is quite low—$500 per month. (Many of these rules, including the level of SGA, are different for people who are blind.) The $500 figure is in addition to "impairment-related work expenses" (costs for items related to the disability that allow the employee to work) or "employer wage subsidies" (payments to another person to assist the employee at work or payments to the employee above his or her productivity level). SSDI cash benefits begin five months after the disability occurs, but can be reinstated immediately if the worker reapplies for benefits within five years of leaving the benefits roll. Medicare benefits begin twenty-four months after the cash benefits.

Once the employee is approved for benefits, the case is reviewed every seven years if no improvement is expected; every three years if improvement is possible; and at determined intervals if improvement is expected. The benefits last for the duration of the beneficiary's life or until age 65 while the person continues to qualify for the program.

SSDI benefits are valuable to those who cannot work any longer, and they provide some financial relief for employers. Disability management policy is more interested in returning people to work than in having them linger as beneficiaries. The work incentive provisions of the Social Security program augment those of the Rehabilitation Act of 1973 and the other laws that assist workers with disabilities. Since 1980, Congress has passed a series of bills that have provided incentives for beneficiaries to leave the Social Security rolls and return to work.

Before that time, beneficiaries feared that they would lose both income security and medical care coverage should their work placement not be successful. The work incentive programs were designed to provide a cushion that would allow beneficiaries to establish themselves in the work force before losing their benefits status. Programs include a trial work period (where income support is maintained), extended eligibility status (during which an employee can retain entitlement to Medicare), and the ability to buy into Medicare at the end of the extended eligibility period, depending upon income. Particularly the possibility that certain SSDI beneficiaries could retain some Medicare coverage while employed may enable small businesses with limited insurance benefits to hire or reinstate people who will need extensive medical services that might be excluded by a benefits plan. After a certain time on SSDI, for the individual who returns to work with earnings of less than 200 percent of poverty level, the Medicare premium is subsidized. As long as the employee's disability persists, he or she may buy into Medicare.

For example, assume that a new employee remains medically disabled, makes at least minimum wage (that is, more than $500 per month), and remains permanently employed. The employee will continue to receive SSDI benefits during the first twelve months of employment. The employee will continue to be eligible for Medicare for the first four years of employment and may buy into Medicare after that time.

In 1980, Frank Bowe, a leader in disability advocacy, criticized the federal government for spending billions to keep people with disabilities dependent and much less to help them remain independent, contributing, and productive members of society. With the provisions embodied in the Americans with Disabilities Act, the services authorized by the Rehabilitation Act of 1973 and other laws, and the recent changes in Social Security legislation, the government has taken very substantial steps toward the independence of Americans with disabilities. Employers can rely on this set of laws to assist them in their quest to retain valuable workers at reasonable costs.

Appendix 2-1
Americans with Disabilities Act Checklist for Title I (Employment)

The following checklist helps determine that the workplace is in conformance with ADA regulations. All questions should be answered "yes" to meet requirements.

Recruitment

	Yes	No
1. Recruitment materials include positive references to persons with disabilities in photos and in written words and cite the company's commitment to nondiscrimination.	☐	☐
2. All positions, including those above entry level, are open to qualified applicants with disabilities seeking opportunities for career advancement.	☐	☐
3. Advertisements for personnel encourage response from qualified persons with disabilities and are placed in forums and in ways that reach these persons (for example, in publications directed to consumers with disabilities and via taped messages for individuals with vision impairments).	☐	☐
4. The company refuses to participate in a contractual or other relationship with an employment or referral agency, a labor union, an organization providing fringe benefits, or an organization providing training and apprenticeship programs that appears to subject qualified applicants to discrimination.	☐	☐

Preselection Criteria

	Yes	No
5. Rooms in which interviews are conducted are accessible to persons with all types of disabilities, including mobility limitations.	☐	☐
6. At least one person is trained to administer tests designed for applicants with impaired sensory, manual, or speaking skills.	☐	☐

	Yes	No
7. Applicants are notified that alternate means of testing are available.	☐	☐
8. Any tests, forms, or selection criteria used relate strictly to a specific job and are consistent with business necessity.	☐	☐
9. Neither applications nor interviewers ask whether an applicant has a disability or questions the nature or extent of a disability (but may solicit information regarding an applicant's ability to perform essential job functions).	☐	☐
10. Equal consideration is given to applicants whose spouse or other family member has a disability.	☐	☐
11. If a particular job raises safety considerations, any eligibility criteria regarding mental or physical abilities developed to ensure safe performance shall include only criteria that are each objectively and demonstrably necessary for safety in the performance of the essential functions of the specific job.	☐	☐
12. No pre-employment medical examinations are required (but may be required after an offer of employment if all entering employees are subjected to the same examination regardless of disability).	☐	☐
13. Information obtained in any medical exam is collected and maintained on separate forms and in separate medical files.	☐	☐
14. Medical history and information is considered confidential and shared only with supervisors and managers concerned with work restrictions and accommodations, personnel who provide first aid and emergency treatment that may be needed, and government officials investigating compliance with the ADA.	☐	☐

Reasonable Accommodations

	Yes	No
15. Reasonable accommodations to the known physical or mental limitations of an employee are provided throughout the employee's term of employment unless the accommodations impose an undue hardship (are significantly difficult or expensive) on the operation of the company's business.	☐	☐

	Yes	No
16. Accommodations suitable for individual employees are determined on a case-by-case basis by supervisors in consultation with the individual involved and after obtaining information and input from appropriate disability-related organizations and other agencies and groups with expertise on such accommodations.	☐	☐
17. Accommodations include, but are not limited to, the following:		
a. Making existing facilities used by all employees readily accessible to and usable by individuals with disabilities.	☐	☐
b. Restructuring a job by assigning nonessential elements to another employee, or introducing other modifications that enable the employee with a disability to perform the essential functions of a position.	☐	☐
c. Allowing constant shifts and part-time or modified work schedules.	☐	☐
d. Reassigning or transferring an employee to another vacant job for which he or she is qualified.	☐	☐
e. Adjusting marginal job requirements, such as the need to hold a driver's license, that are nonessential for performing a specific job.	☐	☐
f. Acquiring or modifying equipment or devices for the disabled, for example, adapting hardware or software for computers to talking calculators for employees with vision impairments, telephone handset amplifiers or telecommunication devices for persons with hearing impairments, and mechanical page turners or raised or lowered furniture for persons with limited dexterity.	☐	☐
g. Providing readers for persons with blindness, interpreters for individuals with deafness, or attendants for those with severe mobility limitations, when feasible.	☐	☐
18. Employees and job applicants are notified of the company's obligation under the ADA to make reasonable accommodations.	☐	☐

	Yes	No
19. A problem-solving approach is used to identify particular tasks or aspects of the work environment that limit performance and could be remedied to provide meaningful equal opportunity to an individual with a disability.	☐	☐
20. The company shows no discrimination toward qualified employees or applicants who have disabilities in any term, condition, or privilege of employment, including—but not limited to—the following areas:		
a. Upgrade	☐	☐
b. Promotion	☐	☐
c. Tenure	☐	☐
d. Demotion	☐	☐
e. Transfer	☐	☐
f. Termination	☐	☐
g. Rehiring	☐	☐
h. Compensation and change in compensation	☐	☐
i. Job assignment	☐	☐
j. Job classification	☐	☐
k. Organizational structure	☐	☐
l. Line of progression	☐	☐
m. Leave of absence	☐	☐
n. Sick leave or any other leave	☐	☐
o. Fringe benefits, including health and other insurance coverage and provisions, available to all by virtue of employment	☐	☐
p. Selection and financial support for training, including apprenticeships, professional meetings, and related activities	☐	☐
q. Employer-sponsored activities, including social or recreational programs	☐	☐
21. The company understands that attitudes toward hiring people with disabilities may frequently be the only change needed.	☐	☐

Appendix 2-2
Regulations to Implement the Equal Employment Provisions of the Americans with Disabilities Act of 1990

PART 1630—REGULATIONS TO IMPLEMENT THE EQUAL EMPLOYMENT PROVISIONS OF THE AMERICANS WITH DISABILITIES ACT

Sec.

Appendix to Part 1630—Interpretive Guidance on Title I of the Americans with Disabilities Act

Authority: 42 U.S.C. 12116.

§ 1630.1 Purpose, applicability, and construction.

(a) *Purpose.* The purpose of this part is to implement title I of the Americans with Disabilities Act (42 U.S.C. 12101, *et seq.*) (ADA), requiring equal employment opportunities for qualified individuals with disabilities, and sections 3(2), 3(3), 501, 503, 506(e), 508, 510, and 511 of the ADA as those sections pertain to the employment of qualified individuals with disabilities.

(b) *Applicability.* This part applies to "covered entities" as defined at § 1630.2(b).

(c) *Construction.*—(1) *In general.* Except as otherwise provided in this part, this part does not apply a lesser standard than the standards applied under title V of the Rehabilitation Act of 1973 (29 U.S.C. 790–794a), or the regulations issued by Federal agencies pursuant to that title.

(2) *Relationship to other laws.* This part does not invalidate or limit the remedies, rights, and procedures

From the *Federal Register* 56 (144), July 26, 1991.

of any Federal law or law of any State or political subdivision of any State or jurisdiction that provides greater or equal protection for the rights of individuals with disabilities than are afforded by this part.

§ 1630.2 Definitions.

(a) *Commission* means the Equal Employment Opportunity Commission established by section 705 of the Civil Rights Act of 1964 (42 U.S.C. 2000e–4).

(b) *Covered entity* means an employer, employment agency, labor organization, or joint labor management committee.

(c) *Person, labor organization, employment agency, commerce and industry affecting commerce* shall have the same meaning given those terms in section 701 of the Civil Rights Act of 1964 (42 U.S.C. 2000e).

(d) *State* means each of the several States, the District of Columbia, the Commonwealth of Puerto Rico, Guam, American Samoa, the Virgin Islands, the Trust Territory of the Pacific Islands, and the Commonwealth of the Northern Mariana Islands.

(e) *Employer.*—(1) *In general.* The term employer means a person engaged in an industry affecting commerce who has 15 or more employees for each working day in each of 20 or more calendar weeks in the current or preceding calendar year, and any agent of such person, except that, from July 26, 1992 through July 25, 1994, an employer means a person engaged in an industry affecting commerce who has 25 or more employees for each working day in each of 20 or more calendar weeks in the current or preceding year and any agent of such person.

(2) *Exceptions.* The term *employer* does not include—

(i) The United States, a corporation wholly owned by the government of the United States, or an Indian tribe; or

(ii) A bona fide private membership club (other than a labor organization) that is exempt from taxation under section 501(c) of the Internal Revenue Code of 1986.

(f) *Employee* means an individual employed by an employer.

(g) *Disability* means, with respect to an individual—

(1) A physical or mental impairment that substantially limits one or more of the major life activities of such individual;

(2) A record of such an impairment; or

(3) Being regarded as having such an impairment. (See § 1630.3 for exceptions to this definition.)

(h) *Physical or mental impairment* means:

(1) Any physiological disorder, or condition, cosmetic disfigurement, or anatomical loss affecting one or more of the following body systems: neurological, musculoskeletal, special sense organs, respiratory (including speech organs), cardiovascular, reproductive, digestive, genito-urinary, hemic and lymphatic, skin, and endocrine; or

(2) Any mental or psychological disorder, such as mental retardation, organic brain syndrome, emotional or mental illness, and specific learning disabilities.

(i) *Major life activities* means functions such as caring for oneself, performing manual tasks, walking, seeing, hearing, speaking, breathing, learning, and working.

(j) *Substantially limits*—(1) The term *substantially limits* means:

(i) Unable to perform a major life activity that the average person in the general population can perform; or

(ii) Significantly restricted as to the condition, manner or duration under which an individual can perform a particular major life activity as compared to the condition, manner, or duration under which the average person in the general population can perform that same major life activity.

(2) The following factors should be considered in determining whether an individual is substantially limited in a major life activity:

(i) The nature and severity of the impairment;

(ii) The duration or expected duration of the impairment; and

(iii) The permanent or long-term impact, or the expected permanent or long-term impact of or resulting from the impairment.

(3) With respect to the major life activity of *working*—

(i) The term *substantially limits* means significantly restricted in the ability to perform either a class of jobs or a broad range of jobs in various classes as compared to the average person having comparable training, skills and abilities. The inability to perform a single, particular job does not constitute a substantial limitation in the major life activity of working.

(ii) In addition to the factors listed in paragraph (j)(2) of this section, the following factors may be considered in determining whether an individual is substantially limited in the major life activity of "working":

(A) The geographical area to which the individual has reasonable access;

(B) The job from which the individual has been disqualified because of an impairment, and the number and types of jobs utilizing similar training, knowledge, skills or abilities, within that geographical area, from which the individual is also disqualified because of the impairment (class of jobs); and/or

(C) The job from which the individual has been disqualified because of an impairment, and the number and types of other jobs not utilizing similar training, knowledge, skills or abilities, within that geographical area, from which the individual is also disqualified because of the impairment (broad range of jobs in various classes).

(k) *Has a record of such impairment* means has a history of, or has been misclassified as having, a mental or physical impairment that substantially limits one or more major life activities.

(l) *Is regarded as having such an impairment* means:

(1) Has a physical or mental impairment that does not substantially limit major life activities but is treated by a covered entity as constituting such limitation;

(2) Has a physical or mental impairment that substantially limits major life activities only as a result of the attitudes of others toward such impairment; or

(3) Has none of the impairments defined in paragraphs (h) (1) or (2) of this section but is treated by a covered entity as having a substantially limiting impairment.

(m) *Qualified individual with a disability* means an individual with a disability who satisfies the requisite skill, experience, education and other job-related requirements of the employment position such individual holds or desires, and who, with or without reasonable accommodation, can perform the essential functions of such position. (See § 1630.3 for exceptions to this definition).

(n) *Essential functions.*—(1) *In general.* The term *essential functions* means the fundamental job duties of the employment position the individual with a disability holds or desires. The term "essential functions" does not include the marginal functions of the position.

(2) A job function may be considered essential for any of several reasons, including but not limited to the following:

(i) The function may be essential because the reason the position exists is to perform that function;

(ii) The function may be essential because of the limited number of employees available among whom the performance of that job function can be distributed; and/or

(iii) The function may be highly specialized so that the incumbent in the position is hired for his or her expertise or ability to perform the particular function.

(3) Evidence of whether a particular function is essential includes, but is not limited to:

(i) The employer's judgment as to which functions are essential;

(ii) Written job descriptions prepared before advertising or interviewing applicants for the job;

(iii) The amount of time spent on the job performing the function;

(iv) The consequences of not requiring the incumbent to perform the function;

(v) The terms of a collective bargaining agreement;

(vi) The work experience of past incumbents in the job; and/or

(vii) The current work experience of incumbents in similar jobs.

(o) *Reasonable accommodation.* (1) The term *reasonable accommodation* means:

(i) Modifications or adjustments to a job application process that enable a qualified applicant with a disability to be considered for the position such qualified applicant desires; or

(ii) Modifications or adjustments to the work environment, or to the manner or circumstances under which the position held or desired is customarily performed, that enable a qualified individual with a disability to perform the essential functions of that position; or

(iii) Modifications or adjustments that enable a covered entity's employee with a disability to enjoy equal benefits and privileges of employment as are enjoyed by its other similarly situated employees without disabilities.

(2) *Reasonable accommodation* may include but is not limited to:

(i) Making existing facilities used by employees readily accessible to and usable by individuals with disabilities; and

(ii) Job restructuring; part-time or modified work schedules; reassignment to a vacant position; acquisition or modifications of equipment or devices; appropriate adjustment or modifications of examinations, training materials, or policies; the provision of qualified readers or interpreters; and other similar accommodations for individuals with disabilities.

(3) To determine the appropriate reasonable accommodation it may be necessary for the covered entity to initiate an informal, interactive process with the qualified individual with a disability in need of the accommodation. This process should identify the precise limitations resulting from the disability and potential reasonable accommodations that could overcome those limitations.

(p) *Undue hardship*—(1) *In general. Undue hardship* means, with respect to the provision of an accommodation, significant difficulty or expense incurred by a covered entity, when considered in light of the factors set forth in paragraph (p)(2) of this section.

(2) *Factors to be considered.* In determining whether an accommodation would impose an undue hardship on a covered entity, factors to be considered include:

(i) The nature and net cost of the accommodation needed under this part, taking into consideration the availability of tax credits and deductions, and/or outside funding;

(ii) The overall financial resources of the facility or facilities involved in the provision of the reasonable accommodation, the number of persons employed at such facility, and the effect on expenses and resources;

(iii) The overall financial resources of the covered entity, the overall size of the business of the covered entity with respect to the number of its employees, and the number, type and location of its facilities;

(iv) The type of operation or operations of the covered entity, including the composition, structure and functions of the workforce of such entity, and the geographic separateness and administrative or fiscal relationship of the facility or facilities in question to the covered entity; and

(v) The impact of the accommodation upon the operation of the facility, including the impact on the ability of other employees to perform their duties and the impact on the facility's ability to conduct business.

(q) *Qualification standards* means the personal and professional attributes including the skill, experience, education, physical, medical, safety and other requirements established by a covered entity as requirements which an individual must meet in order to be eligible for the position held or desired.

(r) *Direct threat* means a significant risk of substantial harm to the health or safety of the individual or others that cannot be eliminated or reduced by reasonable accommodation. The determination that an individual poses a "direct threat" shall be based on an individualized assessment of the individual's present ability to safely perform the essential functions of the job. This assessment shall be based on a reasonable medical judgment that relies on the most current medical knowledge and/or on the best available objective evidence. In determining whether an individual would pose a direct threat, the factors to be considered include:

(1) The duration of the risk;

(2) The nature and severity of the potential harm;

(3) The likelihood that the potential harm will occur; and

(4) The imminence of the potential harm.

§ 1630.3 Exceptions to the definitions of "Disability" and "Qualified Individual with a Disability."

(a) The terms *disability* and *qualified individual with a disability* do not include individuals currently engaging in the illegal use of drugs, when the covered entity acts on the basis of such use.

(1) *Drug* means a controlled substance, as defined in schedules I through V of Section 202 of the Controlled Substances Act (21 U.S.C. 812)

(2) *Illegal use of drugs* means the use of drugs the possession or distribution of which is unlawful under the Controlled Substances Act, as periodically updated by the Food and Drug Administration. This term does not include the use of a drug taken under the supervision of a licensed health care professional, or other uses authorized by the Controlled Substances Act or other provisions of Federal law.

(b) However, the terms *disability* and *qualified* individual with a disability may not exclude an individual who:

(1) Has successfully completed a supervised drug rehabilitation program and is no longer engaging in the illegal use of drugs, or has otherwise been rehabilitated successfully and is no longer engaging in the illegal use of drugs; or

(2) Is participating in a supervised rehabilitation program and is no longer engaging in such use; or

(3) Is erroneously regarded as engaging in such use, but is not engaging in such use.

(c) It shall not be a violation of this part for a covered entity to adopt or administer reasonable policies or procedures, including but not limited to drug testing, designed to ensure that an individual described in paragraph (b) (1) or (2) of this section is no longer engaging in the illegal use of drugs. (See § 1630.16(c) Drug testing).

(d) *Disability* does not include:

(1) Transvestism, transsexualism, pedophilia, exhibitionism, voyeurism, gender identity disorders not resulting from physical impairments, or other sexual behavior disorders;

(2) Compulsive gambling, kleptomania, or pyromania; or

(3) Psychoactive substance use disorders resulting from current illegal use of drugs.

(e) *Homosexuality and bisexuality* are not impairments and so are not disabilities as defined in this part.

§ 1630.4 Discrimination prohibited.

It is unlawful for a covered entity to discriminate on the basis of disability against a qualified individual with a disability in regard to:

(a) Recruitment, advertising, and job application procedures;

(b) Hiring, upgrading, promotion, award of tenure, demotion, transfer, layoff, termination, right of return from layoff, and rehiring;

(c) Rates of pay or any other form of compensation and changes in compensation;

(d) Job assignments, job classifications, organizational structures, position descriptions, lines of progression, and seniority lists;

(e) Leaves of absence, sick leave, or any other leave;

(f) Fringe benefits available by virtue of employment, whether or not administered by the covered entity;

(g) Selection and financial support for training, including: apprenticeships, professional meetings, conferences and other related activities, and selection for leaves of absence to pursue training;

(h) Activities sponsored by a covered entity including social and recreational programs; and

(i) Any other term, condition, or privilege of employment. The term *discrimination* includes, but is not limited to, the acts described in §§ 1630.5 through 1630.13 of this part.

§ 1630.5 Limiting, segregating, and classifying.

It is unlawful for a covered entity to limit, segregate, or classify a job applicant or employee in a way that adversely affects his or her employment opportunities or status on the basis of disability.

§ 1630.6 Contractual or other arrangements.

(a) *In general.* It is unlawful for a covered entity to participate in a contractual or other arrangement or relationship that has the effect of subjecting the covered entity's own qualified applicant or employee with a disability to the discrimination prohibited by this part.

(b) *Contractual or other arrangement defined.* The phrase *contractual or other arrangement or relationship* includes, but is not limited to, a relationship with an employment or referral agency; labor union, including collective bargaining agreements; an organization providing fringe benefits to an employee of the covered entity; or an organization providing training and apprenticeship programs.

(c) *Application.* This section applies to a covered entity, with respect to its own applicants or employees, whether the entity offered the contract or initiated the relationship, or whether the entity accepted the contract or acceded to the relationship. A covered entity is not liable for the actions of the other party or parties to the contract which only affect that other party's employees or applicants.

§ 1630.7 Standards, criteria, or methods of administration.

It is unlawful for a covered entity to use standards, criteria, or methods of administration, which are not job-related and consistent with business necessity, and:

(a) That have the effect of discriminating on the basis of disability; or

(b) That perpetuate the discrimination of others who are subject to common administrative control.

§ 1630.8 Relationship or association with an individual with a disability.

It is unlawful for a covered entity to exclude or deny equal jobs or benefits to, or otherwise discriminate against, a qualified individual because of the known disability of an individual with whom the qualified individual is known to have a family, business, social or other relationship or association.

§ 1630.9 Not making reasonable accommodation.

(a) It is unlawful for a covered entity not to make reasonable accommodation to the known physical or mental limitations of an otherwise qualified applicant or employee with a disability, unless such covered entity can demonstrate that the accommodation would impose an undue hardship on the operation of its business.

(b) It is unlawful for a covered entity to deny employment opportunities to an otherwise qualified job applicant or employee with a disability based on the need of such covered entity to make reasonable accommodation to such individual's physical or mental impairments.

(c) A covered entity shall not be excused from the requirements of this part because of any failure to receive technical assistance authorized by section 506 of the ADA, including any failure in the development or dissemination of any technical assistance manual authorized by that Act.

(d) A qualified individual with a disability is not required to accept an accommodation, aid, service, opportunity or benefit which such qualified individual chooses not to accept. However, if such individual rejects a reasonable accommodation, aid, service, opportunity or benefit that is necessary to enable the individual to perform the essential functions of the position held or desired, and cannot, as a result of that rejection, perform the essential functions of the position, the individual will not be considered a qualified individual with a disability.

§ 1630.10 Qualification standards, tests, and other selection criteria.

It is unlawful for a covered entity to use qualification standards, employment tests or other selection criteria that screen out or tend to screen out an individual with a disability or a class of individuals with disabilities, on the basis of disability, unless the standard, test or other selection criteria, as used by the covered entity, is shown to be job-related for the position in question and is consistent with business necessity.

§ 1630.11 Administration of tests.

It is unlawful for a covered entity to fail to select and administer tests concerning employment in the most effective manner to ensure that, when a test is administered to a job applicant or employee who has a disability that impairs sensory, manual or speaking skills, the test results accurately reflect the skills, aptitude, or whatever other factor of the applicant or employee that the test purports to measure, rather than reflecting the impaired sensory, manual, or speaking skills of such employee or applicant (except where such skills are the factors that the test purports to measure).

§ 1630.12 Retaliation and coercion.

(a) *Retaliation.* It is unlawful to discriminate against any individual because that individual has opposed any act or practice made unlawful by this part or because that individual made a charge, testified, assisted, or participated in any manner in an investigation, proceeding, or hearing to enforce any provision contained in this part.

(b) *Coercion, interference or intimidation.* It is unlawful to coerce, intimidate, threaten, harass or interfere with any individual in the exercise or enjoyment of, or because that individual aided or encouraged any other individual in the exercise of, any right granted or protected by this part.

§ 1630.13 Prohibited medical examinations and inquiries.

(a) *Pre-employment examination or inquiry.* Except as permitted by § 1630.14, it is unlawful for a covered entity to conduct a medical examination of an applicant or to make inquiries as to whether an applicant is an individual with a disability or as to the nature or severity of such disability.

(b) *Examination or inquiry of employees.* Except as permitted by § 1630.14, it is unlawful for a covered entity to require a medical examination of an employee or to make inquiries as to whether an employee is an individual with a disability or as to the nature or severity of such disability.

§ 1630.14 Medical examinations and inquiries specifically permitted.

(a) *Acceptable pre-employment inquiry.* A covered entity may make pre-employment inquiries into the ability of an applicant to perform job-related functions, and/or may ask an applicant to describe or to demonstrate how, with or without reasonable accommodation, the applicant will be able to perform job-related functions.

(b) *Employment entrance examination.* A covered entity may require a medical examination (and/or inquiry) after making an offer of employment to a job applicant and before the applicant begins his or her employment duties, and may condition an offer of employment on the results of such examination (and/or inquiry), if all entering employees in the same job category are subjected to such an examination (and/or inquiry) regardless of disability.

(1) Information obtained under paragraph (b) of this section regarding the medical condition or history of the applicant shall be collected and maintained on separate forms and in separate medical files and be treated as a confidential medical record, except that:

(i) Supervisors and managers may be informed regarding necessary restrictions on the work or duties of the employee and necessary accommodations;

(ii) First aid and safety personnel may be informed, when appropriate, if the disability might require emergency treatment; and

(iii) Government officials investigating compliance with this part shall be provided relevant information on request.

(2) The results of such examination shall not be used for any purpose inconsistent with this part.

(3) Medical examinations conducted in accordance with this section do not have to be job-related and consistent with business necessity. However, if certain criteria are used to screen out an employee or employees with disabilities as a result of such an examination or inquiry, the exclusionary criteria must be job-related and consistent with business necessity, and performance of the essential job functions cannot be accomplished with reasonable accommodation as required in this part. (See § 1630.15(b) Defenses to charges of discriminatory application of selection criteria.)

(c) *Examination of employees.* A covered entity may require a medical examination (and/or inquiry) of an employee that is job-related and consistent with business necessity. A covered entity may make inquiries into the ability of an employee to perform job-related functions.

(1) Information obtained under paragraph (c) of this section regarding the medical condition or history of any employee shall be collected and maintained on separate forms and in separate medical files and be treated as a confidential medical record, except that:

(i) Supervisors and managers may be informed regarding necessary restrictions on the work or duties of the employee and necessary accommodations;

(ii) First aid and safety personnel may be informed, when appropriate, if the disability might require emergency treatment; and

(iii) Government officials investigating compliance with this part shall be provided relevant information on request.

(2) Information obtained under paragraph (c) of this section regarding the medical condition or history of any employee shall not be used for any purpose inconsistent with this part.

(d) *Other acceptable examinations and inquiries.* A covered entity may conduct voluntary medical examinations and activities, including voluntary medical histories, which are part of an employee health program available to employees at the work site.

(1) Information obtained under paragraph (d) of this section regarding the medical condition or history of any employee shall be collected and maintained on separate forms and in separate medical files and be treated as a confidential medical record, except that:

(i) Supervisors and managers may be informed regarding necessary restrictions on the work or duties of the employee and necessary accommodations;

(ii) First aid and safety personnel may be informed, when appropriate, if the disability might require emergency treatment; and

(iii) Government officials investigating compliance with this part shall be provided relevant information on request.

(2) Information obtained under paragraph (d) of this section regarding the medical condition or history of any employee shall not be used for any purpose inconsistent with this part.

§ 1630.15 Defenses.

Defenses to an allegation of discrimination under this part may include, but are not limited to, the following:

(a) *Disparate treatment charges.* It may be a defense to a charge of disparate treatment brought under §§ 1630.4 through 1630.8 and 1630.11 through 1630.12 that the challenged action is justified by a legitimate, nondiscriminatory reason.

(b) *Charges of discriminatory application of selection criteria*—(1) *In general.* It may be a defense to a charge of discrimination, as described in § 1630.10, that an alleged application of qualification standards, tests, or selection criteria that screens out or tends to screen out or otherwise denies a job or benefit to an individual with a disability has been shown to be job-related and consistent with business necessity, and such performance cannot be accomplished with reasonable accommodation, as required in this part.

(2) *Direct threat as a qualification standard.* The term "qualification standard" may include a requirement that an individual shall not pose a direct threat to the health or safety of the individual or others in the workplace. (See § 1630.2(r) defining direct threat.)

(c) *Other disparate impact charges.* It may be a defense to a charge of discrimination brought under this part that a uniformly applied standard, criterion, or policy has a disparate impact on an individual with a disability or a class of individuals with disabilities that the challenged standard, criterion or policy has been shown to be job-related and consistent with business necessity, and such performance cannot be accomplished with reasonable accommodation, as required in this part.

(d) *Charges of not making reasonable accommodation.* It may be a defense to a charge of discrimination, as described in § 1630.9, that a requested or necessary accommodation would impose an undue hardship on the operation of the covered entity's business.

(e) *Conflict with other federal laws.* It may be a defense to a charge of discrimination under this part that a challenged action is required or necessitated by another Federal law or regulation, or that another Federal law or regulation prohibits an action (including the provision of a particular reasonable accommodation) that would otherwise be required by this part.

(f) *Additional defenses.* It may be a defense to a charge of discrimination under this part that the alleged discriminatory action is specifically permitted by §§ 1630.14 or 1630.16.

§ 1630.16 Specific activities permitted.

(a) *Religious entities.* A religious corporation, association, educational institution, or society is permitted to give preference in employment to individuals of a particular religion to perform work connected with the carrying on by that corporation, association, educational institution, or society of its activities. A religious entity may require that all applicants and employees conform to the religious tenets of such organization. However, a religious entity may not discriminate against a qualified individual, who satisfies the permitted religious criteria, because of his or her disability.

(b) *Regulation of alcohol and drugs.* A covered entity:

(1) May prohibit the illegal use of drugs and the use of alcohol at the workplace by all employees;

(2) May require that employees not be under the influence of alcohol or be engaging in the illegal use of drugs at the workplace;

(3) May require that all employees behave in conformance with the requirements established under the Drug-Free Workplace Act of 1988 (41 U.S.C. 701 et seq.);

(4) May hold an employee who engages in the illegal use of drugs or who is an alcoholic to the same qualification standards for employment or job performance and behavior to which the entity holds its other employees, even if any unsatisfactory performance or behavior is related to the employee's drug use or alcoholism;

(5) May require that its employees employed in an industry subject to such regulations comply with the standards established in the regulations (if any) of the Departments of Defense and Transportation, and of the Nuclear Regulatory Commission, regarding alcohol and the illegal use of drugs; and

(6) May require that employees employed in sensitive positions comply with the regulations (if any) of the Departments of Defense and Transportation and of the Nuclear Regulatory Commission that apply to employment in sensitive positions subject to such regulations.

(c) *Drug testing*—(1) *General policy.* For purposes of this part, a test to determine the illegal use of drugs is not considered a medical examination. Thus, the administration of such drug tests by a covered entity to its job applicants or employees is not a violation of § 1630.13 of this part. However, this part does not encourage, prohibit, or authorize a covered entity to conduct drug tests of job applicants or employees to determine the illegal use of drugs or to make employment decisions based on such test results.

(2) *Transportation employees.* This part does not encourage, prohibit, or authorize the otherwise lawful exercise by entities subject to the jurisdiction of the Department of Transportation of authority to:

(i) Test employees of entities in, and applicants for, positions involving safety sensitive duties for the illegal use of drugs or for on-duty impairment by alcohol; and

(ii) Remove from safety-sensitive positions persons who test positive for illegal use of drugs or on-duty impairment by alcohol pursuant to paragraph (c)(2)(i) of this section.

(3) *Confidentiality.* Any information regarding the medical condition or history of any employee or applicant obtained from a test to determine the illegal use of drugs, except information regarding the illegal use of drugs, is subject to the requirements of § 1630.14(b) (2) and (3) of this part.

(d) *Regulation of smoking.* A covered entity may prohibit or impose restrictions on smoking in places of employment. Such restrictions do not violate any provision of this part.

(e) *Infectious and communicable diseases; food handling jobs*—(1) *In general.* Under title I of the ADA, section 103(d)(1), the Secretary of Health and Human Services is to prepare a list, to be updated annually, of infectious and communicable diseases which are transmitted through the handling of food. (Copies may be obtained from Center for Infectious Diseases, Centers for Disease Control, 1600 Clifton Road, N.E., Mailstop C09, Atlanta, GA 30333.) If an individual with a disability is disabled by one of the infectious or communicable diseases included on this list, and if the risk of transmitting the disease associated with the handling of food cannot be eliminated by reasonable accommodation, a covered entity may refuse to assign or continue to assign such individual to a job involving food handling. However, if the individual with a disability is a current employee, the employer must consider whether he or she can be accommodated by reassignment to a vacant position not involving food handling.

(2) *Effect on state or other laws.* This part does not preempt, modify, or

amend any State, county, or local law, ordinance or regulation applicable to food handling which:

(i) Is in accordance with the list, referred to in paragraph (e)(1) of this section, of infectious or communicable diseases and the modes of transmissibility published by the Secretary of Health and Human Services; and

(ii) Is designed to protect the public health from individuals who pose a significant risk to the health or safety of others, where that risk cannot be eliminated by reasonable accommodation.

(f) *Health insurance, life insurance, and other benefit plans*—(1) An insurer, hospital, or medical service company, health maintenance organization, or any agent or entity that administers benefit plans, or similar organizations may underwrite risks, classify risks, or administer such risks that are based on or not inconsistent with State law.

(2) A covered entity may establish, sponsor, observe or administer the terms of a bona fide benefit plan that are based on underwriting risks, classifying risks, or administering such risks that are based on or not inconsistent with State law.

(3) A covered entity may establish, sponsor, observe, or administer the terms of a bona fide benefit plan that is not subject to State laws that regulate insurance.

(4) The activities described in paragraphs (f) (1), (2), and (3) of this section are permitted unless these activities are being used as a subterfuge to evade the purposes of this part.

Appendix to Part 1630—
Interpretive Guidance on Title I of the Americans with Disabilities Act

Background

The ADA is a federal antidiscrimination statute designed to remove barriers which prevent qualified individuals with disabilities from enjoying the same employment opportunities that are available to persons without disabilities.

Like the Civil Rights Act of 1964 that prohibits discrimination on the bases of race, color, religion, national origin, and sex, the ADA seeks to ensure access to equal employment opportunities based on merit. It does not guarantee equal results, establish quotas, or require preferences favoring individuals with disabilities over those without disabilities.

However, while the Civil Rights Act of 1964 prohibits any consideration of personal characteristics such as race or national origin, the ADA necessarily takes a different approach. When an individual's disability creates a barrier to employment opportunities, the ADA requires employers to consider whether reasonable accommodation could remove the barrier.

The ADA thus establishes a process in which the employer must assess a disabled individual's ability to perform the essential functions of the specific job held or desired. While the ADA focuses on eradicating barriers, the ADA does not relieve a disabled employee or applicant from the obligation to perform the essential functions of the job. To the contrary, the ADA is intended to enable disabled persons to compete in the workplace based on the same performance standards and requirements that employers expect of persons who are not disabled.

However, where that individual's functional limitation impedes such job performance, an employer must take steps to reasonably accommodate, and thus help overcome the particular impediment, unless to do so would impose an undue hardship. Such accommodations usually take the form of adjustments to the way a job customarily is performed, or to the work environment itself.

Appendix 2-3
Employer Resources

The following list includes resources available in most states to provide technical assistance to any employer seeking to accommodate an employee with a disability.

National Institute on Disability and Rehabilitation Research
Technology-Related Assistance to the States
States Funded FY 1989/1990/1991

Assistive Technology Service
400 D Street, Suite 230
Anchorage, AK 99501

Contact Person:	Joyce Palmer (907) 274-0138 Program Coordinator
State:	**Alaska**
Lead Agency:	Division of Vocational Rehabilitation
Title:	Assistive Technology Project

Increasing Capabilities Access Network (ICAN)
2201 Brookwood, Suite 117
Little Rock, AR 72202

Contact Person:	Sue Gaskin (501) 666-8868 Project Director
State:	**Arkansas**
Lead Agency:	Department of Human Services Division of Rehab Services
Title:	Increasing Capabilities Access Network (ICAN)

Rocky Mountain Resource and Training Institute
6355 Ward Road, Suite 310
Arvada, CO 80004

Contact Person:	Bill West (303) 420-2942 State Coordinator for Assistive Technology

State: **Colorado**

Lead Agency: Rocky Mountain Resource and Training Institute

Title: Colorado Assistive Technology Project

University of Delaware
Center for Applied Science and Engineering
New Castle County
Newark, DE 19716

Contact Person: Beth A. Mineo, Ph.D. (302) 651-6830

State: **Delaware**

Lead Agency: University of Delaware

Georgia Department of Human Resources
878 Peachtree Street, NE
Room 702
Atlanta, GA 30309

Contact Person: Joy Kniskern (404) 853-9151

State: **Georgia**

Lead Agency: Department of Human Resources

Dept. of Human Services
Vocational Rehabilitation and Services for the Blind Division
1000 Bishop Street, Room 605
Honolulu, HI 96813

Contact Person: Nell Shim (808) 586-5368

State: **Hawaii**

Lead Agency: Department of Human Services

Illinois Technology-Related Assistance Project for Individuals of All Ages with Disabilities
411 East Adams
Springfield, IL 62701

Contact Person: Teri Dederer (217) 785-7091
Project Liaison
Pennie Cooper (217) 522-7985
Executive Director

State: **Illinois**

Lead Agency: Illinois Department of Rehabilitation Services

Title: Illinois Technology-Related Assistance Project for Individuals of All Ages with Disabilities

Department of Human Services
Office of Vocational Rehabilitation Services
Technical Assistance Unit
150 W. Market Street, P.O. Box 7083
Indianapolis, IN 46207-7083

Contact Person: Sandra Metcalf (317) 233-3394
Project Manager

State: **Indiana**

Lead Agency: Department of Human Services

Title: Accessing Technology Through Awareness in Indiana (A.T.T.A.I.N)

University of Iowa
Division of Developmental Disabilities
Iowa City, IA 52242

Contact Person: James Hardy, Ph.D. (319) 353-6386

State: **Iowa**

Lead Agency: University of Iowa

Title: Technology-Related Assistance for Individuals with Disabilities

Kentucky Assistive Technology Service Network
Coordinating Center at Kentucky Department for the Blind
427 Versailles Road
Frankfort, KY 40601

Contact Person: Jan Weber (502) 564-4665
Executive Director

State: **Kentucky**

Lead Agency: Kentucky Department for the Blind

Title: The Kentucky Assistive Technology Service (KATS) Network

Louisiana State Planning Council on Developmental Disabilities
Department of Health and Hospitals
P.O. Box 3455
Baton Rouge, LA 70821-3455

Contact Person: Anne E. Farber, Ph.D. (504) 342-6804

State: **Louisiana**

Lead Agency: Louisiana Planning Council on Developmental Disabilities

Maine CITE
Assistive Technology Coordinating Center
University of Maine at Augusta
University Heights
Augusta, ME 04330

Contact Person: Kathleen Powers (207) 622-3000 ext. 3195
Project Director

State: **Maine**

Lead Agency: Department of Educational and Cultural Services

Title: Maine Consumer Information and Technology Training Exchange (Maine CITE)

Technology-Related Assistance Program
Governor's Office for Handicapped Individuals
300 W. Lexington Street, Box 10
Baltimore, MD 21201

Contact Person: Jay Brill (301) 333-4975
Director

State: **Maryland**

Lead Agency: Governor's Office for Handicapped Individuals

Title: State of Maryland—State Technology-Related Assistance Program

MATP Center
Gardner 529
Children's Hospital
300 Longwood Avenue
Boston, MA 02115

Contact Person: Judy Brewer (617) 735-6380
Director

State: **Massachusetts**

Lead Agency: Commission for the Deaf

Title: Massachusetts Assistive Technology Partnership (MATP)

Governor's Advisory Council on Technology for People with Disabilities
300 Centennial Building, 685 Cedar Street
St. Paul, MN 55155

Contact Person: Rachel Wobschall (612) 297-1554
Executive Director

State: **Minnesota**

Lead Agency: Minnesota Governor's Advisory Council on Technology for People with Disabilities

Title: A System of Technology to Achieve Results (STAR)

Division of Rehabilitation Services
Department of Human Services
P.O. Box 1698
Jackson, MS 39215-1698

Contact Person: Pete Martin (601) 354-6892

State: **Mississippi**

Lead Agency: Division of Rehabilitation Services

Title: Project START—Success Through Assistive/Rehabilitative Technology

Curators of the State of Missouri
UMKC Institute for Human Development
Office of Research Administration
University of Missouri-Kansas City
Kansas City, MO 64110

Contact Person: Carl F. Calkins, Ph.D. (816) 276-1755

State: **Missouri**

Lead Agency: University of Missouri-Kansas City

Montana Dept. of Social and Rehabilitation Services
Rehabilitative Services Division
111 Sanders, P.O. Box 4210
Helena, MT 59604

Contact Person: William D. Lamb (406) 444-2590

State: **Montana**

Lead Agency: Department of Social and Rehabilitative Services

Assistive Technology Project
P.O. Box 94987
Lincoln, Nebraska 68509

Contact Person: Mark Schultz (402) 471-0735

State: **Nebraska**

Lead Agency: Department of Education

Title: Technology-Related Assistance for Individuals with Disabilities in Nebraska

Rehabilitation Division, PRPD
505 East King Street, Room 501
Carson City, NV 89710

Contact Person: Donny Loux, Chief (702) 687-4452
Program Development

State: **Nevada**

Title: Assistive Technology Services, Advocacy, and Systems Change

New Hampshire State Department of Education
Department of Education
State of New Hampshire
Concord, NH 03824

Contact Person: Jan Nisbet (603) 862-4320

State: **New Hampshire**

Lead Agency: Department of Education

State Department of Education
Division of Vocational Rehabilitation
604 W. San Mateo
Santa Fe, NM 87503

Contact Person: Andrew Winnegar (505) 827-3522

State: **New Mexico**

Lead Agency: Department of Education

Title: New Mexico Technology Related Assistance Program (NMTAP)

New York State Office of Advocate for the Disabled
TRAID Project
One Empire State Plaza, Tenth Floor
Albany, NY 12223-0001

Contact Person: Deborah V. Buck (518) 473-4129
Project Manager, TRAID Project

State: **New York**

Lead Agency: Office of Advocate for the Disabled

Title: Technology-Related Assistance for Individuals with Disabilities

Department of Human Resources
Division of Vocational Rehabilitation Services
1110 Navaho Drive, Suite 101
Raleigh, NC 27609

Contact Person: Ricki Cook (919) 850-2787

State: **North Carolina**

Lead Agency: Department of Human Resources Division of Vocational Rehabilitation Services

Title: North Carolina Assistive Technology Project

Department of Human Resources
Vocational Rehabilitation Division
2045 Silverton Road, N.E.
Salem, OR 97310

Contact Person: Gregg Fishwick (503) 378-3830

State: **Oregon**

Lead Agency: Department of Human Resources Division of Vocational Rehabilitation

Title: Technology Access for Life Needs (TALN)

South Carolina Vocational Rehabilitation Department
P.O. Box 15
West Columbia, SC 29171-0015

Contact Person: P. Charles LaRosa
(803) 822-5303

State: **South Carolina**

Lead Agency: Vocational Rehabilitation Department

Developmental Disabilities Council
Department of Mental Health and Mental Retardation
Doctors' Building—Suite 300
706 Church Street
Nashville, TN 37243-0675

Contact Person: E. H. "Buddy" Wright (615) 741-3807

State: **Tennessee**

Lead Agency: Department of Mental Health and Mental Retardation

Title: Tennessee Technology Access Project (TTAP)

Utah State University
Developmental Center for Handicapped Persons
Logan, Utah 84322-6800

Contact Person: Marvin Fifield, Ed.D. (801) 750-1982
Director

State: **Utah**

Lead Agency: University Affiliated Program at Utah State University Development Center for Handicapped Persons

Title: Utah State Program for Technology Related Assistance for Individuals with Disabilities

Department of Aging and Disabilities
Agency of Human Services
103 South Main Street
Waterbury, VT 05676

Contact Person:	Jesse Barth (802) 241-2620 Project Director
State:	**Vermont**
Lead Agency:	Department of Aging and Disabilities
Title:	Assistive Technology Development Grant

Department of Rehabilitative Services
Office of Planning
4901 Fitzhugh Avenue
P.O. Box 11045
Richmond, VA 23230

Contact Person:	Kenneth Knorr (804) 367-2445
State:	**Virginia**
Lead Agency:	Department of Rehabilitative Services
Title:	Developing a Model System for Accessing Assistive Technology

Department of Health and Social Services
Division of Vocational Rehabilitation
P.O. Box 7852
1 W. Wilson Street, 8th Floor
Madison, WI 53707

Contact Person:	Kathy McCleave (608) 266-2179
State:	**Wisconsin**
Lead Agency:	Department of Health and Social Services Division of Vocational Rehabilitation
Title:	State Grants Program, Technology-Related Assistance for Individuals with Disabilities

Chapter 3

Components of a Disability Management Program

Disability management is a complex effort that weaves together many components and many people throughout the organization. It also engages the outside community in dealing with the problems of return to work.

The shape of the disability management program depends on several factors:

• *The characteristics of the organization and its employees.* In smaller worksites one individual or department may carry out the disability management functions. As an organization increases in size and complexity the responsibility for disability management becomes dispersed and the importance of a coordinating committee increases.

• *The types of jobs performed at the worksite.* Often work-related disabilities are a function of the types of jobs at the worksite. The distribution of work-related accidents and illness at a steel mill, for example, looks very different from the distribution at a bank or biotechnology operation. Further, the available jobs determine the accommodation and transitional employment opportunities an employer can offer. Modified work must be congruent with the operations of the organization. Alternatively, a work organization may take on new functions in order to create accommodation for employees with disabilities.

• *Work force characteristics.* The characteristics of the work force determine preventive strategies and help predict the likely areas in need of intervention. A highly educated work force is less likely to need transitional slots than a semi-skilled factory group. Young workers can be expected to recuperate more quickly than older ones.

• *The availability of community resources.* Resource-rich communities are those with the full gamut of social, mental health, and rehabilitation services required to assist persons with disabilities achieve maximum functional performance and vocational potential. The kinds of services typical of a resource-rich community are those provided by a family service agency, mental health center, physical rehabilitation medical service, vocational assessment and training facility, self-help group, budget counseling, and child care facility. In areas without such community resources the workplace itself is pressed to provide or help establish the services. In this instance the task of determining needs and setting priorities takes on extra significance.

Development of a disability management program is evolutionary. Setting all the components in place at once is unrealistic, and may be unnecessary for a small or medium-size employer, for whom the full range of components is not possible anyway. The program should grow and take shape over time, always remaining responsive to the needs of the employer, changes in the workplace and the community, and, most of all, the needs of workers with disabilities.

This chapter defines the components of a disability management program identified in Chapter 1. The components include:

- Needs assessment and baseline data
- A disability management policy
- A coordinating structure
- Provision for early identification and intervention
- Training of key personnel
- Case management for individuals with disabilities
- Work modification options—job accommodation and transitional employment
- Data collection, analysis, and feedback
- Prevention

Needs Assessment and Baseline Data

A detailed status report on existing conditions and services provides an important base in developing and implementing a disability management program. This step establishes priorities and points to areas that require more information before appropriate decisions can be made about the policies and procedures that should be set in place. It helps to develop the best fit possible between the probable needs of the workers with disabilities and the goals of the employer. Completing a needs assessment and collecting baseline data also avoid duplication of services. *Developing a program does not mean reinventing the wheel.* Often it will mean coordinating or reorganizing existing functions. Finally, the baseline data provide information to enable the program to be evaluated for effectiveness in the future.

Needs assessment and development of a baseline data set includes collection and analysis of four types of information:

1. Characteristics of the work force
2. History of disability in the work setting
3. Resources in the community
4. Experience of people in the system

Characteristics of the Work Force

Work force characteristics include age, gender, marital status, level of education, work history and job titles, and ethnicity. This information is usually available in personnel records. It is important because characteristics of the work force highlight the potential services the population will need and may help predict the types of disabilities to which the disability management program will need to respond. Several examples show how this information may be useful:

- Young single minority women with children comprise a major portion of the work force at a hospital. Given this profile, one would expect that there will be a greater occurrence of disabilities unique to women and that many of the problems encountered during disability will concern child care and other child-related issues.
- Results of research (Akabas and Gates 1990) provide evidence that when disability strikes, married workers are at an advantage, because the spouse usually steps in to provide help with daily care. Single workers must seek assistance from outside sources. A largely single employee population will require more backup services in managing disabilities.
- If the work requires heavy physical labor, and low education levels are characteristic of the population, it may be difficult to design alternative work options in response to severe disability.
- Finally, some diseases are more prevalent among certain ethnic groups. For example, black women are particularly vulnerable to high blood pressure.

Preventing disability is a major objective of the disability management effort. Information about characteristics of the work force also assists the development of appropriate preventive strategies. Some types of prevention may be generic—such as stop-smoking campaigns. Others, however, may be targeted to a specific population. For example, if the work force tends to be older, more health care education may be needed to alert the workers to means of accessing better medical care and to help them improve their understanding of their own health needs. If the work force is unusually young, safe-driving instruction and training in the use of safety belts may prevent many disabling conditions.

History of Disability

The history of disability among a work group is important because hard data on various aspects of disability at a specific worksite provide a useful basis for program design and serve as a baseline against which to evaluate program effectiveness. Relevant information, probably available in medical claims, includes:

- *The type of disabilities workers experience.* Are there certain disabilities that occur at a greater rate than expected? Are the disabilities related to the workplace (for example, back injuries among nurses' aides or carpal tunnel syndrome among keyboard operators), life-style (say, drug abuse among musicians), or other identifiable sources (for instance, environmental hazards among asbestos workers)? What is the proportion of workers with permanent, chronic, or worsening disability?

- *Who is out on long-term and short-term disability.* Does disability primarily affect one segment of the work force? Or, are different groups affected differently? For example, do older workers tend to be out longer than younger ones?

- *The length of disability.* What is the average length of disability? Do workers with the same disability vary greatly in the length of time out taken? Do all disabled workers tend to use up short-term disability despite the type of disability? Are there physicians who always treat workers for longer than they seem to need?

- *The type of work employees with disabilities perform.* Do workers with disabilities tend to do the same types of jobs or tasks? Do workers who do the same jobs tend to have the same disabilities?

- *The departments where disabilities occur.* Supervisors play a key role in the return-to-work effort. It is imperative that the disability manager be able to contact the disabled worker's supervisor when necessary.

- *The cost of disability.* One of the primary measures of effectiveness of the disability management program for the employer is the degree to which the effort contains cost or at least shows a favorable cost-benefit ratio. In order to evaluate the success of the program in meeting this goal, detailed cost information must be recorded.

Current disability information provides an understanding of the immediate problems that need to be addressed by the disability management program. Historical data enable disability managers to determine if there are patterns or trends in the occurrence of disability at their site.

Resources in the Community

Community resources (individuals or organizations that can assist the disabled worker in overcoming problems caused by the disability) include health service agencies such as Cancer Care or the MS Society, church groups and their self-help classes, rehabilitation facilities, public assistance associations, neighborhood groups, and family service agencies, including mental health networks.

Sources of information concerning these resources include the United Way, local directories of service organizations, national headquarters of health service providers such as the Arthritis Foundation or the American Heart Association, Family Service America, local hospitals, vocational state rehabilitation agencies and government departments for public assistance and Social Security benefits. They are important because the success of the disability management effort depends on an effective resource network to which workers with disabilities can be referred and from which they can draw entitlements that are not part of the employer's benefits plan (for instance, Social Security Disability Insurance). The employer needs to determine what resources exist and the extent of the services they provide. Then it is possible to determine what resources need to be developed.

Experience of People in the System

Finally, personnel in the system who are currently involved with the problems of workers with disabilities can provide information about how the system operates and what types of assistance are needed. Such data can offer valuable insights into how to modify existing services and implement new program components effectively. Staff need to be asked, "What problems do you have trying to return workers with disabilities to their jobs? What is currently being done to help return? What else would be helpful?"

For most employers, responding to the needs of workers with disabilities is not a new activity. Those at a site who have been involved with helping workers with disabilities can provide valuable information about what has been tried and the success or problems encountered with the assistance offered. EEO, medical, benefits, and risk management personnel, the employee assistance program (EAP) staff, and workers with disabilities and their supervisors are all sources of this information.

In sum, assessing needs and collecting baseline data determines what the organization is currently doing to assist return to work, identifies what additionally needs to be done, provides hard data about patterns of disability over time, and indicates the current status of workers with disabilities, making it possible to assess how best to implement the program at the particular site. The needs assessment and data collection effort not only informs the development of program components but also provides the future basis for evaluating program effectiveness. Appendix 3-1 provides a series of questions that should be asked when developing a needs assessment/data collection effort.

Disability Management Policy

The importance of establishing an explicit disability management policy and the elements of that policy are discussed in detail in Chapter 5. Policy is mentioned here to mark its place in the chronology of the development of a disability management program and to reinforce its significance. Policy is the underpinning of the disability management program. It serves as its constitution, establishing the *rights and responsibilities* of the workers and the employer.

Through the policy, an explicit position is taken by the employer that applies equally and systematically to everyone and is available to all.

It sets in place the *structure* from which all other action is derived. For example, if the policy includes provision of transitional employment for workers with disabilities, then mechanisms must be set in place to evaluate tasks available at the workplace that may be appropriate for workers with various limitations; a means of hooking workers up with the available tasks must be established, a way to supervise and monitor performance to ensure that the work is appropriate and to determine when the worker is able to move on to his or her regular job responsibilities must be designed, and criteria for how long someone can remain in transitional status need to be specified.

Policy *organizes the workplace* by pulling together, into a unified document, elements from the different functions and areas of the workplace. The policies that affect such disparate elements as benefits, operations, training, recruitment, and promotions are all brought together and organized around the goal of meeting the needs of workers with disabilities. The individual policies work in unison and not as separate, unrelated, or contradictory goals of the workplace.

Finally, policy sets the plan for the future. A policy may lay out more than can be implemented immediately. Thus, policy can provide a base for longer-range plans that need to be developed. Top-level management must confront the issues and determine goals before starting on a course of action.

Policy development, therefore, occurs at the start of the process of establishing a disability management program. In setting the structure, providing the organization, and pointing to future directions, policy must be the starting point. It is not something that is deduced at the end.

However, policy is not cast in concrete. It should be both flexible (able to respond to diverse practice situations) and dynamic (able to respond to changes in the system); for example, the Americans with Disabilities Act may require significant changes in employers' hiring policies. Policy should also be interactive with other program components. As program operations reveal that some aspect of policy does not meet a goal effectively, the policy needs to change. For example, policy may state that the term of transitional employment cannot exceed two months. Program operations may show, however, that an additional two to four weeks is needed to overcome recidivism effectively.

Policy is enacted by top management, but it is informed by the needs assessment, which involves input from many different levels and many different departments. Finally, policy needs to be widely communicated and made accessible to all levels of management and workers. This means it needs to be written for all to understand.

Coordinating Structure

The coordinating structure, whether a committee, task force, or advisory board, is composed of representatives from the departments involved in the many aspects of the disability management process. If the work site is unionized, representatives from the union(s) should also be included.

Returning workers with disabilities to work or maintaining workers on the job in the face of the onset or worsening of disability is not, for most organizations or health and welfare trust funds, the responsibility of one department.[1] There is a dispersion of related tasks throughout the

1. Health and welfare trust funds are funds, set aside by the collectively bargained agreement, that are allocated to cover health care, pensions, and other benefits, and are usually placed in a 501C3 trust fund with a board of trustees that represents both labor and management. Frequently, however, the actual administration is more closely related to the trade union than to the employer.

organization. The EAP may attend to the psychological distress experienced by the newly disabled worker, benefits provide income replacement, supervisors assist in developing an accommodation strategy, and medical may oversee a physical rehabilitation program.

Certain problems arise because the disability management activity is allocated to several departments. First, the different departments may not always act in agreement or cooperative fashion. Second, there is no one department or manager to take responsibility for the program. Finally, there is no one department or manager to whom others report. As a consequence, some workers may not receive the optimal assistance available to them, or, in the worst case, some may fall through the bureaucratic cracks and receive no assistance, a situation that increases the likelihood that an individual will never return to work. The role of a coordinating body is to alleviate these problems.

Who is involved? Members of the coordinating committee include representatives from any department that affects workers with disabilities while they are out on disability or once they return to work and from departments that implement prevention strategies to help avoid disability. These departments may include:

- Human resources and its distinctive units
- Benefits
- Medical
- Employee assistance program (EAP)
- Safety
- Training
- Production
- Finance
- Risk management
- Management information system (MIS)
- Engineering/ergonomics
- Legal

If the site is unionized, representatives from the union(s) need to be included. It is also important not to violate union contracts when offering accommodated work. Plans for transitional or accommodated work must be negotiated with the union. The union offers assistance in communicating the program to its members with disabilities.

Representatives from outside organizations are also appropriate in some instances. If a private insurer is the benefits provider, the insurance company might be represented on the coordinating committee. This representative can provide information about benefits and work with the employer to achieve early identification of workers in need of assistance.

Finally, a representative from the United Way or other umbrella organization for local community resources may be a valuable committee member. These individuals can assist in establishing ties with community resources and can be instrumental in developing new resources that may not yet be available within the community, but could be useful in the management of work disabilities.

Responsibilities of the coordinating committee include:

- *Developing administrative procedures and systems* that make the assistance available to workers with disabilities and coordinate intervention strategies. For example, the coordinating committee may establish how a worker receiving disability benefits is referred to the EAP when a claims officer determines the worker is having problems best dealt with by the EAP.
- *Ensuring the efficiency of the system* by making sure that the activities of the different departments involved in the disability management program do not overlap or contradict one another. For example, the medical department should not be encouraging workers to seek accommodated work while supervisors encourage them to stay out until they are able to resume 100 percent of their usual workload.
- *Establishing formal lines of communication* among the different departments to keep each informed of the problems, progress, and changes of the others. In this way the departments can remain responsive to one another.
- *Coordinating activities* that do not fit in any one department. For example, work accommodation can involve the union, industrial relations, the supervisor, and benefits, medical, ergonomics, and safety departments.
- *Reviewing cases that pose problems* the system is having trouble resolving. Suggestions of ways to manage the specific case and determinations as to whether the program needs to be changed to better accommodate the class of problems represented by the troublesome case are appropriate agenda for a coordinating group.
- *Providing a mechanism for commanding resources.* The coordinating committee can allocate and inventory resources available to the program and ensure that these resources are utilized. It can serve as a powerful voice when additional resources are required or the need for change in responsibilities is identified.
- *Furnishing a mechanism to reexamine policy and program procedures.* Committee representatives can see where the program is not working, analyze why there is trouble, and indicate changes in program policy or operation.
- *Setting up a reporting and evaluation mechanism.* The coordinating committee can receive the reports from individual departments on program functioning and then synthesize this information to report to top

management. Thus, it is a key link between those involved in implementation and top management.

Early Identification and Intervention

Early identification of workers with disabilities in need of assistance is one of the most important elements of a disability management program, for three reasons. First, it allows early intervention to help determine whether or not the worker is receiving proper medical care. A study by Akabas and Gates (1990) found that some workers are dissatisfied with their medical care and do not agree with the decisions their physicians make about their ability to return to work. Disability program case managers, through the intake interview, can determine if the worker is being treated, if the worker is satisfied with the treatment, and whether or not the treatment is perceived as helping in recovery. The potential value of treatment is enhanced when a request for a second medical opinion or change in medical supervision is initiated during an early review.

Second, early identification helps case managers to intervene before problems become too big to be resolved easily. Problems experienced during disability are not limited to physical recovery. Workers with disabilities are often beset by financial problems, personal or family concerns, and problems in returning to work. Catching these issues at their start helps to reduce their impact.

Finally, intervening early can affect how workers with disabilities perceive themselves. Consider the worker who is in a serious car accident that requires a lengthy recovery and will surely leave her unable to lift heavy file folders, which is part of her job as a legal secretary. The only contact she has with her workplace following the accident is her benefits check. She hardly hears from her supervisor or co-workers. The longer she is out, the more intense becomes her feeling that return to her job is impossible. In her isolation from the workplace she begins to think of herself as disabled, protected from total poverty only by the benefits check she receives biweekly. She loses the motivation to return.

Early intervention can change this scenario. It can reassure the worker that the employer wants her back and will find a place for her. It can also help short-circuit the mind-set that turns a worker with a disability into a disabled person. Intervening early fuels the motivation to return by reinforcing the value of the worker to the workplace and offering a way to realize that ability—not disability—determines the worker's employment future. Thus, early identification of workers in need of assistance enables early intervention to resolve problems before they become insurmountable and thus facilitates return to work.

Although the concept of early identification and intervention appears straightforward, it is not. The difficult question that must be considered revolves around the definition of "early." At New England Medical Center intervention occurs *at the time of an accident.* A worker does not go home if he or she is hurt on the job but receives immediate medical treatment and, depending on the severity of the injury, may be sent back to work immediately. For sites without medical services, such a response may not be feasible.

In most cases, the optimal time for intervention is not clear. When does a medical problem become a disability instead of a transient illness where return to work is probable? It is obviously a poor use of resources to intervene when someone suffers from the flu and will be out for less than two weeks. But, what if someone suffers from emphysema, and though recovery is relatively fast, enabling the person to return to work within three or four weeks, the impact of the disease affects job performance?

Some guidelines to help decide when to intervene can be gleaned from past research and from the organization's own experience with workers compensation cases:

- *Look at the diagnosis.* Despite the expected return-to-work date, certain diagnoses may be associated with potential problems in returning to work. For example, a cancer patient who must undergo chemotherapy after return to work or a worker returning after an exacerbation of arthritis may require assistance overcoming the stress of maintaining the job in the face of disability.
- *Look at the return-to-work date set by the physician* or the established recovery period. If the date is greater than three months, ambiguous, or suggests permanent disability, the individual is a candidate for assistance through the program.
- If the employee with the disability approaches the case manager or the supervisor, whether for a specific problem or a vague concern, the worker may need assistance through the program.

Training of Key Personnel

The ecosystems approach to disability management assumes that introducing the program will have an effect throughout the organization. Clearly, staff from the departments directly involved in disability management are affected as their job tasks change and their roles expand to include the new activity. To carry out the new tasks these staff members need to be trained. For example, claims officers from the benefits department need to be trained in early identification and referral procedures. Affirmative action people need to be trained in how to analyze jobs for their suitability for providing accommodated work and how to assess the workers referred to them in light of the available jobs.

Members of the coordinating committee may also require training. The training may be to provide the skills for facilitating the group process in instances where committee representatives are unfamiliar with working in a group. Or, the training may revolve around the new skills needed as the consequence of expanded job roles.

The program, however, does not operate in a vacuum. For example, the way the supervisor and co-workers respond to absorbing the workload of workers out on disability and their acceptance of them after their return are influenced by the information available to co-workers about the disability, strategies for coping with workers upon their return, and the level of managerial commitment conveyed through the program to assist return. Information, commitment, a cache of coping strategies and the skills to carry them out, therefore, are the core of the training focus for these groups.

The decision of whom to train and what the substance of the training should be depends on the size of the firm, its structure, and the level of expertise available. The same tasks may be the responsibility of different departments in different organizations. For example, some employers may have sophisticated EAPs to handle case management and referral; others may have staff social workers or vocational counselors responsible for intervention; for others, benefits personnel may need to learn this skill. Guidelines on whom to train and the substance of the training, however, include:

- *All staff directly involved in the disability management program* need, at a minimum, a thorough orientation that describes the entire program and not just the one piece for which the individual or department has responsibility. As in all productive enterprises, everyone must understand how he or she fits into the total picture if they are to be motivated to behave productively.
- *Top management team.* The disability management initiative can be expected to cause some concern among certain groups in the organization, such as supervisors, safety personnel, and risk managers. It is important for top management to evidence commitment to the concept. An orientation to the disability management plan should be arranged so that the organization's leadership is familiar with its objectives, procedures, and personnel.
- *All staff who must perform new tasks.* New tasks could range from being part of the coordinating committee to case management to identify-

ing program participants. Job descriptions may have to be changed in line with the task assignments and training.

• *All staff who must follow new procedures.* In some instances the tasks a person performs will remain relatively unchanged. For example, a claims officer may still review claim forms to determine eligibility for benefits, but, as part of the program, if a claimant meets certain criteria, the claims officer may be required to refer the claimant to the disability case manager. How do the new criteria get conveyed to the claims officer? Who explains to whom they are to be applied? How does that referral take place? Does the claims officer deal directly with the case manager, or does the claims officer go through her supervisor or the coordinating committee? If the claims officer handles the referral directly, does she call the case manager with the information, send a copy of the claimant's file, or send some other summary sheet with information selected by the case manager? In what time frame is the claims officer responsible for making sure the case manager receives the information—the same day, within two days, within a week?

• *Supervisors who are currently, or may later be, responsible for returning disabled workers.* The supervisor is the key link between the disabled worker and the disability management job done. Thus, the supervisor's sensitivity to problems the disabled workers face and initiative in developing strategies to help them overcome them are fundamental to successful return.

• *Any outside service providers who need to understand the employer's system to serve the firm effectively.* These providers may include, for example, insurance companies' and community resources' personnel. At a minimum these organizations need to be provided with an overview of the program and an understanding of how it affects them.

The training may be done in-house or may require the help of outside consultants. Once the program has been designed, it is necessary to review in-house expertise. Can staff develop appropriate forms for recording information, constructing assessment instruments, analyzing the organization to determine the best referral system, and so on? Those areas that cannot be handled by existing staff may need the assistance of outside consultants.

Finally, training is not a one-shot deal. Initially, the training requires an intensive effort because the program needs to be introduced and a considerable amount of new information needs to be transmitted. However, seeing a worker with a disability through the program from onset of disability to successful return to work or work readjustment may take months. As those who are involved in the program go through the first cycles of returning people to work they will need feedback and continued explanation on how the program operates. This feedback, explanation, or clarification is part of the training effort. Further, new staff, or those newly assigned to jobs that involve disability management tasks, require training updates.

Case Management

The core of disability management programs is the case managers. Case management is the most effective way to realize the many benefits to the organization and the individual provided by disability management programs, for three reasons. First, the differences among cases cannot be overlooked. People with the same disability respond differently to the pressures of returning to work. The interplay of work history, family circumstances, and emotional stability, for example, with prior work experience and with the problems of physical recovery influence successful return to work. Given two employees who suffered strokes of equal severity, the younger person may work harder on rehabilitation than the older, and the better-educated employee is likely to have more work options than the one with minimal education.

Second, many of the people helped through the program are vulnerable and overwhelmed. The personal contact with a case manager often provides a focus and motivation for staying on the job or returning to it. Participants in a demonstration program in our own research frequently cited the support of the case manager as a primary reason for returning to work (Gates, Taler, and Akabas 1989).

Third, case management, through working on the individual level, provides a systematic approach to marshaling resources on behalf of the worker with a disability. An intake interview that systematically determines needs in the physical and emotional realms of the life of an individual with a disability is provided in Appendix 6-1. By looking at the various aspects of an individual's adjustment, the case manager applies a bio-psycho-social assessment to the situation.

The role of the case manager is to identify the needs of the disabled worker. To keep the job or return to work, the worker with a disability may need assistance in a wide range of areas. The intake interview is the first opportunity to identify needs. The interview provides information on the potential problem areas a worker faces during the period of disability or readjustment to work, including the following:

- *Accommodation at the workplace*. The worker may not know that transitional employment opportunities that offer a shorter workday, workweek, or different work assignments, or accommodated work that provides for reduced tasks or change in how the work is performed, may be possible. Or the employee may not know how to go about negotiating such options.

• *Medical care.* Some workers report dissatisfaction with their physician's treatment or think the treatment is not helping them to recover. These people need assistance in talking to their doctors about their recovery. Also, returning to work depends on the physician's consent. Often, however, a worker with a disability does not know the criteria used to determine a return-to-work date, or if that date could be changed given the nature of the job to which he or she is returning. The case manager can help a worker talk to a physician about what his or her job entails and how that may affect returning to work.

• *Family and financial problems.* Disability brings reduced earnings. This can cause severe family and financial problems. Workers with disabilities frequently need assistance in sorting through these problems, budgeting, or applying for financial help from appropriate government agencies.

• *Benefits and program information.* It never occurs to many workers to learn about the benefits to which they are entitled or the services available to them should they become disabled. When disability strikes, they are confused about their rights and unaware of support services. This lack of information makes successful return more difficult.

Through follow-up conversations the case manager brings into sharper focus the nature of specific problems and catches new problems as they develop.

The case manager also acts as a liaison in the system. To solve the problems faced by workers with disabilities, case managers need to activate interactions throughout the firm, and sometimes in the community as well. The case manager must be ready to call a worker's supervisor, any department that affects the worker's return, such as benefits or medical, or the physician. When benefits are not provided in-house, the case manager may need to work with outside insurers. The case manager must also obtain the involvement of union representatives when work modification is needed. In addition, he or she must know the resources available in the community and how to refer workers to the appropriate agency or organization.

The disability management program has been described as pulling together resources dispersed throughout the firm and the community to meet the needs of individual workers. The problems faced by workers touch upon a wide range of work areas. The case manager must rally the representatives from these areas to work together to bring the employee with a disability back to work.

The complexity of the job and the number of skills called upon in case management demand the attention of a professional. It is not possible to train nonprofessionals in all the counseling and other required skills. Social workers, rehabilitation counselors, nurses, and psychologists are appropriate personnel to carry out the case manager's role. Alternatively, a liaison person who is familiar with benefits or other human resources activities can act as a referral agent, working along with a case manager or provider from an outside consulting organization that specializes in rehabilitation services. (This is more thoroughly detailed in Chapter 6.)

Work Modification

Returning employees to work is a primary goal of disability management programs. The worksite, therefore, must be prepared to provide jobs for returning workers who may be limited in their level of functioning. Two classes of alternatives need to be considered:

1. *Physical changes to the worksite*. Changing the physical location of someone's work, access to the work, design of the workstation, and the like can make the difference between being able to return or remaining on disability. For example, a wheelchair-bound draftsman can no longer sit at the drafting table that requires a stool; providing a drafting table at the proper height for the wheelchair enables the worker to get back to his job. The concept of fitting the environment to the tasks that need to be performed is not a new one. Ergonomics has long provided a basis for understanding the interaction between work setting and functional capacity. Accommodated work is an extension of the existing approach.

2. *Changed work*. While some workers may be assisted by physical modification of the workplace, others may require a change in the tasks their jobs entail, or the way the tasks are completed. For example, a nurse's aide suffers from a lower back injury. She is unable to lift patients for several months but can perform the other parts of her job. The hospital could redefine her job during her recovery period to eliminate lifting and include those tasks she is able to complete, if only on a part-time basis. There are a number of alternatives that can be provided to address the different needs of workers with disabilities, including these:

- Temporarily modify the tasks required in a person's usual job.
- Temporarily provide a new job until the person is able to return to his or her usual work.

- Permanently modify the tasks required in a person's usual job.
- Permanently provide a new job.
- Allow part-time work or time off during the day for rests, visits to the doctor, or rehabilitation.
- Provide helpers to disabled workers to assist with the parts of their jobs that have become problematic for them.

The alternatives an employer selects depend on the type of work that needs to be done and the worker's functional limitations. For example, some jobs are difficult to modify. A truck driver cannot do her job without sitting at a steering wheel. If sitting at a steering wheel is not possible, a new job would be needed. Existing work contracts also shape the alternatives an employer can provide. Unionized sites must include union representatives in defining accommodated work to avoid contract conflicts.

With creative thinking it is possible to develop effective strategies to meet the needs of the particular site and specific disability. Marks and Spencer stores in England exemplify one creative solution to finding work for people with disabilities, in their case for mentally retarded people. All jobs at the store were broken down into their separate tasks. Those tasks that were appropriate for a retarded employee to perform were collected and reassigned to such a worker. The outcome was that a retarded individual was successfully employed at each store and the underemployment of the remaining work force was reduced by reassigning the less demanding tasks to a retarded person. This action enhanced the overall productivity of the stores involved.

The number of alternatives, ranging from physical accommodation to permanently finding new jobs, may appear formidable. In fact, however, research finds that often very simple, low-cost changes have a significant impact (Collignon 1986). Replacing a chair, staggering work hours, permitting several breaks during the day are changes not difficult to set in place, and the cost of doing so is a fraction of the cost of paying months of benefits payments to a valuable employee to stay home and not work.

There are situations where, because of the type of work available within an organization, or because of the severity of the disability, accommodation by the employer is impossible. In such situations, employers have usually provided out-placement services for the person with a disability, have referred the individual for retraining, either paying directly for the instruction or referring the employee to the state vocational rehabilitation agency, or have provided disability retirement benefits for the former employee.

In the last case, the employer may wish to contact the Social Security Administration to help document the individual's eligibility for Social Security Disability Insurance (SSDI). If the right to this benefit can be established, an important financial resource is available to the person. Most long-term disability insurance packages are written (or should be written) as supplements to SSDI benefits. The employer achieves a direct cost savings when SSDI eligibility is verified.

Data Collection, Analysis, and Feedback

Data—the word smacks of numbers and statistics that no one is sure how to collect or how to interpret. Ultimately, the quality of a disability program depends on the quality of the available information. Without adequate program data, it is not possible to assess the needs of the company, monitor how well the program is operating, refine the program, and evaluate its effectiveness. In other words, reliable program data are essential to keep track of what is going on.

Developing data collection procedures involves the following:

- *Determining what is already in place.* Most companies collect some data about employees with disabilities, such as number of days absent. Along with the kind of information, the *way* the information is collected needs to be assessed. Is the information entered directly into a computer? If so, how are computer files set up? Do staff fill out standardized forms to summarize data or are data reported differently by each person? Scattered information that is never coordinated understates the cost of disability and limits the response to it.

- *Determining who uses the data and how.* Program data are important for knowing what is going on. Case managers need to know the status of their cases. The coordinating committee needs to know how well each department is functioning. Others also need to know about program operation. Top-level management, supervisors, frequently used community resources, unions, and insurance companies may all need to know about the effectiveness of their contribution to the program. Further, the form of the information each needs may vary—some require detailed information about individual cases or actions; others need summary data.

- *Determining additional program data that need to be collected.* It is unlikely that data collection prior to program implementation is sufficient for monitoring and evaluating the program. Additional data needs must be made explicit. For example, additional data may be required about the types and costs of disabilities, the problems encountered during disability, the tasks appropriate for accommodated work return, and the range of services provided by existing community resources. More specifically, categories of data that need to be collected include these:

—*Baseline data.* As previously discussed in the section on needs assessment, it is important to determine what the firm is currently doing so that the program does not duplicate functions and to establish a starting point from which to evaluate program effectiveness.
—*Record keeping of ongoing activities of the case manager and the coordinating committee.* Systematically recording intake data, assessing problems, and recording case manager interventions are required to keep track of what happens to individual cases. Case managers must have a way to record basic demographic information about their clients, systematically identify problems in order to select an intervention strategy, and know how long it has been between contacts, which referrals have been made and their outcomes, new problems that have developed, and the like. Individuals' records also provide the basis for assessing the effectiveness of community resources by documenting the success of a referral in solving a problem. (The interview form provided in Appendix 6-1 collects most of the necessary information about individuals, and The Workplace Center at Columbia University has a software package that analyzes the problems of workers with disabilities and can calculate the distribution frequency of those problems.)
—*Follow-up to determine program effectiveness.* It is important to evaluate how well workers assisted through the program readjust to the workplace. Are they still on the job three months after return to work? How are their performance and level of satisfaction? Are there problems with supervisors or with co-workers? Follow-up to determine the effect of implementing the program on involved staff is also needed. If new tasks have been assigned to staff, how well are they being performed? What impact have the new roles had on the department's operation?
—*Process activities.* Like a road map, a log of process activities shows how far you have come and how far you have to go. The destination is fulfillment of the policy. The debates of policy issues and the discussions of problems in implementation delineate the path to reaching program goals. Records of these meetings document decisions and avoid future wrong turns by recording past solutions.
—*Cost-benefit data.* A primary objective for the company is to control the costs associated with disability. Adequate cost-benefit assessment requires information such as the amount of benefits payments, costs of associated medical care, levels of productivity, and lost days of work.
—*Special studies.* Each worksite has some problems that are unique. For example, workers may be prone to a particular class of disabilities, or characteristics of the work force may indicate that certain

problems are more likely for those out on disability. Disability managers may find they require more information about these special issues and must conduct a study to gather specific data required.

—*Evaluation of community resources.* The success of the intervention depends, to a great extent, on the quality of the services provided by community resources. Disability managers need to know the range of services offered, the eligibility criteria for service, and the effectiveness of the organization in assisting workers. Monitoring this information, over time, allows the organization to make productive use of community resources.

• *Determining how data will be collected and stored.* Once the extent of data needs is identified, the best way to collect and store data must be decided. Will information be computerized? Do forms need to be developed to standardize data collection? Who is responsible for gathering data? Are log books needed to record process data, such as the minutes from meetings and correspondence? How should case records that detail the case manager's intervention be kept? What should be the form of a community resource manual? Who will have access to the data? How will confidentiality be maintained? These questions begin to shape the tasks of data collection and storage. Chapter 7 contains more explicit information on data systems related to disability management.

Prevention

Thus far, the focus of the discussion has been on rehabilitation and accommodation. Early identification, case management, and work modification are aimed at overcoming the problems once disability has occurred. One of the most effective strategies for managing disability, however, is to teach workers how to avoid injury and illness. Prevention is a way both to maintain a healthier work force and to reduce the cost of disability by reducing the need for benefits and health care payments. A disability management program, therefore, should include primary prevention. Some prevention efforts are mandated by law. Occupational safety requirements set by OSHA have had a significant impact on reducing work-related accidents and illness. A worksite may have unique conditions that increase the probability of certain disabilities, or the work force may have characteristics that suggest that certain disabilities will be more prevalent. Data collection helps the disability manager assess where disability is occurring. Sources of information include medical claims and the information collated by risk management, safety, and medical personnel. Prevention strategies can then be developed to deal with the problem areas identified.

Conclusion

This chapter introduced the components of a disability management program. An ideal program includes all of the components, but an organization can have a significant impact on disability with a far less sophisticated response. Some companies are too small for each of these components to be separated from each other. That is, one individual or department may be responsible for one, several, or all components. Further, the scope of program components may vary depending on the size and needs of the employer, the needs of the employees, and political and economic constraints, such as union contracts, budgets, and the resources available in the community. Regardless of who carries out the functions or the extent to which they are realized, the content of each component must be considered and taken into account to implement an effective disability management program. Succeeding chapters discuss the components at greater length, giving details of how to set the components in place.

Appendix 3-1
Questions to Assess the Extent of Disability Management Practices at the Company

General Information About the Company Important to the Disability Management Effort

1. Profile of the company
   a. How large is the company?
   b. How many sites are there, how many employees are at each site, and where are the sites located?
   c. What types of jobs do people hold?
   d. Is there a union(s) at the company?
      - Are there clauses in the contract related to disability?
      - Does the union provide disability coverage?
      - How does the union contract affect job accommodation?
2. Profile of disability at the company
   a. What are the most frequent types of disabilities and their rates of occurrence?
   b. Who is out on long-term and short-term disability, and what are the lengths of time out?
   c. What type of disability insurance is available?

Experience of Workers Absent Because of Illness or Injury

1. *When* are disabled or ill workers first identified?
2. *Who* first identifies the worker (i.e. benefits department, supervisor, other)?
3. *When* does the worker begin receiving disability benefits?
4. Is the worker contacted by the company during the period of disability, other than through receipt of benefits payments?
5. If the worker is contacted during the period of disability, what is the nature of that contact?
   a. What is the purpose of the contact?
   b. When does it occur?
   c. Who makes the contact?
6. Is assistance offered to the worker through the workplace to help with problems that arise as a consequence of disability? What types of services? Medical/health-related? Family/personal? Financial? Work-related?
   a. Is there a formal assessment process to determine what type of assistance is needed, or is it up to the worker to request help?

b. Is assistance provided in-house, or are workers referred to outside providers?
c. Whom does the worker contact, or who contacts the worker about possible assistance (that is, is the worker assigned to a case manager)?
d. What workplace interventions are available?
   - Modified tasks?
   - Modified routines, such as number of hours worked, number of breaks during the day?
   - Transitional employment?
   - Technological assistance?
   - Physical facilities change?
   - Job retraining?
   - On-site medical care?
   - On-site rehabilitation services?
e. To what extent can the worker participate in the process (that is, participate in job accommodation/modification decisions)?

7. What happens when the worker returns to work? Is there any follow-up to determine if readjustment to work is satisfactory? What happens when problems persist?
8. How is the experience of workers who are out on disability different from those of workers who do not leave work following the onset or worsening of illness or disability? Are there differences in availability of services or how problems are identified?

Disability Management Components Already in Place

1. What is the current level of awareness and concern about disability management at the company?
2. Does anyone collect, analyze, and study data about disability?
3. Is there an explicit, formal disability policy?
   a. If there is no formal policy, what are the implicit attitudes of the employer toward:
      - Job protection?
      - Availability of accommodated work return?
      - Pay for accommodated work?
      - Criteria for eligibility for accommodated work?
      - Responsibility for costs of hiring replacement or temporary employees?
      - Procedures when conflicts or problems occur as a consequence of discrimination/disclosure?
2. Who is responsible for disability management (for example, benefits, EAP)?
3. Is there departmental coordination of all departments that might affect the disability management process?
   a. If so, how does coordination occur (that is, coordinating committee,

responsibility of disability manager, informal discussions among staff, and so forth)?

b. If there is a coordination committee, who is on it, to whom do the committee members report, how do issues get to the committee, and so on?

4. What services are provided by outside vendors?
5. How are those needing disability management services identified?
6. Are workers assigned to case managers?
   a. If so, who are the case managers (claims officers, social workers, rehab specialists, nurses, psychologists, others)?
   b. What is the role of case managers (for instance, assessment, service delivery, monitoring, evaluating, coordinating)?
7. Is training provided to supervisors, co-workers, or management for return-to-work or job maintenance issues? If so: Who is trained? Who does the training? What is training about? When and where does the training occur?
8. Is the disability management process coordinated with organizations outside the workplace that affect return to work or job maintenance?
   a. Is there contact with physicians about accommodated work return?
   b. How are unions involved?
   c. How are relationships with outside resources developed?
   d. Are outside insurance carriers involved?
9. Are there wellness/prevention programs available to employees?
   a. If so, what is the focus of these programs?
   b. How are they related to disability issues?
10. Has there ever been a formal needs assessment to characterize the labor force and the history of disability at the company?
11. Are adequate data about the program and workers maintained?
    a. How is information collected, stored, and accessed?
    b. What types of reports are generated?
    c. Who is responsible for data collection?
12. Are disability management activities monitored and evaluated for effectiveness?
    a. Are benefits reviewed?
    b. Is cost-effectiveness determined?

Chapter 4

Preparing to Implement Disability Management: An Organizational Perspective

One of the first ideas most of us learn in science is that objects at rest tend to remain at rest. One of the first ideas most of us learn in organizations is that organizations have great difficulty changing. In short, inertia rules the roost! The phenomenon of resistance to change, be it in inanimate objects, individuals, or organizations, is a reality that must be confronted and overcome to establish a disability management program. This chapter offers a framework for analyzing the existing situation and developing a strategy for effective change. It applies the concept of field theory initially described by Kurt Lewin.

How Organizations Operate

Think about organizations in which you have participated. Typically a great deal goes on among the individuals who make up the organization, in the organization itself as an entity, and in the organization's external environment. A set of individuals with very different agendas make up the organization. Some have production goals, others profit goals; others are more concerned about maintaining the organization as a system. Often these goals are determined by the title and departmental affiliation of the individual.

The structure of an organization frequently reflects the kind of work the company is engaged in or the technology it uses. For example, team participation may be structurally embedded in an organization that delivers a service such as health care. Individualism may characterize the sales agency of an insurance company. A hierarchical pattern may exist at a bank where decisions on sizeable, risky loans are made. A decision-making process marked by agreement among peers may develop at a company creating new computer software.

Futhermore, organizations exist in different environments, and these environments are constantly changing. A particularly relevant example is the passage of the Americans with Disabilities Act of 1990. Until its passage, only federal contractors had to be concerned with federal law requirements regarding employment of people with disabilities. With the ADA's passage, all firms with twenty-five or more employees faced such requirements. By 1994, organizations of fifteen or more will come under coverage. Those who opposed the ADA argued that, especially in small companies, this change might require a significant reorganization of their mode of operating, involving recruitment, division of work, and organization of physical space.

Obviously, organizations are open, fluid systems. Formally, they have specified chains of command and relationships that are detailed on organization charts. These are shadowed by more informal arrangements of friendship groups and work alliances that often are more influential than the structured order. All systems develop their own cultures, which define norms, values, and habitual interactions among the actors. These realities must be understood and responded to if any new initiative is to take hold.

Field Theory

Field theory interprets organizational behavior as a field of countervailing forces. At any particular time, and in relation to any particular issue, the existing pattern reflects the fact that those forces are in dynamic balance. Those who like the existing situation and those who would like to change it in any specific direction are relatively equal. For example, as regards organizational policy toward those who become disabled, the policy is maintained at its current level because those who support the present means of dealing with the issue are in the majority, while those who would seek change in any direction are balanced by those who would seek change in the opposite direction.

But that type of stability is not static. The policy is constantly confronted by changes within the organization and between it and its environment that may influence the field of forces. Increasing cost of health care may be one force for change. A labor market in which the skills required by the organization become short in supply may be another force for change. Interest within the organization in improving the response to affirmative action mandates may be another force for change. A new human resources director who comes from an organization that dealt differently with the disability issue may alter the forces. Downsizing of the organization may also mean change, as may a new technology that reduces the physical demands of the work. In most organizations, especially in today's rather turbulent economic environment, many of these forces are oscillating at the same time.

These forces for change begin to place the system under stress, encouraging readjustment that allows equilibrium to occur at a different point (or policy). Clearly, in a field of forces that cover many variables, their influence can exert pressure for change in different directions. Suppose that you would like to accomplish a particular change, for example, establish a return-to-work policy for employees experiencing the onset of disability in an organization with no such policy currently. There will be "driving forces" promoting change and "restraining forces" standing in the way of change. To achieve the desired change (that is, a new stability that incorporates a return-to-work policy), the driving forces that favor the policy must increase, the restraining forces that oppose it must decline, or some combination thereof must occur.

Most observers report that the greater the stress on the system, the more likely it is to be amenable to change. For anyone trying to orchestrate change, the implication is clear. If the problem you have identified is not causing sufficient stress within the organization, you may have to increase its visibility (and therefore stress) before the forces for change are sufficiently powerful to accomplish the desired end.

Key Actors

Several other ideas complement the concept of force field analysis. The analysis assumes "key actors"—those in the organization who have some involvement in the issue of interest or have decision-making power regardless of the issue. Key actors are able to influence the decision and action processes. It is important to know where each key actor will stand on the issue of interest. Is his or her position likely to be positive, negative, or neutral—will the actor facilitate, serve as a barrier, or stand by as an observer during the change process?

Consistently, commentators on organizational behavior have affirmed Adam Smith's contention that self-interest is the driving force of our endeavors. Even the biologists have failed to dispute this conclusion. They had long heralded the altruism of the animal kingdom that appeared in, for example, insect colonies (where every member cooperates to feed and protect the queen bee, the mother of them all). Recent research suggests, however, that each creature's instinct to maintain its gene pool is what keeps every member cooperating, not altruism at all.

So, it is important to understand the self-interest of each of the key actors and to marshal that self-interest into a coordinated, cooperative effort. We humans, however, are sufficiently complex that self-interest may subsume values that seem to contradict self-interest. For those who would influence others, it helps to be tuned in to their core belief system. Fortunately for anyone interested in promoting assistance to organizational members who develop disabilities, the sought-after outcome does not contradict most individuals' basic values.

Key actors usually see a proposal as in their own self-interest if they think it will decrease organizational uncertainty, increase their own autonomy, or ally them with a prestigious idea or group. They are also moved by what their "friends" are doing on the issue, and by what "debt" they feel to the initiator. Having a record of doing things for others within the system is helpful to anyone who wants to influence organizational policy. It then is possible to draw on your "social capital" or "debts" to gain support for your issue of interest.

The Change Agent

Every change process requires a change agent. Frequently, the change agent operates behind the scenes. In fact, chances of successfully influencing a system are vastly improved when the change agent does not seek personal recognition. This does not mean that the change agent is without self-interested motivation or that the change agent will not benefit measurably from the change. Organizational rewards come in many different guises—new reporting channels, changes in assignment, reputation as an expert, participation on significant task forces, additional resource allocations, powerful "friends"—each with much to recommend it. In short, a successful change agent is always rewarded, though not necessarily equally with the *recognized* agent of change.

Every organization is filled with well-intentioned persons who have been bruised trying to change it. Remember, *inertia rules the roost.* Preparing the system for change is no guarantee that change will occur. Even with the road map that this chapter provides, the path is filled with potential ruts. Before proceeding, the change agent needs to assess the territory (where the key actors stand), check out the roadblocks (restraining forces), pick a destination (goal) that can be reached within the constraints of the vehicle (resources available) and its gas supply (promoting forces), and then take a test run (pilot study) as quietly as possible.

Strategic planning is the absolutely essential roadbed (promoting forces) for effective change.

One expert recently described the changes in human resources policy that have accompanied the economic belt tightening. He advised establishing an atmosphere that indicates that the organization values its employees. Within that context, he identified flexible benefits, giving employees more choice, managing costs better, getting employees involved, line management decision making, and accountability as the ingredients of a preferred tactical approach to human resources policy. Establishing disability management fits well with this tactical approach.

Operationalizing Organizational Change

To consider the process of establishing a disability management program, imagine this scenario. The organization is at rest, but under stress. It has a generous benefits program that covers medical care, short- and long-term disability, and retirement. Its labor force is filled with tenured and committed employees who are highly skilled and aging. Organizational policy has been to retire, on long-term disability (LTD), all employees who develop disabilities serious enough to keep them out of work for a year. Moreover, policy has required that individuals be able to fulfill 100 percent of the functions of the job on return to work.

Several organizational actors begin to be concerned about the disability policy, including the affirmative action officer, the director of the employee assistance program, the risk manager, and the benefits director. Any one of them may become the change agent. Figure 4-1 suggests the range of potentially interested organizational members by their task roles and their possible attitudes toward a change in disability policy within the organization.

In any organization one person may occupy a number of the roles listed in Figure 4-1 and may be in conflict over the disability issue because of those seemingly contradictory roles. In large organizations there may already be a significant number of persons with disabilities, and they may constitute a strong and convincing influence for change. It is possible that an employee with a disability or one with a disabled family member may become the spark for change. In the development of employee assistance programs it was often recovering alcoholics who played significant roles in the establishment of EAPs. At the very least they made the issue of chemical abuse visible in the organization and urged a helping response to those experiencing substance abuse and other mental health problems.

An analysis of Figure 4-1 indicates that there are positive, negative, and neutral key actors in relation to concerns about disability issues. The

Figure 4-1. Key actors and their disability-related concerns.

Key Actor	*Disability-Related Concerns*
CEO	Considers the present benefits package too costly to maintain on an ongoing basis
Human Resources VP	Shares the CEO's concern about rising benefits costs and seeks productive channels of control that will not disrupt employee relations
Industrial Relations Manager	Concerned that any change in the benefits package will disrupt the carefully developed and trusting labor-management relationship and increase the adversarial stance of the union
Benefits Manager	Notes that LTD premiums and health care costs have been mounting faster than the inflation rate and feels some responsibility to develop a cost containment initiative
Medical Director	Feels that the best way to prevent disability is to be sure that no employee who is not in perfect health is working
Affirmative Action Officer	Aware of passage of the ADA and implications that present policy may violate regulations
EAP Director	Sees employees with disabilities who do not want to retire but cannot perform former tasks 100 percent
Risk Manager	Notes that the costs of workers compensation have been mounting faster than the inflation rate and that the problem will escalate when a new state benefits structure goes into effect next year
Safety Director	Believes that the aging of the work force constitutes an unacceptable risk for the organization and is urging a reduction in the retirement age
Line Managers	Feel pressure to produce and want all employees to be able to carry out all job functions without limitations
Union President	Regards any change in benefits as a give-back to be fought with all the strength the union can muster; disability issues consume major pieces of his time, and members seek support in establishing early retirement rights

positive views are held, in our mythical company, by the affirmative action officer, the benefits manager, the EAP director, and the risk manager. Each may play the role of change agent. More neutral views are held by the CEO and the vice-president of human resources. They are concerned about cost but have not necessarily identified the disability arena as a place of responsibility or one that needs change. Negative views are held by the industrial relations manager, the medical director, and the safety director, as well as by line managers and the union president.

The positions outlined in Figure 4-1 typify the ones likely to be held by key actors in most organizations. Although individual ideology may vary, it is one's organizational role that usually determines his or her typical position. For example, the CEO is likely to be concerned about many issues and would not necessarily focus on disability unless some force within the organization brought the issue to priority status. To a lesser extent, the same holds true for a human resources vice-president. Line managers, on the other hand, like stability and consistency so that they know how to plan the next day's work. A change in the way things are done disrupts that equilibrium and is most immediately problematic for them. Hence, in most organizations they tend to be the most "conservative." Yet they are also the key to change in most settings, since the day-to-day management of the operation is in their hands.

The other potentially negative positions may be the most amenable to redirection. It is possible that the organization has no union, in which case those two potential restraining forces (the industrial relations manager and the union president) will not exist. Or, the union president may know what the EAP director knows—that members would like to return to work before they are able to perform all the functions of their positions 100 percent. If so, and the union president can be won over to a disability management initiative, the industrial relations manager is likely to follow happily. Alternatively, the industrial relations manager may be convinced that the early retirement theme has become excessive and that it is a fair issue to bring to the bargaining table and expect some acceptance from the union president. The industrial relations manager under that scenario may be willing to test the waters with a pilot study.

The views of the safety director and the medical director are more ambiguous. They appear to hold positions based on preconceived notions, not an unusual situation. Data that would support an alternative conclusion (for example, the fact that it is the new, and probably young, employee who is now likely to sustain a serious work accident) may be all that is needed to help them become neutral, or even driving forces for disability management. The experience of other companies, as well, can provide convincing evidence for a reassessment of their positions. Friendship with the change agent, or with one of those who constitute the "team" of driving forces, may also be sufficient to move them into that column.

Any and all of these tactics are equally possible influencers. It is clear, therefore, that the change agent must begin to understand every actor involved and each individual's own self-interest and values, as well as formal and informal organizational ties. In any force field, as indicated earlier, there are many key actors, all of whom have some interest and stake in an identified problem and proposed change to resolve it. At least one of those actors is critical to the decision-making process (that is, no change can occur without his or her consent). Other actors are facilitators—they can help make the change possible.

Before going public with a proposal, a change agent would be well advised to carefully analyze the positions of the various key actors. It is equally important to identify what leverage—social capital, data, friendships, other influential contacts, resources—is available to enhance the driving forces, limit the restraining forces, and win over the critical actors so that the proposed change can go forth. Figures 4-2 and 4-3 provide a format for carrying out such an analysis. Figure 4-2 calls for listing all the key actors that the change agent can identify. Colleagues already part of the team should be listed as well. Figure 4-3 offers a format for analyzing each key actor's own force field. Once completed, these analyses provide the basis for formulating a strategy for attaining disability management goals.

Example

Analyze Figure 4-4 under the assumption that the benefits manager is the person who has decided to be the change agent. Also assume that the work force does not belong to any union, thereby eliminating the industrial relations manager and the union president from the list of key actors. In the benefits manager's analysis, as demonstrated in the figure, the training director becomes a key actor, particularly because he or she is seen as positively disposed to a disability management change. We know that in any organizational change, success is often tied to a good training program that prepares personnel to perform their new functions. Applying our concept of self-interest, we are assuming, therefore, that in this scenario the training director will support the change because it creates significant demand for training.

Example

In completing the key actor analysis shown in Figure 4-5, the change agent should be as specific as possible.

Figure 4-2. Identifying key actors.

Key Actors	*Indicate Critical or Facilitating*	*Indicate Positive (+), Neutral (0), Negative (–)*
1.		
2.		
3.		
4.		
5.		
6.		

A similar form is completed for *each* key actor identified in the force field. As the reader can see, the benefits manager identifies several forces operating on the human resources vice-president that will influence him to support disability management—what benchmark companies are doing in this arena, the vice-president's friendship with (and therefore trust of) the benefits manager, and his awareness of the ADA regulations and his own values. But forces interfering with his support are also identified—concern about his own boss's position, his work schedule, his fear that change may cause intradepartmental relationships to be upset, and his ambivalence about the impact of disability management over the long run. Following identification of these various forces, the benefits manager is able to discern strategies that might shift the balance in favor of support by the human resources vice-president for disability management. On the form, these are listed as initiatives that might increase the promoting forces or reduce the restraining forces.

Clearly, certain issues are more amenable to change than others; certain issues have greater potency than others; certain issues cannot be predicted because of their uncertain nature. The exercise in developing a force field analysis of the situation in relation to key actors helps the change agent understand whether or not the goal is realizable. Too many neutral and negative key actors, too strong restraining forces with little identifiable impetus to overcome them, too weak or uncertain driving forces all suggest that, at best, a great deal of work will be required to

Figure 4-3. Force field analysis for key actor.

Key Actor: ______________________________

Check one: _____ Critical Actor _____ Facilitating Actor

Check one: Currently _____ Positive
_____ Neutral
_____ Negative

Driving Forces (for change)	*Restraining Forces (against change)*

What may increase these?	*What may reduce these?*

Figure 4-4. Identifying key actors (filled-in example).

Key Actors	*Indicate Critical or Facilitating*	*Indicate Positive* (+), *Neutral* (0), *Negative* (–)
1. CEO	Critical	0
2. Human Resources VP	Critical	0
3. Affirmative Action Officer	Facilitating	+
4. EAP Director	Facilitating	+
5. Risk Manager	Facilitating	+
6. Medical Director	Facilitating	–
7. Safety Manager	Facilitating	–
8. Line Managers	Facilitating	–
9. Training Director	Facilitating	+

prepare the system for change. An alternative or partial goal may be advisable.

Obviously, the converse is equally true. If the analysis identifies that most key actors are positive or neutral, that there are few unpredictable forces, and that those in favor have high credibility and interest, the change agent may wish to move ahead quickly. In that case the force field analysis identifies what needs attention and what the agent can and cannot control. In short, it suggests a path for action.

Assessment of Data Needs

The discussion thus far suggests the value of data in moving the position of those who are neutral or negative toward a proposed change in a more positive direction. Employing organizations are a wealth of what might be called social booking information—data on various aspects of the work situation, family, personal history, and health experience of most employees. These data are rarely organized in such a way as to provide the framework necessary for developing a disability management initiative. The framework is there, however, and, increasingly, computer technology

Figure 4-5. Force field analysis for key actor (filled-in example).

Key Actor: Human Resources VP

Check one: X Critical Actor ___ Facilitating Actor

Check one: Currently
___ Positive
X Neutral
___ Negative

Driving Forces (for change)	*Restraining Forces (against change)*
Awareness that several of their benchmark companies have disability management programs	Uncertainty about the CEO's position on disability management
Respect for and friendship with benefits manager	Has been assigned major responsibility for recruiting staff for a new office opening in two months
Knowledge that the ADA will require efforts to maintain employees with disabilities at work	Concern over the scare tactics often used by affirmative action department
Humane basic values	Fear of intradepartmental struggle between medical and benefits person
	Believes turnover is in the firm's long-run interest and that it is easier to release those with "golden" packages

What may increase these?	*What may reduce these?*
More information on the programs in benchmark companies and on ADA regulations	Positive clarification from the CEO
Knowledge that employees with disabilities want to stay at work	Recruitment problems because of shortage of skilled workers
	Developing support from medical and safety directors

makes it accessible to those who know what they want to know and where the data are that will answer their questions easily, as shown in this case study.

Case Study

At one employer, of just over 5,000 employees, one of the authors was able to identify, with the director of management information (a potentially valuable key actor), where information was stored that would provide a complete data set to understand the economic and social impact of disability on employees and production. Data came from such varied sources as "Unconfidential Employee Data File," "Work History File," "Medical Department File," "Benefits Claim File," "Payroll File," and "Departmental Staffing File." These files were combined into a single system, dubbed the "Early Intervention System." It provided a profile of all employees, identified who develops disabilities, including cause, department, and work impact, and revealed health care and other benefits costs of disability.

A review of the data available also helped identify gaps in the collection of information. As a result, a form and reporting system were implemented to record the occurrence of workplace accidents from both the employee and supervisory points of view. (For examples of these forms, see Appendixes 7-1 and 7-2.) This eventually provided the basis for a systematic prevention effort.

The dispersed nature of supporting data in organizations is a primary explanation for lack of attention to the disability issue. In most settings, the cost of disability is disguised by dispersal of the evidence. The fact that most of the data are already embedded in existing systems makes it relatively cheap to acquire. Although the change agent can point to numerous disability management studies in the management literature, with positive results, it is always powerful to be able to answer questions specific to the setting in which the issue is being considered. Data not only provide important support for the proposal to develop a disability management program, but also establish a base line against which to measure the outcome of such a program.

Coordinating Committee

Preparing the organization for disability management is a process which moves almost imperceptibly from the lonely task of pre-analysis carried out by the change agent into the process of implementing disability management. The first component of disability management, namely, a needs assessment as indicated in Chapter 3, is also part of the organizational preparation effort. After that, when the process is truly underway, the next component is designation of a coordinating committee.

Selecting a coordinating committee is a delicate activity that requires thoughtful preparation. It should be undertaken once critical actors have agreed to pursue the disability management effort. The coordinating committee serves as the body that engages all parts of the organization's system in attending to the disability issue. Its membership should include:

- The critical actors or an empowered representative
- Those with a responsibility for any aspect of the program, including anyone who may exert formidable opposition, in order to neutralize that influence
- Someone who can bring financial resources to bear in the interest of disability management (for instance, a representative of the comptroller's office)

Some member of the coordinating committee should be designated as the chair. This probably should not be the same person responsible for case management of the disability program, although that person should be on the committee in either an official or ad hoc status. Since the coordinating committee is actually the legislature for the program, its leader should be an individual with policy responsibility. The coordinating committee presides over the significant decisions that must be made at the inception of the program. Its first responsibility is to develop, approve, and communicate the policy that will frame the disability management program.

But the coordinating committee is also the mediator of the ongoing program. It is responsible for resolving issues of interpretation of policy on accommodation, payment, return to work, and other aspects of the disability management program. Because of these ongoing responsibilities, the committee should be scheduled for regular meetings, at the beginning probably on a weekly basis. One of the major goals of a disability management program is to shorten the period of disability-driven absence from work. Expeditious attention to program issues is essential if the program is to fulfill its potential human and economic savings.

Once the coordinating committee is in operation, the organization is "on board" for the disability management initiative. Whether the committee is two people who meet together, precipitated by the onset of disability of one employee in a small firm, or a large-scale effort that involves numerous departments and is served by a facilitator especially employed for that project, its responsibilities are clear—to smooth the way for effective implementation of a creative effort at maintaining, or returning to work, employees who face the onset or functional worsening of their disabling condition. Chapter 5 describes the kind of policy issues that constitute the first agenda of the committee.

Chapter 5

Laying Out the Policy on Disability Management

Policy is the linchpin of any management program. It is essential to develop a clear policy, communicate it throughout the work system, and reinforce it with procedures and the allocation of resources. There should be no doubt in anyone's mind concerning the intent of management. The requirements for a good policy statement are like those for a good news story—it should contain all the information relevant to the situation, namely, who, what, when, where, and how:

- Who does the policy cover?
- What does it provide?
- When (under what circumstances) is it activated?
- Where does it apply?
- How will it be implemented?

A policy statement informs the system and all its actors (workers, supervisors, managers of those departments that are especially involved in disability issues, like benefits, the employment assistance program [EAP], EEO, medical) as to what can be expected. It provides a guide to behavior and offers the basis for understanding the consequences that will flow from any particular action.

A good policy statement starts with a sense of philosophy and values. It moves on to objectives. It ends with a set of particular ingredients and implementation procedures. Although a policy statement is just one component of a disability management program, it should subsume all other components mentioned in Chapter 3. It should be based on a needs assessment and provide for coordination, early identification, case management, transitional employment, training, data collection and analysis, and prevention.

New policy statements should be compatible with all other policies in a program. Nothing causes a policy to be ignored so surely as when it contradicts existing, accepted, and valued policies. In the case of disability management policy, for example, benefits, medical leave, and the collective bargaining contract itself may all need to be examined in light of policy development. So, too, it is vital that policy be viewed as a constantly evolving phenomenon; flexibility is crucial. These generalizations will become clearer as we turn to the specifics of disability management policy.

This chapter describes the ingredients in a disability management policy. It is designed to help with the multiple decisions that must be made in fashioning a position on the issue of disability. This includes developing objectives, establishing procedures for eligibility and early identification, and selecting the particular model.

Philosophy and Values

The absence of a policy is a policy in itself. When there is no written disability management policy, the unspoken policy is to encourage employees who become disabled to drop out of the labor force, wallow at home, overutilize medical care, and draw payment to stay home while they await total recovery. If total recovery does not occur, the unspoken policy dictates early termination or retirement.

This unspoken policy carries with it a parallel philosophy and set of values. It suggests that management does not care about its employees, that workers are regarded as replaceable parts in the production process, and that physical prowess is the most important characteristic of a good and valued employee, rather than length of service, experience, skill, knowledge, commitment and team participation, or any combination thereof.

Any human resources manager would blanch at committing such a philosophy or policy to paper. Yet, without writing an alternative policy, that unspoken position is the message that the system carries to its employees. Unfortunately, in some corporate cultures the message is not unintended. There is a general view that employees out on disability are somehow shirkers, ready to defraud the organization given the least chance. Can such an unwritten message carry anything but an invitation to abuse the system?

On the other hand, a written policy can have a positive impact on an organization and its environment. The philosophy and values appropriate to the disability issue are no different from those that have been identified consistently as encouraging the development of a productive work force. They are results-oriented and rest on these ideas:

- Recognition that employees are the organization's most valuable asset
- Commitment to the growth, development, and protection of that asset through employees making their own voluntary selection among available options
- Creation of a safe and healthy workplace and a climate that empowers worker participation
- Expectation that attention to these issues will improve morale and, therefore, productivity
- Understanding that the work force and management are in a partnership arrangement to achieve these conditions, and that mutual rights and responsibilities result

To this list of values proved to augment productivity can now be added one derived from disability management—accommodation of employees who experience the onset or worsening of a disabling condition, or whose change of assignment makes a pre-existing disability more dysfunctional.

Such a policy statement creates a culture based on positive attitudes. It enlists everyone in the disability management mission. It promotes the maximum yield from the organization's labor force. Although management often gives lip service to these principles, disability management hinges on action, not just words. It is essential, therefore, to *act* according to these principles if disability management is to have any significant impact. It is necessary to:

- *Show* that management cares by initiating contact with persons experiencing disability.
- *Offer* growth experiences by training and promoting employees regardless of disability.
- *Mitigate* the conditions that seem to result in accidents and illnesses that cause disabilities.
- *Share,* with workers and/or the union, decision-making power concerning disability issues.
- *Provide* workplace responsiveness through accommodation to the needs of persons with disabilities.

Policy Objectives

Too often a policy is issued and organizational actors have no way of evaluating its meaning in relation to their own responsibilities and achievements. A policy statement that includes objectives provides concrete guideposts against which outcomes can be measured. Individual and organizational objectives are necessary if the policy is to serve as a guide for action.

Individual Objectives

Individual objectives vary depending on the person's role in the disability management process. For the person experiencing the disability, the objectives may be maintaining the job or returning to work in a manner that optimizes the choices for the individual and the organization. Employees want to feel needed and important to the enterprise. A policy of immediate contact, for example, can prevent development of feelings of helplessness and disconnectedness from one's job and co-workers, often termed *disability mentality*.

A methodology that maximizes the participation of all interested parties—the person with a disability, and management and union representatives—is an essential ingredient for achieving successful outcomes. Measures of successful outcome for the individual employee facing disability include:

- Reduction in the recovery time from injury or illness
- Minimization of the permanency and severity of disability
- Prevention of loss of skills
- Keeping the job and protecting income

There are many other objectives that require individual action. Although most of these can be measured in organizational outcomes, there is a set that concerns primarily the behavior of supervisors. These include:

- Achieving work accommodation within the employee's own department most of the time
- Agreeing on an individual written rehabilitation contract, including a return-to-work schedule
- Reducing the number of workers out on disability in any particular department by eliminating or reducing the causes of accidents and industrial illnesses
- Minimizing the charges to the department for disability benefits

Organizational Objectives

As stressed throughout this book, disability management is organizationally desirable because it satisfies both humane and cost-containment objectives. Instead of constantly allocating funds to support disability, the organization reroutes them to improve treatment. Instead of casting off human resources as if they were depreciated machines, the program enhances the organization's human assets by promoting rehabilitation and prevention. Important evidence of organizational success, therefore, is reduced cost of disability and increased morale, commitment, and well-being within the company.

Under ideal circumstances, instituting a disability management program saves the employer money at no cost to the employee. It reinforces the work ethic and maintains valuable employees. It also assists the employer in achieving compliance with the regulations of the Americans with Disabilities Act of 1990.

Specific indicators of accomplishment of these objectives include these positive changes:

- Contact established with employees facing disability within the first week of disability in all situations where significant lost time is likely
- Reduced lost time due to shortened periods of absence from work following disability, made possible by arranging return to accommodated work during recovery rather than allowing long periods of idleness
- Appropriate work opportunities available for all those interested in keeping their job or returning to work, including cooperation from line supervisors in designating such employment opportunities
- Fewer employees seeking representation by lawyers and fewer adversarial workers compensation cases
- Reduced costs of medical care, workers compensation, and sickness and accident payments
- Increased use by claimants of care providers suggested by the medical department or case manager
- Favorable cost of rehabilitation care for those treated through the case management effort compared with those who select their own private providers
- Increased coordination of employee care among the organization, community physicians, other providers, and, when indicated, union representatives, thereby improving the quality of care, employee morale, and company image
- Reduction in the number and severity of accidents, industrial illnesses, and disabilities caused by trauma, as well as reduction in lost-time claims owing to recidivism
- Effective cooperation between representatives of the union and management on achieving the goals of the disability management program, and thereby improved labor-management relations (when the employees are under collective bargaining agreements)

Disability Management Procedures

Disability management requires action. A policy statement should indicate what those actions will be—in short, how the organization will be altered to implement the policy. The kind of provisions required include:

- Designating the amount of time allowed to elapse prior to contact with a newly disabled worker
- Specifying the conditions under which job accommodations will be made
- Agreeing on the length of time an employee's job will be guaranteed for his or her return
- Identifying the incentives and disincentives to be applied to gain cooperation from supervisors and newly disabled employees for program objectives
- Assigning responsibility for coordination and communication of disability management
- Establishing relationships with attending physicians and other community providers
- Developing data sets that will allow the program to function as well as monitor and evaluate its activities
- Analyzing precipitators of disability and developing responsive preventive actions, including ergonomic interventions
- Providing a dispute resolution mechanism

Issues

Each of these provisions raises issues that must be resolved before a disability management program can be finalized. As well, there are other important questions that warrant attention from decision makers. Following is a discussion of these issues and the advantages and disadvantages of alternative options. Wherever possible, specific questions that an organization might consider in the decision process are identified.

Eligibility

Identifying who will be the target of the disability management initiative and under what circumstances is the first issue to be faced by a planning committee. It raises the question of whether all individuals who exceed a given disability period (say, anyone who passes the one-week mark) will become targets, or whether particular diagnoses are of sole interest.

If intervention occurs too early in the disability cycle, more people are contacted than need be. For example, among those already out for a week, the vast majority will return to work within the first month, making it cost-ineffective to contact everyone at the one-week mark. Yet early intervention is vital to prevent development of a disability mentality (I'm disabled, no one wants me, I better hang on to those benefits checks, there's no hope of my getting back to work). Further, because the vast majority of persons are out for only a brief period, major costs can be saved by cutting even those brief periods, if only by a day each.

A solution to this dilemma is to use some criterion for contacting employees who lose time that combines diagnosis and time out with a physician's indication of expected date of return to work. Certainly, anyone whose disability is likely to extend beyond a month, by diagnosis (for example, cancer, stroke, head trauma), physician's expectation, or the actual passage of time, is a candidate for intervention during the first week. Efforts directed at optimizing return-to-work plans are indicated.

Once these screening criteria are determined, other issues must be resolved in establishing policy. A series of questions arise in relation to the conditions under which an individual is included in the disability initiative:

- *Will participation in a rehabilitation regime be mandatory for those seeking continued benefits?* Several state workers compensation laws already carry such a provision. Organizations can certainly build this requirement into their own short- and long-term disability plans. Such a requirement, to have a neutral impact, must be accompanied by provisions for accommodated and transitional work opportunities.

- *Will employees be required to accept task assignments outside their usual work?* Even if it represents a status reduction? In situations where new task assignments must be accepted, there is usually a provision to maintain former earnings levels, at least for a designated period of not less than one year.

- *What are the minimum number of hours required for an employee to be included in the accommodated work program?* Does someone have to work every day or just a few days a week? How many hours per day will be required? Although the basic principle in return to work is to eliminate paying employees for staying at home, until workers can perform several hours of work a day, several days a week, work requirements may be viewed as punishing rather than rehabilitative.

- *What is the maximum period of time (if any) that an employee will be allowed to remain in a transitional work slot?* Will this differ if an employee is being maintained at full wages? At reduced wages? Experiencing a disability should not be allowed to turn into a reward. Most organizations have a pool of special assignments that they use as transitional positions. If transitional work assignments are particularly pleasant or easy, or given to those employees who did not like their usual work, there is a tendency to welcome these provisional opportunities. As a result, many companies limit occupancy of these positions to three months to avoid filling them up and having to create more. Of course, some employees will never be able to return to their former jobs. For them, permanent accommodated or alternative assignments must be developed outside the "special assignment pool."

• *What criteria should be applied to decide to retire someone on disability rather than attempt return to work?* The dividing line between accommodating a worker with a disability and separating him or her from the work force should be determined on the basis of what is good for the employee in the first instance. There are situations where a disability is best resolved by retraining the person for work that is within his or her capacity, but outside the present employer's opportunities. There are other circumstances where the disability is of sufficient severity that, coupled with the individual's age, education, and the available opportunities in the labor market, no meaningful work is possible. Both these situations suggest termination or retirement rather than return to work.

Early Identification

A disability management policy must include directives for all persons in contact with an employee at the onset or worsening of a disability. This may include supervisors, who often are the first to be aware of an accident or illness that creates a disability. Performance appraisal of employees may also alert a supervisor to deteriorating performance. Or the employee may volunteer the onset of a disabling condition.

The supervisor can use the deteriorating job performance as a signal to refer the employee to the EAP. Although often the assumption is that declining productivity is linked to a substance abuse problem, EAPs report that this is the true cause less than a quarter of the time. The onset of physical or emotional disability, which warrants early attention, may be the problem. EAPs can be particularly effective in identifying early stress situations that can cause future disability. As a case-finding mechanism, the EAP, particularly when it is in-house, is unsurpassed. That unit has the potential, as well, to carry forth the coordinating function of the disability management policy.

Coordination—Assignment of Responsibility

The employee who initiates interest in the disability management issue varies by setting. As indicated, sometimes EAP personnel identify the need for disability management from the content of their caseload. Often risk management becomes concerned about the escalating costs of workers compensation. Safety may stimulate interest when a review of their data identifies the need for better prevention. Many other possibilities present themselves according to the culture and circumstances of a particular organization. Disability will continue to be everybody's business, and therefore nobody's business, unless responsibility is clarified at the policy level.

The policy statement should specify the structure and assign responsibility for the disability management function. Options range from appointing a special coordinator with a clinical background to designating a claims examiner or someone in the human resources department. In small settings, disability management becomes yet another responsibility of the sole personnel practitioner in the organization, or the administrative assistant to the director. While there are specific skills required to administer the activity, they can be learned through experience and training. The necessary (although not necessarily sufficient) condition is that someone be in charge.

Make or Buy?

Initiating a disability management program requires a significant organizational effort. The "make or buy" decision concerns whether the organization should utilize its own personnel to establish and operate the program (make) or whether it should contract with an outside specialist for such services (buy). There are advantages to each option. A company that "makes" its own disability program is better able to reflect its corporate culture and distinctive interests. It can respond swiftly to changing situations. For large organizations, especially ones with technology unique to the setting (for example, a steel mill) or with a structure of social and medical services already in place, the make decision appears superior.

Yet, even some large organizations may think that they are not equipped to establish and monitor such an initiative, or do not wish to allocate resources and attention to this unfamiliar turf. For them and for small companies (under 1,000 employees), it may be cost-effective and programmatically beneficial to "buy." Many private vendors of rehabilitation services are willing to accept such a challenge. (Further discussion of this issue can be found in Chapter 6 on case management.)

The variables an organization should review in arriving at the make-or-buy decision include:

- Past behavior (prior contracting makes it easier to contract a new function)

- Availability of providers and other resources in the local community (in a resource-rich community it is easier to find a provider, yet easier to run an in-house program)
- Interest in centralizing or decentralizing the function (a minimum size is necessary for a "make" decision to be economically viable, while an organization with many satellite sites may wish to "buy" services locally)
- How specialized the jobs and labor force of the organization are (if there are unique jobs, it is harder to engage an outside provider who has the necessary knowledge)
- Value of introducing a third party—in this case, a provider (this is sometimes an advantage when there is an adversarial mind-set; organizations with long histories of litigation around disability issues may wish to start their new initiative with a "buy" decision and move later, once a new culture is established, to a "make" situation)
- Whether or not the workplace is organized (unions often prefer the work to be done inside)

All these issues need consideration in the make-or-buy decision process. And the decision itself does not have to be an either-or one. A mix is possible in which the program is administered in-house and the resources for actual treatment are harnessed by a contractor. (This is an especially viable model for a small business.) In other cases, central locations may be handled better in-house, while small, dispersed field sites are easier served through a local provider.

Several other points related to the make-or-buy decision must also be considered:

• *Self-insure or insure through a carrier.* If the employer provides benefits through an insurance carrier, the insurance policy can be written to incorporate the main components of the disability management program. The employer may wish to have a liaison role to monitor program quality, but does not itself have to "make" a program.

A self-insured employer, however, has a strong incentive to "make"—to handle the entire process in-house and reap all the savings that such administrative control can provide. In a study of disability management programs that surveyed 1,000 employers (Akabas and Krauskopf 1989), there was a high correlation between being self-insured and having a disability management program.

• *Extent of medical care and social services offered at the workplace.* Organizations that have an extensive medical department or employee assistance program in-house have a significant head start on "making" a disability management initiative. An effective program, even under a "buy" decision, would need to coordinate with these in-house resources, causing sufficient duplication of effort to commend the "make" decision. (Without these in-house resources, the cost advantage may lie with a contracted provider.)

- *Centralized or decentralized model.* In situations where the benefits administration is centralized, there is some advantage in "making" an organizational disability management program. A more decentralized operation, either because it has multiple smaller units, or because it leaves decision making in the field, is better served by allowing each unit to arrive at its own decision, and this probably argues for the "buy" option.

Incentives and Disincentives

To accomplish disability management objectives, there is a need to discourage certain negative tendencies (like staying home longer than necessary because benefits are endangered once a person with a disability returns to work) and encourage positive ones on the part of such key organizational actors as supervisors (like welcoming back a supervisee with a disability because that results in an immediate unit cost savings for the supervisor by transferring disability benefits costs to a central pool). At the very least, policies need to be enacted to affect positively the behavior of supervisors and workers with disabilities.

Supervisory Cooperation

Supervisors, who play a central role in disability management, are often caught between the proverbial rock and hard place. They are asked to accommodate workers who, for a time at least, may not be able to perform their customary tasks, yet they are expected to meet the usual production requirements for their unit. One can understand and empathize with the supervisor who waits an extra week before encouraging the return of a worker with a disability, hoping that the additional time will bring the employee closer to being able to perform his or her usual work. But such behavior sabotages the return-to-work goal.

A carrot-and-stick approach is needed to encourage supervisors to support return-to-work programs. Use of his or her own performance appraisal to encourage a supervisor to maintain communication with employees with disabilities and encourage them to return to work is an effective strategy. Charging benefits payments back to a supervisor can provide a powerful disincentive to leave a disabled worker at home. At the same time, offering to pay such benefits from a central pool rather than from an individual supervisor's budget in situations where the employee is returned to partial work can help to overcome supervisory reluctance.

There are many additional incentives for supervisors to support a disability management initiative. For example, it is difficult to recruit replacement labor on a temporary basis. If a supervisor is not allowed to fill a job when an employee is out on disability, the supervisor has an incentive to identify accommodations. Some companies make accommodating employees with disabilities one of the criteria on which a supervisor is evaluated. When merit raises are tied to positive evaluations, the drive toward accommodation is noticeably enhanced.

Other features that can be built into a performance appraisal include evaluation of a unit's reduction in accident time and other lost-time activities. Safety audits and holding supervisors responsible for employee training help to promote prevention. Supervisors should be responsible for complete investigation of the circumstances of any accidents, and there should be a comparative analysis of the accident "experience" of each supervisor. Building safety into performance review is likely to encourage safety promotion and other prevention initiatives. Supervisors also have an incentive to participate in early case identification, since it is always easier to remedy a problem before it becomes serious, difficult, and costly. The incentive to participate is even greater if the budget implications for the supervisor are positive.

Steelcase, one of the world's largest office equipment manufacturers, has an interesting early identification program that depends on supervisors. It recognizes that it is possible that a disability may cause an employee to become dysfunctional and subject to a disciplinary process. The Employee Performance Improvement Committee, headed by the plant manager, explores the situation of any employee who accumulates a specified number of points for work infractions before termination is considered. A counselor meets with the employee to explore the problem and be available to present the employee's perspective at the committee meeting. When disability is identified, therapeutic intervention rather than termination is recommended.

Supervisors require two sorts of information in order to carry out their roles in disability management—information as to what accidents are occurring in their areas, and information about how to work with an employee who encounters a disability. Inadequate training and information flow can make the disability management role of supervisors extremely frustrating and burdensome, resulting in unconscious and conscious behavior that impedes the disability management initiative.

Employee Cooperation

It is necessary as well to use incentives to encourage employees to return to work as soon as appropriate. As alluded to throughout, the onset of disability is a fearsome experience. James A. Hatherley of Liberty Mutual Insurance Company noted in 1991, "Beyond their injuries, injured workers are worried about their jobs, their families, and their ability to pay their bills. Failure to respond to these urgent fears and needs in a timely manner only reinforces their mistrust of their employer. . . ." If they are expected to cooperate in the disability management procedure, workers facing disability need to be made "whole." Their income and opportunity should remain unaffected by the onset of disability.

How to accomplish this challenges most employers. The nature of the benefits and work-accommodation structure holds the key. The self-insured employer need only pay out the difference between the disability benefit and the usual salary of the employee. The same is so for the organization that provides benefits through a carrier, with one major hitch—policies must be written so that benefits continue while other than usual work is being performed or while usual work is being performed at reduced productivity.

Such provisions are not uniformly available. In many states, for example, the workers compensation law does not allow for full payment of benefits when partial earnings are received. (In some, it does not allow for any payment when work of any kind is resumed.) Somehow, the worker who is eligible for benefits must receive a sum equal to the usual pay to have an incentive to return to work before full recovery.

This is particularly difficult to accomplish when the task to which the individual is to return carries a lower rate of pay than his or her former job, or when the employee is unable to work full time, even when the only lost time is that involved in fulfilling the medical regimen. Nonetheless, the accommodated task, because it is only temporary, can be paid at a higher rate than others are receiving for the same task. The important restriction is that this action must be a clear provision of formal policy, known to all parties. Assurance that a benefit is uniformly provided helps co-workers accept what might otherwise be considered favoritism.

Providing release time for medical care is another incentive to employees to return to work. It carries the message, "We want you back, but we also want to take care of you." Pilkerton Glass in England is the largest glassmaker in the world. In the early days of glassmaking, the material would shatter frequently, causing serious injury to the tendons and ligaments of workers. Pilkerton developed an in-plant rehabilitation service to care for such employees. Now that glassmaking is a much safer operation, the rehabilitation service at Pilkerton is devoted to in-house rehabilitation for back injuries and cardiovascular diseases. Workers lose hardly any time from work because they know that the best care in the community is available at the plant!

A lengthy period of job guarantee was identified earlier as an incentive for supervisors to find accommodated work for a supervisee experiencing disability. Here we are faced with a dilemma. A short period of job guarantee is an incentive for employees to return to work. (For example, Wang Laboratories guarantees jobs for thirteen weeks. Although recovered employees may return after that time, there is no guarantee of returning to the same job beyond the thirteen-week period. Wang has found this to be a significant incentive for "recovery" by thirteen weeks.) Some limitation on the time allowed to return to work is essential. The particular amount of time that will balance supervisor and supervisee incentives may differ depending on the culture of the company and the nature of its work.

Transitional Employment and Job Accommodation

One of the keys to making employees "whole" and providing incentives for them to return to work is the nature of the jobs available when they return to the workplace unable to perform their usual work. In considering appropriate assignments, the focus must be on the functional capacity of the employee rather than on the diagnosis or disability. The goal should be to provide work that will be useful to the organization *and* serve as a rehabilitative assignment for the employee. Such assignments should be for a limited time period. In workplaces covered by union contracts, these jobs should be considered outside the contract for purposes of seniority, bumping, and other job protection measures provided in the collective bargaining agreement.

Some employers create a special pool for jobs for such functions as recycling, cleaning, clerical operations, training, safety, housekeeping, and inspection. Even the smallest employer has such easily overlooked tasks. This work is often valuable, but neglected when organizational planning is attentive solely to production and the "bottom line." Because employees on accommodated jobs would not be able to do their usual work, and would therefore be at home if transitional spots were unavailable, the cost of these needed but ignored assignments is only the difference between the worker's disability or compensation benefit and usual pay. For the average employee this comes to about $200.00 per week. Almost any work performed is likely to be worth more than that.

Weirton Steel, in cooperation with its union, devised a particularly creative alternative employment situation to encourage early return to work. The company realized that the mill was becoming computerized, and that this would require new skills among all its employees. Each person out on disability was allowed to draw full pay if he or she attended a computer class at the mill for the period of disability, or up to sixty days, whichever was shorter. Those who experienced disability returned to work more skilled than their nondisabled co-workers, and Weirton carried out essential training at minimum cost.

Steelcase found another solution. Its employees use work gloves in large volume. These require frequent cleaning and repair, which Steelcase originally contracted out. They decided that the work would be an ideal transitional job and established a glove-servicing activity on-site as an assignment for employees recovering from disability.

Other employers have set up similar "subcontracting shops" within their own operation, where the work can be tailored to the rehabilitation goal of the worker. Given a work force of serveral thousand, the pool of those out on disability usually possesses the variety of skills and abilities needed for most jobs within the organization. And if those employees can be accommodated at work, they keep in contact with peers in the lunchroom, the parking lot, and other plant locations and so avoid the onset of a disability mentality.

Dispute Resolution Mechanism

Even the best-written of policies will not eliminate disagreement on how they should be interpreted. Every policy statement on disability management should designate an individual, or title, that will be charged with conflict resolution. In organizations with collective bargaining contracts and arbitration provisions, it is possible to treat disagreements on disability through them. Lacking a grievance procedure, organizations may wish to structure a multistep appeal process and designate a respected health provider as the final arbiter. (This is a rarely used provision once a culture develops that encourages and accepts optimal timing on return to work as the expected outcome of disability.)

Remember the Other Players

There are many other actors in the disability management effort that need attention. While not part of the policy agenda, their interests are worthy of note. As policy is enacted, attention to their interests is necessary so that they promote the goals of disability management rather than impede them. These other actors include the union, attending physicians and other community providers, and attorneys who represent compensation claimants.

In unionized workplaces, as has been mentioned, the union can have a positive impact on disability management goals, provided it is included in the planning. A disability management policy must be flexible, which means that exceptions to usual policy may have to be incorporated in the plan. Sometimes these exceptions affect the terms of the collectively bargained agreement, a situation known to be viewed with suspicion by even the most cooperative union. Yet, because disability can affect anyone, at any time, provisions that take care of disability are in everyone's interest. The union can understand that, and can sell a disability policy to its members, given the opportunity. Unions welcome such policies because disability is often a thorny issue that demands inordinate time and energy from union leaders. Moreover, members out on disability may have little else to concentrate on than how little protection they feel they have received from the union. In short, a worker out on disability is often a temporarily disgruntled union member, seeking extensive attention from the leadership.

Community providers and physicians may be unwittingly obstructive of disability management policy. They are unclear about the demands of jobs and, therefore, may overprotect their patients with regard to appropriate return-to-work dates (as discussed in Chapter 9). They are fearful of malpractice suits and anxious to "keep their patients happy" so that they will continue to seek their services. Research has confirmed that a doctor's word is "sacred," and 90 percent of all workers return to work on the date the doctor initially projected for return. But physicians have little information about the workplace, what their patients' usual work is, and what accommodations are possible.

Several steps can be taken to achieve support from community providers for disability management efforts. Communication is basic. Physicians want to learn, and to provide good care to their patients. The employer can help them accomplish that objective by including them in case management discussion (see Chapter 6). Adding questions about rehabilitation and work accommodation on the physician report form, and providing more choices concerning date of likely return to work, will help doctors think about these issues.

Some employers invite doctors known to treat a significant number of their employees to tour the workplace. In situations where there is an HMO, this is certainly a course to be recommended. Depending on how large the work site is, the employer may wish to develop a newsletter for physicians (issued as needed) that covers new developments in the specific disability situations most likely to occur within the organization. It is also possible to offer special training programs to community physicians on occupational rehabilitation. Good relationships with the medical and social service providers within the employer's community are relatively easy to establish and absolutely essential to effective disability management policy.

Lawyers, too, may obstruct disability management efforts. Building a case for a claimant that depends on keeping someone out of work, and using excessive medical care, is irresponsible behavior that is hurtful to the long-run interests of the client. Most workers want to work, and even unexpectedly large settlements are inadequate compensation for the loss of that role. Nor do settlements compensate for the expected inflation that may eventually eat up most of an unemployed client's gain. Helping clients receive prompt and fair compensation is responsible practice. Peer review within the legal community should disavow those situations where excessive representation is destructive to workers' well-being. If necessary, employers should press these issues before the appropriate review bodies.

Conclusion

Disability affects different companies differently. In a small business, its onset, though infrequent, will be dramatic and personal. In a larger organization, disability is an issue which tends to be brushed aside. Employers seem to relinquish control and allow the response to disability to fragment in a way that they would never allow in the production process.

Disability management policy is a response to both situations. It is part of a continuum of concern for employees. It reinforces the work ethic, changes the balance between indemnity and prevention, and maintains valuable employees. It views the worker as a committed partner rather than an employee about whom management should be suspicious. It recognizes that a worker who is dedicated on Monday does not adopt a "beat the system" stance on Tuesday just because he or she suffers an illness or injury. It concedes that the skills and potential contribution of such a worker continue to have value despite the onset of disability. It provides an opportunity to ensure quality care and to move the organization from insurance coverage to real involvement in employee health. It confirms that it is less costly to prevent than to go back and fix. It instructs supervisors that they are expected to develop all workers, including those with disabilities, and it ensures that career building will not be interrupted because of the onset of disability.

There are no quick ways to achieve such outcomes. What is required is sustained effort, clearly enunciated and consistently enacted—in short, a disability management policy.

Appendix 5-1
Logic Company: Model Policy and Guidelines for a Disability Management Program

Logic Company confirms that its most valuable asset is its employees. An important goal of the company, therefore, is to return employees who are out of work because of a disability to productive and rewarding jobs at the earliest appropriate time.

Information, assistance, and access to proper medical and rehabilitation resources will be provided to help employees recover so that they may return to work.

In order to coordinate all issues related to managing disability, a task force will be formed, which will report to the vice-president of human resources. The core group will consist of representatives from the medical department, benefits, industrial relations, and other appropriate operations managers and union representatives. This task force will be responsible for developing and coordinating policies and procedures.

All efforts will be made to return an employee to his original job or to a comparable job that is open and at the same pay rate. Workplace accommodations will be explored that will permit such a job return. If this is impossible either because there are no such jobs open or because the employee's disability, even with reasonable accommodations, does not permit the same type of employment, other job options will be identified. If an employee must return to a job at a lower salary than his predisability wage, for a period not to exceed the first year, and under the discretion of the company physician, the disability wage replacement programs, either short-term or long-term disability, will make up the difference between the current wage and the employee's original standard earnings. The Earnings Protection Plan or Long-term Disability Plan (LTD) will supplement the employee's salary *on the new job* only to an amount *not greater than* the disability payment the employee would have been eligible to receive (when the salary *for the new job* is less than the original standard earnings).

Assuming appropriate documentation of disability from the employee's physician or the medical department, an employee's job will remain unfilled for a period not to exceed six months for a sickness and accident claim. In a workers compensation claim it can remain open for as long as appeals are pending. During this period, the cost of hiring temporary employees will be borne by the line manager's budget.

The company encourages the development of part-time and/or transitional employment as a strategy for assisting employees to return to work as early as appropriate. In these instances, the employee will receive sickness and accident or worker's compensation payments supplemented by the percentage of the full-time wage or salary reflected in the actual hours worked. The employee's wage or base salary will increase, therefore, as he or she returns full-time to the normal occupation. No employee will earn more than his or her original wage or base salary, however, unless the job to which the worker returns has a higher rate than his or her original position.

Earnings Protection Plan or LTD payments, which begin at the end of short-term disability, will continue to be available only if the employee is cooperating with the treatment plan prescribed by the medical department. Such a plan will be developed during the short-term disability period in cooperation with, and with the full participation of, the employee.

Disagreements regarding treatment requirements or return-to-work recommendations will be reviewed by the medical director, the employee's representative(s), such as an outside physician, or another physician determined by the medical department to be competent in the field. If necessary, a referral to a third-party physician selected by the medical department, which shall apply the criterion of "recognized competence," will be considered in determining appropriate treatment and course of action. Employees must be participating in an approved rehabilitation program for continued coverage.

If no job is available, the company will attempt to find or develop training programs in appropriate skills to increase the possibility of the employee's finding a job either within Logic Company or in another company. Benefits will be continued during training periods as they would have been under present workers compensation or sickness and accident coverage.

Efforts will be made to identify prevention programs that will reduce the possibility of employees' developing disabilities. These efforts may include health promotion programs and ergonomic interventions. Early voluntary referral to the medical department by supervisors or union representatives will also be encouraged for employees who appear at risk of disability.

Parallel efforts will be made to establish alternative job opportunities for employees who develop disabilities. These will include transitional, time-limited employment in a special section set aside to perform previously contracted-out work, new jobs that will enhance the safety of employees and the smooth functioning of production, and such other opportunities that may be developed by the Disability Task Force.

Special disability management staff will be identified, in the medical department, who will have case management responsibilities for those employees who have been out of work for six days and training responsibilities for those employees and union members who carry additional responsibilities in the disability management system.

Procedures

The six guidelines that follow apply to all the following disability management procedures:

1. Employees are encouraged to return to work.

2. Reducing the cost of disability payments and medical care is in the interest of all employees, the union, and the management of the company.

3. No employee shall lose seniority contractual rights or benefits as a result of return to work.

4. Disability management should save the company money at no cost to the individual employee with a disability.

5. Any new job created for a person with a disability will not become part of seniority rights and will remain exclusively for purpose of affirmative action for those with disabilities. These jobs may be held on a part-time or full-time basis. As well, accommodation on formerly held jobs may involve part-time work.

6. Unless unable to do so because of the severity of injury, all employees sustaining on-the-job accidents shall complete an accident report at the time they receive emergency care.

On day of absence, an employee or a family member must notify the supervisor. The supervisor will discuss the needs of the employee and possible return to work with the caller and record the information in the employee's record. If an employee fails to call, it is the responsibility of the supervisor to follow up with a call to the employee to ensure uniform information gathering, confirm medical reports, or open other sources of information.

Within the first week that the employee remains out of work, the employee's supervisor will notify the disability management staff. This staff will contact the employee and send him or her all material describing medical documentation requirements and benefits procedures. At this time disability management staff will begin an assessment process that will identify appropriate resources necessary to facilitate the employee's recovery and return to work.

From then until work return, disability management staff will coordinate these services. Regular contact will be maintained with the supervisor to involve him or her in the employee's progress and to assess and alleviate, jointly, any problems that may inhibit the employee's return.

At the appropriate time, disability management staff, in cooperation with the supervisor and other team members as indicated by the particular needs of the person with the disability, will be responsible for negotiating reasonable job accommodation, including part-time or transitional employment and changes in task assignment, shift, or equipment.

By month four, any long-term rehabilitation or social or medical interventions should be planned and agreed to by the employee. The employee's adherence to this plan will permit him or her to receive disability payments. Disability management staff will also help the employee apply for Social Security disability benefits should it appear that the employee will be unable to return to any kind of work or that the total disability will last more than six months.

Each employee on disability payments will be required to maintain current medical documentation regarding the disability and further documentation attesting to adherence to the rehabilitation plan. The disability management staff will be responsible for periodic review of long-term cases, and will plan work-return strategies, as described above, at the appropriate time.

Training programs for supervisors and union representatives will be planned and offered at regular intervals to describe the disability management program and supervisory roles, including that of acting as an early referral source.

Disability management staff will also provide literature and training programs for employees, describing the disability management system and any new programs or policies that are part of it.

Chapter 6

Case Management as a Disability Management Tool

Case management is an essential element in dealing effectively with workplace disability. The appointment of a case manager by an employer usually signifies a serious commitment to disability management and return to work.

This chapter delineates the scope of case management and traces this new, powerful, and popular intervention strategy. Case managers are described in relation to their background and practices (relevant to specific populations). Four different models of case management are reviewed briefly. Guidelines are offered for selecting a case management firm should the employer decide to contract for the service from an outside vendor. The costs and benefits of case management are also considered.

Although case management is just one of nine specific components (identified in Chapter 1) of a disability management initiative, it is the case manager (often in cooperation with others) who is involved in or directly responsible for the other eight components. That is, the case manager participates in establishing relevant policies and procedures, is involved in case finding and early intervention, serves on the coordinating committee, is the principal liaison with community agencies, designs and participates in the training of key actors, implements the data collection and evaluation scheme, and advises on matters of safety and prevention. The company programs described in Chapter 8 affirm that case managers perform all these tasks and more, depending upon circumstances, and are the focal point of the disability management program. The case manager also serves as the system "navigator," facilitating the personal contacts and flow of information between the various parties involved in the complex enterprise of disability management. The case manager, however, has a primary focus on helping the individual confronted by the onset or worsening of disability.

Scope of Case Management

Case management has recognized antecedents in the professional traditions of social work, nursing, psychology, and rehabilitation counseling. There is little in the case management approach that is new or different from what has been practiced for decades in such disciplines. What is new, however, is the emphasis on case management as a discrete, valued function that can make an impressive impact on the individual and on the various systems of care.

Case management has traditionally been used in social work to help people coordinate their use of social services. More recently, case management has been used to ensure quality and achieve cost-effectiveness in delivery and use of health care and mental health services. Medical case management has been described as one of the major health care strategies to emerge during the 1980s. Rehabilitation and facilitation of return to work on behalf of employees with a serious or catastrophic illness or disability is a relatively new arena for the practice of case management. Some commentators have referred to this development as the "second generation" of case management.

In recent years case management has been extended to a variety of sites (private case management firms, mental health centers, insurance companies, corporate settings, hospitals) on behalf of individuals in need of multiple and costly services (neonatal infants, AIDS victims, cancer and stroke patients, head injury patients).

Over the last ten years numerous authors (Merrill 1985; Kaplan 1990; Akabas and Krauskopf 1989; Austin 1983; Moxley 1989; Sanborn 1983; Weil and Karls 1989; Henderson 1988) from an array of disciplines (social work, health care, mental health) have offered various definitions of case management. Although these definitions may differ in some respects, the most important element of the various definitions is the same—namely, case management is *a method of coordinating and integrating a range of social, health, and rehabilitation services to enhance the functioning and quality of life of the individual, improve the quality of care, and conserve costs.* While the organizational setting may dictate certain variations on this theme, there is general agreement that the case manager provides the following:

- *Case identification.* The case manager is immediately notified when an employee has a serious work injury or disabling illness and qualifies for short-term disability or workers compensation.
- *Client assessment and planning.* The case manager meets with the disabled worker to assess the employee's needs and disability status and

begins to make specific plans for treatment, job accommodations, and timely return to work. The case manager usually records his or her assessment and writes an individualized plan laying out the future course of action, all with a view toward timely, appropriate return to work. (The basis for an effective case management process is provided by the intake interview, shown in Appendix 6-1.) The case manager meets with the supervisor and the company or treating physician, convenes the coordinating committee, and refers the employee to a local rehabilitation service agency, the employee assistance program (EAP), or other community-based agency.

- *Provision and implementation of services.* The case manager assists in the design of job accommodations, performs a vocational assessment, counsels, supports, and works to motivate the employee, and helps the family identify benefits and resources that may be relevant to its needs.

- *Monitoring, evaluation, and follow through.* The case manager maintains contact with the employee, oversees provisions of all services by outside vendors, records data as to progress and outcome, and follows the employee's adjustment after the return to work.

- *Advocacy.* The case manager "lobbies" on behalf of the employee with the supervisor, union representative, or company physician; closely monitors the provisions of community services to ensure that the employee receives high-quality service at a reasonable cost; and works with community groups to establish services needed by employees (a drug treatment clinic, a hospice, a work-hardening program that helps an employee slowly increase work capacity during the return-to-work process).

The Popular Appeal of Case Management

The tremendous growth in the use of case management services has been documented by two surveys. In 1986 the Washington Business Group on Health found that only 40 percent of 181 large companies surveyed had a case management program. By 1988, just two years later, all but two of 88 companies surveyed had such a program—and one of those two was planning to implement a program within the next two years (Schwartz and Heckard 1988).

In her survey, Kaplan (1990) noted that case management became a popular concept during the 1980s because of its dual focus: On the one hand, it enhances client functioning; on the other, it contains costs. Serious illness and disability can create overwhelming multiple problems for the employee and his or her family. Add to these problems the complexity of the social service and health care systems and their cost, the role that case management can play can be appreciated.

In both the public and private sectors, case management evolved as a discrete service to accomplish the following objectives:

- Ensure continuity of care across services at any given point or over time as the individual moves from one status or setting to another; for example, when an employee is discharged from an in-patient psychiatric center to a community provider.
- Ensure that services are responsive to the full range of the individual's needs as those needs change over time; for instance, a head-injured person may need residential, social service, and employment assistance over many years.
- Help individuals gain access to entitled benefits by dealing with such questions as eligibility criteria and documentation requirements, such as the referral of an employee on long-term disability to the Social Security Administration for disability benefits.
- Ensure that services provided match the individual's needs and are provided in a proper, timely, and nonduplicative manner; for example, making sure that an employee on workers compensation receives vocational services from a public or private rehabilitation agency.

Case managers may become counselors for persons facing disability, helping them sort through options and emotions that follow the onset of their condition. Advocacy on behalf of employees, once they have decided on their preferred course of action, can also be a case management role.

The Practice of Case Management

Karen Kaplan (1990), director of the National Center for Social Policy and Practice, emphasizes that:

> The basic premise of case management is simple: It is the delivery of the right services at the right time. Done correctly, case management works because it helps ensure top quality care delivered in a timely fashion. It allows the use of appropriate specialized services that maximize recovery.

Timely delivery, in itself, can be a cost-containment device. It reduces or eliminates the expensive search for the elusive "cure" and helps employees move quickly through the most costly stages of return to work.

Who Are Case Managers?

Case management is evolving as a professional function offered by a variety of disciplines, including social work, nursing, medicine, rehabilitation counseling, and psychology. The "discipline of choice" is usually determined by the organizational setting, the needs of the clientele, and the objectives to be achieved. If the organizational setting is a large insurance company, and the primary need of the clients is medical case management with an emphasis on quality health care and cost control, nursing is more likely to be the discipline of choice. An employee assistance program concerned with the needs of mental health and substance abuse clients, with the objective of personal and family adjustment, is more likely to opt for a social worker. A large employer who wants a case manager familiar with vocational evaluation techniques and job accommodations to facilitate the return to work may prefer a vocational rehabilitation counselor.

Who Receives Case Management Services?

A variety of factors determine who receives case management services, including diagnosis and severity of the disabling condition, complexity of the individual situation, and the likelihood of high cost. Usually one or more of the following conditions characterizes the recipient of case management. He or she is:

- Undergoing extensive medical or mental health treatment
- Receiving short- or long-term disability benefits
- Involved in a particularly difficult and long-term workers compensation case
- Experiencing the worsening of a condition that causes functional problems in performing the usual job tasks

Case Management and Catastrophic Illness

Catastrophic case management usually consists of early identification and referral of potential high-cost cases to specialized treatment centers, ongoing assessment of the treatment process, and transitional planning. Case management programs may use a diagnostic screen to flag potential high-cost cases because a relatively small number of disabling conditions account for the majority of high-cost cases covered by the company's health insurance plan. Common high-cost conditions include neonatal complications, AIDS, major head trauma, spinal cord injury, cardiac disease, stroke, and cancer.

Sometimes case management is directed solely at containing medical care costs and ensuring quality. This occurs in circumstances where the individual with a disability is unable to maintain or resume work. The John Hancock Insurance Company has found that case management on behalf of patients with AIDS can result in high-quality, appropriate care and at the same time conserve resources. In spring 1986, a patient with cryptococcal meningitis due to AIDS was referred to the John Hancock Case Management Service. The patient was receptive to case management, so the case manager first arranged for an initial evaluation by a local nurse specialist. With input from the patient's physician, the nurse determined that the patient needed long-term intravenous administration of antibiotics and assistance with personal care at home.

The case manager used the nurse's recommendations to develop a cost-effective home care plan that included negotiated rates for nursing care and equipment rental for intravenous therapy. The case manager also coordinated communication among everyone involved in treating and caring for the patient, including the physician, the home care agency, the equipment company, family, friends, and local AIDS organizations. Because the patient had just been notified that his building was to be torn down, the case manager helped the patient find a new apartment in a subsidized building where he could live and receive care with another AIDS patient.

When the patient's condition deteriorated and he was no longer able to care for himself safely, the case manager worked with the home care agency to increase services. The case manager recommended home health visits beyond the 120-visit limit provided for under the patient's benefit plan, so that the patient could remain at home and thus avoid expensive hospitalization or nursing home placement. Thus, the case manager helped the patient achieve his wish of remaining at home during treatment and the terminal stages of his illness. Net savings were projected at $158,000.

The success of a case management plan hinges on how well it is formulated and how much cooperation can be obtained from the patient, workplace representatives, family, and health care providers. These two factors depend primarily on the caliber and degree of empathy of the case management professional and the resources and authority he or she can bring to the situation.

Case Management and Mental Health/Substance Abuse

Cases involving psychiatric conditions and substance abuse, until quite recently, were not managed, largely because most case managers are nonspecialized registered nurses, and it was felt that they did not have the training to manage mental health or substance abuse cases. There is now a decided trend, however, in the direction of providing case management to psychiatric and substance abuse cases, often contracting with a specialized firm employing psychologists, social workers, and substance abuse counselors.

Recently, for example, Teamsters Local 705, with approximately 1,100 employers, implemented an integrated employee assistance and managed mental health program. Local 705 had seen its in-patient mental health admissions jump 68 percent from 1988 to 1989. Much of the increased cost came from unmanaged extended in-patient adolescent care. In late 1989 the local contracted with Assured Health Systems, a nationwide EAP firm with eighteen locations in the Chicago area, for mental health case management services. Similarly, IBM Corporation, with approximately 300,000 employees nationwide, has recently contracted with American Psych Management for mental health and substance abuse case management services. In this arena, return-to-work plans are a vital aspect of case management, especially in relation to long-term follow-up.

Case Management and Long-Term Disability

Long-term disability (LTD) plans provide employees with a specific percentage of their income in the event of serious disablement. Most LTD plans provide benefits for two years if the employee cannot do his or her regular job. Thereafter, to remain eligible for benefits, an employee usually must be unable to do any reasonable job, giving consideration to the person's training, education, experience, and prior economic status.

At Northwestern National Life Insurance (NWNL), when an LTD claim is approved, the case is automatically reviewed by a committee composed of representatives of claims administration, rehabilitation services, and the Social Security coordinator. The committee determines the services necessary to facilitate return to work or receipt of Social Security disability benefits. If return to work is feasible, a case manager, usually a vocational rehabilitation counselor, is assigned to work with the disabled employee with that goal in mind.

A successful LTD rehabilitation outcome relies on an individualized case management plan and active participation by the employee with a disability. At NWNL, the case manager intervenes immediately following receipt of the case file from the coordinating committee. The initial contact with the employee provides an explanation of the employee's rights and responsibilities under the LTD contract. The rehabilitation assessment includes a comprehensive review of the individual's mental, emotional, and physical status, family concerns, financial needs, work history, and legal considerations. The case manager also assesses the individual's level of motivation and attitude toward reemployment.

The case manager may refer the employee to specialized treatment centers, arrange for a vocational evaluation and job accommodations, and offer support and encouragement throughout the rehabilitation process. The case manager also consults with the employer, supervisors, and other members of the company (medical, human resources, benefits staff) who may be involved in facilitating the employee's return to work. A successful case management effort, once again, must keep the employee's heart as well as head focused on returning to work. This requires a case manager who listens well, interprets needs to workplace supervisors, and serves as liaison and advocate in helping the person with disability negotiate the difficult goals of returning to work with temporarily or permanently diminished capacity. The goal always is to make the best use possible of existing ability and avoid paying someone to stay home.

Case Management and Workers Compensation

Workers compensation claims are a good illustration of a point made previously—a very few cases generate the most significant costs. Ninety percent of all workers compensation claims may be due to simple, straightforward "sprains and strains," "object in the eye," and "aches and pains," which may involve only a few days of absence from work. The few cases of traumatic multiple injuries, amputations, cumulative trauma disorder, and chronic back pain syndrome, however, can lead to lengthy absence from work and high costs in relation to medical care, rehabilitation, and wage replacement.

Travelers Insurance has implemented a nationwide case management approach to workers compensation claims. Travelers' approach aims to reduce medical and claims costs through provider discounts, proactive and retrospective utilization management (in the latter, case management is reviewed to identify situations in which alternative actions might have improved the outcome), early intervention with potential problem cases, and return-to-work programs in close cooperation with employers as well as employees.

During the early 1980s the Naval Systems Divison of FMC Corporation decided to deal with its workers compensation costs by getting disabled employees back to work at the earliest appropriate time through active case management. FMC's workers compensation return-to-work program combines immediate, consistent case management with job accommodations. From the day an injury occurs, the occupational health nurse and the case manager maintain direct contact with the employee, the employee's supervisor, and the employee's treating physician.

The case manager undertakes a complete case review of every workers compensation claim. Employees may be brought back to work on modified schedules and retrained for new work tasks; machines, workstations, and jobs are modified to accommodate the employees' functional limitations.

What Will Enhance the Success of a Case Management Program?

Employers who have implemented effective case management programs believe there are certain critical generic ingredients that need to be considered, including the following:

- The company must ensure that the case management strategy reflects and is consistent with the company's values and corporate culture, particularly its approach to human resources. The corporate philosophy will determine the relative priority of such factors as access to quality care, cost containment, cost-effectiveness, and positive employee relations.
- Top management support is essential to the success of the case management effort.
- Specific case management goals that are realistic and attainable should be established.
- The case management program should be integrated with the company's short- and long-term disability and workers compensation programs.
- Open and ongoing lines of communications must be created and maintained. Communications must be multilevel and multidirectional, flowing among case managers, employees, supervisors, union representatives, hospitals, physicians, community agencies, and other resources.
- An evaluation component should be built in early to determine whether the program is achieving its goals and objectives. It is important to identify and analyze both successes and failures. The company, in fact, may learn more from an objective assessment of case management failures than from their successes.
- The total program requires careful ongoing monitoring and a comprehensive annual review.
- Flexibility should be encouraged. A case management program must have the capacity to continually adapt to changing employer and employee needs and environmental trends.

Models of Case Management Programs

Different arrangements may be utilized to make case management programs available to employees. One of the first decisions for an employer is whether to administer the program internally ("make") or acquire case management services from an external organization ("buy"). Internal programs usually involve the appointment of a case manager who is assigned to the human resources, medical, or benefits department. External case managers may be employed by an insurance company, an independent case management firm, or some other service provider (such as a hospital, rehabilitation center, or social service agency).

Internal Case Management Programs

An increasing number of large corporations are creating their own case management departments—Sears, Honeywell, Herman Miller, AT&T, 3M, General Motors, to name a few. The major advantages of an internal program are that control over benefits decisions are retained within the company, the program can be custom-tailored to match the company's philosophy and policies, such a program usually allows quick response to new policies, and coordination with other departments involved in the employee's return to work is facilitated. The internal case manager also has immediate knowledge of the corporate culture and a better understanding of the nature of the employee's job, the employee's history with the company, the company's traditional willingness to accommodate returning workers, the individual's supervisor and his or her likely response to an employee with a disability, and the potential use of benefits to fund the necessary rehabilitation services.

Once the decision has been made to "make" an internal program, the next step is deciding what focus the program will have. This decision will affect where the program is placed organizationally and who staffs it. For example, the case management program may be aimed at workers compensation or non–workers compensation cases, or both. The program may be limited to active employees or may be extended to dependents covered under an employee's health benefit plan or to retirees. To achieve the greatest success in the early stages, the program may be targeted at areas in which the employer is experiencing high medical care costs. Pilot efforts can be expanded once the kinks in the system are worked out.

After determining the program focus, the company must next decide how the program will fit into existing policies and procedures. Chapter 5 discussed the development of a policy statement at length. The early case-finding mechanisms are vital to the case management activity. Ideally the case manager is notified automatically whenever a disability occurs among the work force. As noted previously, some companies utilize a list of diagnoses that automatically prompt case manager intervention. In other instances, the case manager may learn of a case when the employee is absent for a certain length of time.

Supervisors may be charged with responsibility for identifying employees with disabilities. The benefits department is another logical point of identification. Also, employees may be encouraged to self-identify their need for case management services. The EAP may see an employee whose physical and emotional problems warrant an intense, extensive case management response. The program is structured to allow the case manager to intervene quickly once he or she learns of an employee (or a dependent) who needs attention. The case manager often meets with the employee or the family within hours or days of initial referral, assesses the case, and develops a recommendation for services.

If the services are all covered under the employee's benefits plan, the case manager may simply make recommendations to the employee or family, and they will make the ultimate decision. It is important that the case manager not pressure the employee or family into choosing one course of action over another. If the employee feels forced into selecting an option, and is not happy with the result, then he or she may lose motivation to return to work, or in a worst-case scenario, may be tempted to take legal action against the company.

If the services are not all covered by the benefits plan, the case manager often considers whether the extra expense can be justified by the enhanced possibility of the employee's returning to work, or of the dependent or retiree's having a fuller or speedier recovery. Usually "plan exceptions" are reviewed by the coordinating committee, which makes the final determination.

It is vital that all relevant parties be included in the planning and implementation process. Case management decisions often affect supervisors, medical personnel, union representatives, benefits staff, human resources staff, and workers compensation specialists. All of them need to be involved in the process. Appendix 6-1 shows a tried and true first-interview protocol for a case manager. It allows the interviewer to identify needs and perceptions of employees facing the onset of disability or serious illness. It also provides a road map for the case manager concerning the kinds of services the individual will need to overcome identified problems. The interview was developed by the Workplace Center of Columbia University as the outcome of case management activities in almost a dozen locations throughout the country with over 250 clients representing a range of occupations and employers.

Independent Case Management Programs

As mentioned earlier, it is common and probably more feasible for all but large employers to "buy" external case management. The major advantages of an external case management program are that the program is ready-made, so it can be implemented quickly, and its greater specialization allows staff to have more expertise about local facilities and about rarer, more serious diagnoses such as AIDS and mental health problems. An established case management firm also brings with it experiences with other employers that may suggest options and alternatives that would not have occurred to the in-house staff. Many employers also would prefer to delegate authority to offer or deny case management services to an external agent, thus avoiding direct involvement in any disputes and conflicts that arise.

A decentralized company or one with relatively few catastrophic cases and the desire to minimize administrative staff and overhead will probably want to use an outside case management program. Also, if employees are unaccustomed to having the company involved in their personal lives, the company may want to start with an outside vendor.

Buying a program is not a now-and-for-all-time commitment. It can be a good way of initiating case management and learning how the initiative fits into the employer's overall human resources strategy. Ultimately, the employer may aim toward a culture that carries the message "We care." An in-house effort may help promote such an image.

The past decade has seen an enormous rise in the number of independent case management enterprises in the United States, from small one- or two-person companies to major corporations with offices nationwide. The services provided by these companies vary tremendously. Some provide only coordination of care and utilization review. Others offer direct rehabilitation services such as vocational evaluation, work hardening, and counseling. Contact with the employee or provider may be by telephone only or may involve several personal contacts over time. If one case management company does not provide a needed service, it may contract with yet another one that does.

Independent case management firms charge for their services in a variety of ways, most commonly on an hourly basis. Rates differ widely but are usually competitive within a given community or region. The vendor and employer often negotiate over what services can be charged at the standard rate, what services should not be billed explicitly (such as marketing or administrative time), and what services should be billed at some other rate (for example, paperwork and travel time are often billed at half the standard rate). Another method is to charge a percentage of total paid claims or to charge on a monthly per employee basis.

Figure 6-1, developed by William Hembree for *Business and Health,* summarizes the advantages and disadvantages of each approach. In the final analysis, of course, most employers determine whether to establish an internal program or contract with an external vendor on the basis of cost considerations. Employers with thousands of employees in a few

Figure 6-1. Choosing the best case management program.

Internal Program	*External Program*	*Combination*
Less costly	Often national in scope	Greatest flexibility
More extensive than external	Avoids overhead costs, salaries, space allocations	Allows use of sources as needed, development of internal capacities for core services
More flexibility, fast response to creative ideas	Already developed	Retains caring, sensitive, hands-on approach
Better sense of ownership and involvement	More streamlined in decentralized situations	Best return on investment in situations with local involvement
Better understanding of corporate culture, organizational climate	Better accommodates small employer	
Potentially more effective	Often can be implemented more quickly	
Better opportunity to monitor quality of care	May shift any ill will created to external vendor	
Employee appreciation not mitigated or attributed to others	Can be part of other health services	
Case management communication becomes part of overall communication process	Usually uses sophisticated evaluation protocols	

Reprinted from *Business and Health*, July/August 1985.

major installations may have a number of high-risk cases, and thus it would be more cost-effective to hire or appoint their own staff. Smaller employers, or those in dispersed locations, may not have a sufficient number of high-risk cases to justify the administrative expense. They would choose to contract with local providers or a national case management firm with sites around the country.

Insurer-Based Case Management Programs

Virtually all major health and disability insurance companies have found it economically compelling to include case management services in their insurance packages. Insurance-based case managers provide the same array of services as the independent companies. Those who purchase insurance from a carrier usually pay for case management services with their insurance premiums. Companies that do not purchase insurance pay for the services as they are used (fee-for-service arrangements). Fees vary, but are usually charged on an hourly basis of up to $130 per hour.

Provider Case Management Programs

Case managers have been used in social service agencies for many years. A more recent trend, however, is the provision of case management services by public and private health service providers. The goals of these case managers are somewhat different from those already described. Since they are not hired or employed by the employer or the insurer, these provider-based case managers tend to be more focused on the relationship between the patient and the health care providers. The goals of provider-based case management are usually twofold:

1. To help the patient identify and access all the relevant and necessary services for which he or she is eligible
2. To help the facility or agency provide the best care in its domain

These case managers may be patient advocates within the health service provider's facility, or at the outside agency or service provider's place of business. The case manager's activities include finding financing for the services the client needs, helping the patient sort out treatment alternatives, coordinating care interventions among a variety of physicians and other medical specialists, locating community services to help the client once he or she leaves the facility, arranging assistance for the client's family.

Site-based case managers are generally paid by the facility or agency for which they work. Financing for their services may come from insurance reimbursement, directly from the client, or from public sector revenues if the case manager works for a public agency.

The National Rehabilitation Hospital (NRH) in Washington, D.C., for example, has a full-time case manager. The role of the hospital case manager includes the following major activities:

- *Communication and coordination between the hospital, insurers, employers, public agencies, family physicians, and so forth.* The NRH case manager is the single contact point within the hospital for the referral source, who is often the primary payer. The case manager informs insurance case managers and others as to the patient's status and treatment progress.
- *Organization and coordination of the individualized medical treatment plan.* For example, the case manager facilitates the treatment process by ensuring that team conferences are conducted in a timely manner and that records and reports are completed and distributed to interested parties.
- *Patient and family relations.* The case manager is the first person to greet the patient and family members when they arrive at the hospital. The case manager explains the treatment plan in detail and clarifies his or her role.
- *Transition planning.* The case manager assists when a patient progresses from inpatient to outpatient status or day hospital treatment, moves on to another facility, or goes home and potentially back to work.
- *Hospitality services.* The case manager assists families from out of town to find hotel and other accommodations and facilitates local transportation services for patients and family members.

Guidelines for Selecting a Case Management Program

Whether you hire an internal case manager, select a case management company, or receive such services as part of an insurance package, outcomes depend on the quality of the service provided. The relative newness of case management as a discrete service means there is an unfortunate absence of agreed-upon standards for assessing the quality of service and a lack of nationally accepted credentials for judging qualifications.

Before a company can begin to evaluate case management providers, it must first review its own human resources strategy with particular attention to its disability and return-to-work policies, as indicated earlier.

A written policy serves as a benchmark against which candidates may be evaluated. (The questions relevant to company strategy are detailed in Chapter 5.)

The employer should set out the specific criteria and requirements it will utilize in screening prospective case managers. Several employers (Weyerhaeuser, General Motors, Burlington Industries) utilize a request for proposal (RFP) format (see Chapter 8) to communicate their needs and requirements to prospective case management vendors. The RFP usually requires all applicant agencies to respond to a standard set of questions and criteria. This allows for a uniform evaluation of comparative data. Many of these questions and criteria are equally relevant to selecting an in-house coordinator:

- Areas of specialization
- Staff professional and educational background
- Detailed description of all direct services and support activities, including, for example, how issues of visits to the employee's home, selection of treating physicians, worksite negotiations, and follow-up activities are handled
- Fee schedules, cost estimates, and reimbursable charges (waiting and travel time, telephone, report preparation)
- Convenience of office location and hours of operation
- Size of the case manager's caseload and their various areas of responsibility
- Procedures for use of subcontractors and specialists, and their availability
- Policies to ensure privacy and confidentiality
- Extent and type of liability insurance
- Timeliness of referral response
- Timeliness of written documentation of case activity and progress
- Financial viability and bank references
- References from organizations comparable to yours with which the vendor has dealt

For an outside provider, agreement should be reached on terms of case selection, documentation requirements, reevaluation procedures (a formal annual review is customary), and conditions under which the contract may be terminated. Performance expectations should be understood, for example:

- Prompt referral response
- An individualized, goal-oriented, written plan of service

- Prior approval from the employer before the plan of service is changed
- Timely reports that are well documented, understandable, and properly organized
- Measures of cost-effectiveness, outcome, or impact
- Quality review and professional accountability (an internal quality control system)

A detailed review of proposals in response to the RFP should be followed by interviews that include the case managers who will be serving the company's employees.

In assessing competing companies (or candidates for in-house programs), the employer should take the time necessary to become thoroughly familiar with each one and to investigate references extensively, including employers whom they have served but may not have included on their list of "satisfied clients." It is equally important that the employer make time and employees available to the representatives of the case management firm so that they come to know the employer's critical "four P's"—personnel, policies, procedures, and practices—as well as the general "style" of the employer's operations. A professional and ethical case management company or candidate will also be assessing the company to determine if there is sufficient common ground, agreed-upon expectations, and shared values to support a long-term relationship.

Membership in relevant professional associations and licenses in those states requiring such licensure are, of course, absolutely essential, but are not sufficient conditions for selection. It is also important that the prospective case manager demonstrate knowledge of the local labor market, job trends in the community, labor laws, union agreements, and relevant community service organizations.

Measuring the Costs and Benefits of Case Management

It is important to know that the popularity and extension of case management is *not* based on proven cost-benefit evaluation. There is much anecdotal evidence about significant savings achieved by use of case management services. To date, however, there have been too few comprehensive, objective studies of case management to estimate how cost-effective it is with confidence. There are three basic reasons for this situation:

1. It is simply very difficult to measure the costs and benefits of a case management program precisely. The estimate of cost savings hinges on many assumptions about what would have happened without the intervention of the case manager. Although sometimes it is evident, as when a case manager arranges for a patient to be transferred out of a more intensive level of medical care into a less intensive one, in many instances it is not so clear.

2. Many of the cost-effectiveness studies have been done by management companies themselves, which have a vested interest in finding that their own services produce high benefit-to-cost ratios. One important and respected study was conducted by researchers at Brandeis University (Henderson 1987). They examined the experience of people with spinal cord injuries, head injuries, cancer, AIDS, and high-risk infants. Their study found that case management was cost-effective only in one third of the 244 cases studied, and only for infants as a group. Projected long-term savings were found, however, in 60 percent of the cases.

3. No two clients or case management programs are exactly alike. The findings in any study depend on a wide array of variables, including client characteristics, quality of the services provided, timing of intervention, training and experience of the case manager, and creative use of benefits that are not in the original benefits plan. Each company needs to evaluate and refine its own disability management effort according to their experience and the results achieved.

The first step for any company wanting to evaluate its own program is to gather data on what has happened to its employees and dependents in the absence of case management (that is, the needs assessment component). How long do people with different diagnoses stay in an acute care hospital or rehabilitation facility? What benefits do they use, at what cost? How long do they stay out of work? Demographic data also need to be collected (for example, the age, sex, race, diagnosis, health condition, and job type of employees referred for case management).

It is very helpful if the case management program is established in such a manner as to make it easier to collect data as people move through the system. When the case manager begins to work with each employee, he or she needs to begin to track the time spent on each person and any other outlays of time or money to purchase equipment or services. How long this procedure is followed depends on whether the company wants to track savings over the short or long term. The case manager may only follow the case until it is closed, that is, the case manager's services are no longer needed. In some instances, however, long-term savings are realized after case closure, making follow-up studies informative.

Companies that purchase case management services probably will not have a choice about how to measure the costs and benefits of the service. But they should scrutinize how the case management company performs its own assessments and make their own adjustments. It may be helpful, if the company is considering awarding a major contract, to have an outside cost-benefit expert make an independent assessment of the case management company's methodology and the procedures it utilizes to assess the costs and benefits of the service. It is vital to include all of the cases in determining the cost-to-benefit ratio—not just the successful ones. Employers need to ensure that the methods used to determine what would have happened without the intervention are based on objective indicators.

The McDonnell Douglas Corporation recently completed a very comprehensive, longitudinal evaluation of the costs and benefits of their EAP. This study is particularly important in relation to its sophisticated design, its relevance to disability case management, and its findings. The study identified that the company's EAP saved $4 for every dollar it spent. The study, which was carried out by an outside contractor, included a total of 20,000 employees who were followed for over three years.

The McDonnell Douglas study focused solely on the money saved in reduced health claims and lower absentee rates among EAP "graduates." "Soft" benefits such as increased employee morale and loyalty and improved relations with supervisor, or other potential savings, were not included in the study. The evaluation, which was conducted by the consulting firm of Alexander and Alexander, confirmed that employees who used the company's EAP services for chemical dependency or mental health problems had fewer absences, generated fewer medical claims, and remained with the company longer than their counterparts who were undergoing treatment for the same problems but did not use the company-sponsored EAP.

In 1988, McDonnell Douglas' EAP spent $1.3 million to treat 1,032 employees. Over three years this investment yielded a savings of $5.1 million in reduced medical claims and $800,000 in reduced absenteeism. All costs were adjusted for inflation and were converted to 1988 dollars. Beyond the bottom-line figures, the study revealed that the greatest EAP benefit occurred "down the line." In the year following initial diagnosis and the initiation of treatment, employees with chemical dependency problems who did not go through the EAP had a significant increase in absenteeism and eventual termination.

Conclusion

The enthusiasm of the proponents of case management needs to be balanced by the recognition that this relatively new approach to human service coordination and cost containment has all the "growing pains" of any new movement. In practice, case management is neither as successful as its more zealous supporters claim nor as misguided as its most severe critics fear. The key to case management is a focus on the individual employee and his or her needs. When those needs are well attended, desirable outcomes are likely. The interview protocol in Appendix 6-1 provides a framework for considering the issues of job, medical care, family, and financial concerns that must receive attention in a case management effort.

While case management is a promising new tool for disability management, it is a "new" tool. Case management needs to be tested, and much remains to be learned about what works under which circumstances, and what does not. We believe that case management is the key to successful disability management.

Appendix 6-1
Intake Interview for the Early Intervention Program

Date ______________________
Claimant's ID # ______________
Claimant's phone # ____________

I. *Job Questions*

To help you think about what kinds of services would be most valuable to you, I'd like to find out about what it's like for you to not be working right now.

1. In general, how much, if at all, do you miss being at work? Do you miss being at work [READ EACH CATEGORY. CHECK THE APPROPRIATE RESPONSE.]
   ____ a. Very much?
   ____ b. Moderately?
   ____ c. A little?
   ____ d. Not at all?

2. A job can be an important part of a person's life in many different ways. I'm going to ask you about different aspects of what a job offers; these aspects include financial rewards, a way of organizing the day, a way of gaining recognition and respect from others, a chance to socialize with others, a reason to feel good about yourself, something to think about, and a way to learn new things. For each one, please tell me whether this has been very important, somewhat important, or not important for you. [READ EACH CATEGORY AND CHECK THE APPROPRIATE RESPONSE. REMIND THE CLAIMANT THAT THE RESPONSES ARE VERY IMPORTANT, SOMEWHAT IMPORTANT, OR NOT AT ALL IMPORTANT.]

	Very Important	*Some-what Important*	*Not at all Important*
a. Financial rewards	____	____	____
b. A way of organizing the day	____	____	____

Note: A modified form of this individual intake interview, and an expert system that produces suggested interventions to remedy identified problems, comprise the INSTASCAN software assessment package available from The Workplace Center, Columbia University School of Social Work, 622 West 113th Street, New York, NY 10025.

	Very Important	*Somewhat Important*	*Not at all Important*
c. A way of gaining recognition and respect from others	____	____	____
d. A chance to socialize with others	____	____	____
e. A reason to feel good about yourself	____	____	____
f. Something to think about	____	____	____
g. A way to learn new things	____	____	____

3. How much do you want to return to your job? Do you want to return [READ EACH CATEGORY AND CHECK THE APPROPRIATE RESPONSE.]
   ____ a. Very much?
   ____ b. Moderately?
   ____ c. A little?
   ____ d. Not at all?

   [IF THE ANSWER IS VERY MUCH OR MODERATELY, SKIP TO QUESTION 5. OTHERWISE CONTINUE TO QUESTION 4.]

4. If you don't completely want to, which of the following are reasons that might keep you from returning? [WORKER MAY RESPOND TO MORE THAN ONE; CHECK ALL THAT APPLY.]
   ____ a. Just don't feel well enough right now; definitely want to return as soon as I can
   ____ b. Scared of bringing on a recurrence of the disability
   ____ c. Didn't like my job anyway
   ____ d. Like being at home
   ____ e. Too much pressure at work
   ____ f. Worried that I won't be able to perform my job
   ____ g. Other (specify) ________________________________

5. How likely or unlikely do you think it is that you will be able, at some point, to return to your present job? [READ EACH CATEGORY AND CHECK THE APPROPRIATE RESPONSE.]
   ____ a. Very likely
   ____ b. Somewhat likely
   ____ c. Somewhat unlikely
   ____ d. Very unlikely

   [IF VERY LIKELY, SKIP TO QUESTION 7. OTHERWISE CONTINUE WITH QUESTION 6.]

6. What makes you say that? Is it because [READ EACH CATEGORY AND CHECK THE APPROPRIATE RESPONSES.]

_____ a. Your doctor said so
_____ b. Your supervisor (foreman) said so
_____ c. You don't think you will ever fully recover
_____ d. Your job is not being held for you
_____ e. Other (specify) ______________________

7. Has anyone contacted you or have you contacted anyone from work since you left? Yes _____ No _____

   [IF NO, SKIP TO QUESTION 9. IF YES, CONTINUE TO QUESTION 8.]

8. Who have you contacted or who has contacted you? [READ EACH CATEGORY AND CHECK ALL THAT APPLY.]
   _____ a. Management (including personnel)
   _____ b. Supervisor (foreman)
   _____ c. Co-workers
   _____ d. People you supervise
   _____ e. Union representative
   _____ f. Other (specify) ______________________

9. How much do you think your employer or supervisor (foreman) wants you to come back to work? [READ EACH CATEGORY AND CHECK THE APPROPRIATE RESPONSE.]
   _____ a. Wants you to come back
   _____ b. Doesn't care whether or not you come back
   _____ c. Doesn't want you to come back
   _____ d. Job is finished/no job to go back to

10. How flexible do you think your employer is willing to be to accommodate any changes you may need to do your job once you are able to return? These changes may include, for example, doing different tasks, coming to or leaving work at different times, working with different people, and the like. [READ EACH CATEGORY AND CHECK THE APPROPRIATE RESPONSE.]
    _____ a. Very flexible
    _____ b. Somewhat flexible; depends on what you are asking for
    _____ c. Somewhat inflexible
    _____ d. Very inflexible
    _____ e. Job is finished/no job to go back to

11. How much do you think most of your co-workers want you to return to work? [READ EACH CATEGORY AND CHECK THE APPROPRIATE RESPONSE.]
    _____ a. Want you to come back
    _____ b. Don't care whether or not you come back
    _____ c. Don't want you to come back
    _____ d. Job is finished/no job to go back to

12. I'd like to get a sense of what your work involves. Please describe the activities on which you spend the most time. Begin with the one on which you spend the greatest portion of your time, and then continue. [PROMPTS: TYPING, HAMMERING, DATA ENTRY, FILING, LOADING, OPERATING MACHINE.]

    a. ______ d. ______
    b. ______ e. ______
    c. ______ f. ______

13. Now, please describe to me the physical requirements of your work, such as standing, moving about, sitting, lifting, carrying, pushing, pulling, and the like. Again, begin with the one on which you spend the greatest portion of your time, and then continue.

    a. ______ d. ______
    b. ______ e. ______
    c. ______ f. ______

14. Now, please describe the mental factors, such as decision making, clarity of thought, concentration, attention, judgment and the like that your work requires. Again, begin with the one on which you spend the greatest portion of your time, and then continue.

    a. ______ d. ______
    b. ______ e. ______
    c. ______ f. ______

15. If you were to return to work in your present condition, are there any of the activities, physical or mental, that you just described that you would be unable to do? Yes ____ No ____

    [IF NO, SKIP TO QUESTION 22. IF YES, CONTINUE TO QUESTION 16.]

16. Which ones? ______

17. Does your work require that you do these activities daily or weekly?

    ____ Daily
    ____ Weekly

    [IF THE RESPONSE IS DAILY, CONTINUE TO QUESTION 18. IF THE RESPONSE IS WEEKLY, SKIP TO QUESTION 19.]

18. What percentage of your usual workday did you spend doing these activities that you cannot do now? ______

    [SKIP TO QUESTION 20.]

19. How much of your week do you spend doing these activities?

    ______

20. Do you think it could be worked out for you to go back to your job and just not do those activities or do them differently? Yes ____ No ____ Job no longer available ____

    [IF THE RESPONSE IS NO, CONTINUE TO QUESTION 21. IF THE RESPONSE IS YES, SKIP TO QUESTION 22.]

21. Why not? ____

    ____

    [SKIP QUESTION 22 IF THE CLAIMANT CANNOT RETURN TO HIS OR HER FORMER JOB.]

22. Besides the specific parts of your job that might be hard for you to do, is there anything else about your normal workday that might need to be changed so you could return to work now? Second, if a change is needed, who would be involved in, or approve, that change. Now, let me read you a list of possible changes and please tell me, if you think they apply to you, who would be involved in the change, and how likely you think it is that the change will be made. [READ EACH CATEGORY AND CHECK YES OR NO. IF THE RESPONSE IS YES, ASK WHO WILL BE INVOLVED AND CHECK ALL THAT APPLY. ALSO ASK IF THE CHANGE IS LIKELY OR UNLIKELY.]

    Change the length of the workday: Yes ____ No ____
    [IF YES] Who is involved?
    ____ a. Management (including personnel)
    ____ b. Supervisor (foreman)
    ____ c. Co-workers
    ____ d. People you supervise
    ____ e. Family
    ____ f. Union representative
    ____ g. Other (specify) ______________________

    Is it:
    Likely change will be made? ____ Unlikely change will be made? ____

    Change work hours to avoid rush hour travel? Yes ____ No ____
    [IF YES] Who is involved?
    ____ a. Management (including personnel)
    ____ b. Supervisor (foreman)
    ____ c. Co-workers
    ____ d. People you supervise
    ____ e. Family
    ____ f. Union representative
    ____ g. Other (specify) ______________________

    Is it:
    Likely change will be made? ____ Unlikely change will be made? ____

Provide more breaks or rest periods during the day? Yes ____ No ____
[If YES] Who is involved?
____ a. Management (including personnel)
____ b. Supervisor (foreman)
____ c. Co-workers
____ d. People you supervise
____ e. Family
____ f. Union representative
____ g. Other (specify) ____________________

Is it:
Likely change will be made? ____ Unlikely change will be made? ____

Allow time off during the day for medical care? Yes ____ No ____
[IF YES] Who is involved?
____ a. Management (including personnel)
____ b. Supervisor (foreman)
____ c. Co-workers
____ d. People you supervise
____ e. Family
____ f. Union representative
____ g. Other (specify) ____________________

Is it:
Likely change will be made? ____ Unlikely change will be made? ____

Change any of the tasks that you do? Yes ____ No ____
[IF YES] Who is involved?
____ a. Management (including personnel)
____ b. Supervisor (foreman)
____ c. Co-workers
____ d. People you supervise
____ e. Family
____ f. Union representative
____ g. Other (specify) ____________________

Is it:
Likely change will be made? ____ Unlikely change will be made? ____

Change the location of your work? Yes ____ No ____
[IF YES] Who is involved?
____ a. Management (including personnel)
____ b. Supervisor (foreman)
____ c. Co-workers
____ d. People you supervise
____ e. Family
____ f. Union representative
____ g. Other (specify) ____________________

Is it:
Likely change will be made? _____ Unlikely change will be made? _____

Change how you get to work? Yes _____ No _____
[IF YES] Who is involved?
_____ a. Management (including personnel)
_____ b. Supervisor (foreman)
_____ c. Co-workers
_____ d. People you supervise
_____ e. Family
_____ f. Union representative
_____ g. Other (specify) _______________

Is it:
Likely change will be made? _____ Unlikely change will be made? _____

Change who you work with? Yes _____ No _____
[IF YES] Who is involved?
_____ a. Management (including personnel)
_____ b. Supervisor (foreman)
_____ c. Co-workers
_____ d. People you supervise
_____ e. Family
_____ f. Union representative
_____ g. Other (specify) _______________

Is it:
Likely change will be made? _____ Unlikely change will be made? _____

Provide help from other people? Yes _____ No _____
[IF YES] Who is involved?
_____ a. Management (including personnel)
_____ b. Supervisor (foreman)
_____ c. Co-workers
_____ d. People you supervise
_____ e. Family
_____ f. Union representative
_____ g. Other (specify) _______________

Is it:
Likely change will be made? _____ Unlikely change will be made? _____

[IF ANY OF THE RESPONSES TO QUESTION 22 ARE YES, CONTINUE TO QUESTION 23. IF ALL RESPONSES TO QUESTION 22 ARE NO, SKIP TO QUESTION 24.]

23. Do you have any ideas how to begin approaching these changes?
Yes _____ No _____ [IF YES] What would you suggest? ______________
____

24. While you are out, who, if anyone, is doing the work you usually do? [READ EACH CATEGORY AND CHECK THE APPROPRIATE RESPONSE.]
_____ a. Nobody; work not getting done
_____ b. Co-workers/supervisor
_____ c. Someone else hired termporarily
_____ d. Someone else hired permanently

25. What year did you start working for the employer you were working for at the onset of your disability? ______________

26. All in all, how happy would you say you have been with your job or usual work? Would you say you were [READ EACH CATEGORY AND CHECK THE APPROPRIATE RESPONSE.]
_____ a. Very happy?
_____ b. Happy?
_____ c. Unhappy?
_____ d. Very unhappy?

[IF THE WORKER WAS UNHAPPY OR VERY UNHAPPY, CONTINUE TO QUESTION 27. OTHERWISE, SKIP TO QUESTION 28.]

27. What kinds of things are you not completely happy with, and do you have a sense that any of those things have contributed to your disability? Let me read you a list of things and you tell me if it is something you are not completely happy with and, if so, if it contributes to your disability. [TWO RESPONSES ARE NEEDED FOR EACH CATEGORY. READ EACH CATEGORY AND FIRST ASK IF IT IS SOMETHING THE CLAIMANT IS NOT COMPLETELY HAPPY WITH. IF IT IS, PLACE A CHECK IN THE FIRST COLUMN. NEXT ASK IF IT CONTRIBUTES TO THE CLAIMANT'S DISABILITY AND CHECK THE APPROPRIATE RESPONSE.]

	Not Completely Happy	*Contributes to Disability*	*Does Not Contribute to Disability*
a. Work environment (noise, ventilation, dirt, crowding)	_____	_____	_____
b. Salary	_____	_____	_____
c. Relation to co-workers	_____	_____	_____
d. Relation to supervisor	_____	_____	_____
e. Tasks	_____	_____	_____

	Not Completely Happy	Contributes to Disability	Does Not Contribute to Disability
f. Routine (hours of work)	______	______	______
g. Repetition	______	______	______
h. Pressure	______	______	______
i. Hazards	______	______	______
j. Fatigue	______	______	______
k. Boredom	______	______	______

28. Is there anything you want to change about your job or usual work?
Yes ____ No ____

[IF THE RESPONSE IS YES, CONTINUE TO QUESTION 29. IF THE RESPONSE IS NO, SKIP TO QUESTION 30.]

29. What would you like to change? ______________________________

II. *Health Questions*

Now let's talk about your health and how you are feeling these days.

30. What exactly does the doctor tell you is wrong with you?
____

31. Is this the first time you have been out on this diagnosis?
Yes ____ No ____

[IF NO, CONTINUE TO QUESTION 32. IF YES, SKIP TO QUESTION 33.]

32. How many other times have you been out on this diagnosis? ________

33. I'd like you to tell me what the main symptoms of your illness or injury are—what are the main things that you're feeling as a result of your condition? [PLACE RESPONSES IN APPROPRIATE CATEGORIES. CHECK ALL THAT APPLY.]
____ a. Tiredness/weakness
____ b. Headaches
____ c. Other pain
____ d. Dizziness
____ e. Numbness of body part(s) (where?) ________________
____ f. Nausea/vomiting
____ g. Depression
____ h. Difficulty breathing
____ i. Difficulty thinking/disorientation

_____ j. Blurred/impaired vision
_____ k. Difficulty walking
_____ l. Lack of appetite
_____ m. Sleeplessness
_____ n. Other (what?) ______________________________

34. Do you consider yourself to be [READ EACH CATEGORY AND CHECK THE APPROPRIATE RESPONSE.]
_____ a. Severely disabled?
_____ b. Moderately disabled?
_____ c. Slightly disabled?
_____ d. Not at all disabled?

35. Are there any situations or circumstances that make your condition or your symptoms worse? Yes _____ No _____

[IF THE RESPONSE IS YES, CONTINUE TO QUESTION 36. IF THE RESPONSE IS NO, SKIP TO QUESTION 37.]

36. What are they? ______________________________
____

37. Are there any situations or circumstances that make your condition or your symptoms better? Yes _____ No _____

[IF THE RESPONSE IS YES, CONTINUE TO QUESTION 38. IF THE RESPONSE IS NO, SKIP TO QUESTION 39.]

38. What are they? ______________________________
____

39. What would you say is the most difficult symptom that you are experiencing? ______________________________

40. Are you being treated for your disability? Yes _____ No _____

41. Do you feel like the treatment is helping you? Yes _____ No _____

42. Do you think you will be able to return to work while the treatment is still going on? Yes _____ No _____

[IF THE RESPONSE IS NO, CONTINUE TO QUESTION 43. IF THE RESPONSE IS YES, SKIP TO QUESTION 44.]

43. Why not? ______________________________

III. *Medical Questions*

Now, let's talk about your medical condition and what the doctor says.

44. To what extent, if any, did you talk with your doctor about what kind of work you do? Did you talk with your doctor [READ EACH CATEGORY AND CHECK THE APPROPRIATE RESPONSE.]
    ____ a. To a great extent?
    ____ b. To a moderate extent?
    ____ c. Only a little bit?
    ____ d. Not at all?

45. How much do you think the doctor understands about your job and the activities it involves? Do you think your doctor [READ EACH CATEGORY AND CHECK THE APPROPRIATE RESPONSE.]
    ____ a. Understands everything about your job?
    ____ b. Understands most of the things about your job?
    ____ c. Understands only a little bit about your job?
    ____ d. Does not understand at all about your job?

46. Did you discuss with the doctor returning to your usual job?
    Yes ____ No ____

    [IF YES, CONTINUE TO QUESTION 47. IF NO, SKIP TO QUESTION 52.]

47. What did he or she say? [READ EACH OF THE FOLLOWING CATEGORIES, THEN ASK THE WORKER TO SELECT THE BEST RESPONSE.]
    ____ a. Said I could return right away
    ____ b. Said I could probably return within a month
    ____ c. Said I could probably return within two months
    ____ d. Said I could probably return some time after that
    ____ e. Couldn't say at this point if or when I could return
    ____ f. Said I definitely can't return to work
    ____ g. Other ________________________________

48. Do you agree with the doctor's judgment? Yes ____ No ____

    [IF NO, CONTINUE TO QUESTION 49. IF YES, SKIP TO QUESTION 50.]

49. Why not? ________________________________

50. If the doctor doesn't think you should return now to your usual work, did you discuss the possibility of returning to some modified form—part-time or a different job, or something else? Yes ____ No ____

    [IF YES, CONTINUE TO QUESTION 51. IF NO, SKIP TO QUESTION 52.]

51. What did he or she say? ____________________________________

52. How satisfied or dissatisfied are you with the medical care you have been getting? [READ EACH CATEGORY AND CHECK THE APPROPRIATE RESPONSE.]
    _____ a. Very satisfied
    _____ b. Somewhat satisfied
    _____ c. Somewhat dissatisfied
    _____ d. Very dissatisfied

    [IF THE CLAIMANT IS SOMEWHAT DISSATISFIED OR VERY DISSATISFIED, CONTINUE TO QUESTION 53. OTHERWISE, SKIP TO QUESTION 54.]

53. What additional care or services would you like? [READ EACH CATEGORY AND CHECK THE APPROPRIATE RESPONSE.]
    _____ a. Longer visits to doctor
    _____ b. Answers to all your medical questions
    _____ c. Fuller explanation of your condition
    _____ d. Referral for a second opinion
    _____ e. Options for your treatment
    _____ f. More frequent visits to doctor

IV. *Family and Finance Questions*

Now I would like to get some information about you and your family.

54. With whom do you live? [READ EACH CATEGORY AND CHECK ALL THAT APPLY.]
    _____ a. Spouse
    _____ b. Parents
    _____ c. Children (how many?) _____
    _____ d. Siblings
    _____ e. Alone
    _____ f. Other (specify) ____________________________________

55. What is your marital status? [READ EACH CATEGORY AND CHECK APPROPRIATE RESPONSE.]
    _____ a. Single
    _____ b. Married
    _____ c. Separated
    _____ d. Divorced
    _____ e. Widowed

    [IF CLAIMANT IS MARRIED, ASK QUESTION 56. OTHERWISE, SKIP TO QUESTION 57.]

56. Is your spouse currently working? Yes _____ No _____

57. Now, let me suggest some things that people do when they are not at work and tell me if any are things that you are doing too. I am going to read a list of activities. Please tell me both if you are involved in the activity now and if you were involved in the activity *before* your disability. I am interested in how much time you spend or did spend at each activity. Do you or did you spend a lot of time, a moderate amount of time, just a little bit of time, or no time at all? [READ EACH ACTIVITY AND CHECK THE APPROPRIATE RESPONSE FOR THE ACTIVITY NOW AND PRIOR TO THE DISABILITY.]

Visiting your doctor

Now do you spend
____ a. A lot of time?
____ b. A moderate amount of time?
____ c. A little bit of time?
____ d. No time at all?

Before your disability did you spend
____ a. A lot of time?
____ b. A moderate amount of time?
____ c. A little bit of time?
____ d. No time at all?

Exercising/rehabilitation routines

Now do you spend
____ a. A lot of time?
____ b. A moderate amount of time?
____ c. A little bit of time?
____ d. No time at all?

Before your disability did you spend
____ a. A lot of time?
____ b. A moderate amount of time?
____ c. A little bit of time?
____ d. No time at all?

Resting in bed

Now do you spend
____ a. A lot of time?
____ b. A moderate amount of time?
____ c. A little bit of time?
____ d. No time at all?

Before your disability did you spend
____ a. A lot of time?
____ b. A moderate amount of time?
____ c. A little bit of time?
____ d. No time at all?

Doing household chores

Now do you spend
____ a. A lot of time?
____ b. A moderate amount of time?
____ c. A little bit of time?
____ d. No time at all?

Before your disability did you spend
____ a. A lot of time?
____ b. A moderate amount of time?
____ c. A little bit of time?
____ d. No time at all?

Taking care of the children

Now do you spend
_____ a. A lot of time?
_____ b. A moderate amount of time?
_____ c. A little bit of time?
_____ d. No time at all?

Before your disability did you spend
_____ a. A lot of time?
_____ b. A moderate amount of time?
_____ c. A little bit of time?
_____ d. No time at all?

Sitting around the house

Now do you spend
_____ a. A lot of time?
_____ b. A moderate amount of time?
_____ c. A little bit of time?
_____ d. No time at all?

Before your disability did you spend
_____ a. A lot of time?
_____ b. A moderate amount of time?
_____ c. A little bit of time?
_____ d. No time at all?

Other activities (specify) ________________________________

Now do you spend
_____ a. A lot of time?
_____ b. A moderate amount of time?
_____ c. A little bit of time?
_____ d. No time at all?

Before your disability did you spend
_____ a. A lot of time?
_____ b. A moderate amount of time?
_____ c. A little bit of time?
_____ d. No time at all?

58. Right now, is there someone at home or elsewhere who assists you in your daily activities? Yes _____ No _____

[IF THE ANSWER TO QUESTION 58 IS YES, CONTINUE TO QUESTION 59. IF THE ANSWER IS NO, SKIP TO QUESTION 62.]

59. Who is the primary person who does that? [READ EACH CATEGORY AND CHECK THE APPROPRIATE RESPONSE.]

At Home
_____ a. Spouse
_____ b. Child
_____ c. Parent
_____ d. Sibling
_____ e. Other (specify) __________

Elsewhere
_____ a. Spouse
_____ b. Child
_____ c. Parent
_____ d. Sibling
_____ e. Other (specify) __________

60. Has that person altered his or her schedule much since you went out on disability? For example, did he or she take time off from work, or from other activities? Would you say that person has altered his or her schedule [READ EACH CATEGORY AND CHECK THE APPROPRIATE RESPONSE.]

_____ a. A lot?
_____ b. A moderate amount?
_____ c. A little bit?
_____ d. Not at all?

61. Has this made your relationship [READ EACH CATEGORY AND CHECK THE APPROPRIATE RESPONSE.]
_____ a. Better?
_____ b. No different?
_____ c. Somewhat worse?
_____ d. Worse?

[IF CLAIMANT HAS ANSWERED QUESTIONS 59–61, SKIP TO QUESTION 67.]

[FOR THOSE WHO ANSWERED NO TO QUESTION 58, CONTINUE HERE WITH QUESTION 62.]

62. Do you need help with your daily activities? Yes _____ No _____

[IF THE RESPONSE IS YES, CONTINUE TO QUESTION 63. IF THE RESPONSE IS NO, SKIP TO QUESTION 67.]

63. Is there someone who you think could assist you? Yes _____ No _____

[IF THE RESPONSE IS YES, CONTINUE TO QUESTION 64. IF THE RESPONSE IS NO, SKIP TO QUESTION 67.]

64. Who is that person? _______________________________________

65. Have you spoken to that person about it? Yes _____ No _____

[IF THE RESPONSE IS NO, CONTINUE TO QUESTION 66. IF THE RESPONSE IS YES, SKIP TO QUESTION 67.]

66. Do you think we should talk about asking them to help you?
Yes _____ No _____

67. I'd like to get an idea of how the people in your family feel about the possibility of your returning to work. Who, if anyone, is worried most about your returning to work? [READ EACH CATEGORY AND CHECK THE APPROPRIATE RESPONSE. HAVE THE WORKER SELECT ONLY ONE RESPONSE.]
_____ a. Spouse
_____ b. Parent
_____ c. Child
_____ d. Sibling
_____ e. Other (specify) _______________________________
_____ f. No one is worried

[IF NO ONE IS WORRIED, SKIP TO QUESTION 71. OTHERWISE, CONTINUE TO QUESTION 68.]

68. How worried is that person? Would you say that person is [READ EACH CATEGORY AND CHECK THE APPROPRIATE RESPONSE.]
    ____ a. Very worried?
    ____ b. Moderately worried?
    ____ c. A little bit worried?
    ____ d. Hardly worried at all?

69. What is the reason for his or her worry? [READ EACH CATEGORY AND CHECK THE APPROPRIATE RESPONSE.]
    ____ a. Fear that you will get sick/hurt yourself again
    ____ b. Likes having you at home
    ____ c. Thinks you work too hard
    ____ d. Knows you were not happy at your job anyway, and this is a good opportunity to get away from it
    ____ e. Other (specify) ____________________

70. Do you think that this family member's worry affects you in deciding when to go back to work? Would you say that it [READ EACH CATEGORY AND CHECK THE APPROPRIATE RESPONSE.]
    ____ a. Affects you a lot?
    ____ b. Has a moderate effect?
    ____ c. Affects you slightly?
    ____ d. Hardly affects you at all?

71. Are there members of your family that are in favor of your returning to work as soon as possible? Yes ____ No ____

    [IF THE RESPONSE IS YES, CONTINUE TO QUESTION 72. IF THE RESPONSE IS NO, SKIP TO QUESTION 74.]

72. Who, if anyone, is most supportive of your returning to work as soon as possible? [READ EACH CATEGORY AND CHECK THE APPROPRIATE RESPONSE. HAVE THE WORKER SELECT ONLY ONE RESPONSE.]
    ____ a. Spouse
    ____ b. Parent
    ____ c. Child
    ____ d. Sibling
    ____ e. Other (specify) ____________________

73. Would you say that this person [READ EACH CATEGORY AND CHECK THE APPROPRIATE RESPONSE.]
    ____ a. Supports you a lot?
    ____ b. Supports you a moderate amount?
    ____ c. Supports you a little bit?
    ____ d. Hardly supports you at all?

I just have a few more questions. A lot of people have trouble with finances while they are out on disability. I'd like to ask you some questions about that.

74. What is your weekly take-home pay? $ ____________________

75. What percentage of your household's total income was your salary when you were working? ____________________

76. Who else contributes to your household income? [READ EACH CATEGORY AND CHECK THE APPROPRIATE RESPONSE.]
____ a. Spouse
____ b. Parents
____ c. Children
____ d. Sibling
____ e. Other (specify) ____________________

77. How satisfied were you with your salary? Would you say you were [READ EACH CATEGORY AND CHECK THE APPROPRIATE RESPONSE.]
____ a. Very satisfied?
____ b. Somewhat satisfied?
____ c. Somewhat dissatisfied?
____ d. Very dissatisfied?

78. How many other people depend on you as their major source of income? This can include a spouse, children, elderly relatives, and anyone else who is financially dependent on you. ____________________

79. Do you have less money now than before your disability?
Yes ____ No ____

[IF YES, CONTINUE TO QUESTION 80. IF NO, SKIP TO QUESTION 81.]

80. Has your financial situation been affected [READ EACH CATEGORY AND CHECK THE APPROPRIATE RESPONSE.]
____ a. A lot?
____ b. A moderate amount?
____ c. A little bit?
____ d. Not at all?

81. While you are out on disability, how does your family's income compare to what it was before? ______ [TRY TO GET PERCENTAGE BY WHICH IT WAS REDUCED. IF WORKER SAYS THAT HE OR SHE HAS NO FAMILY OR LIVES ALONE, GET INFORMATION ABOUT THE CLAIMANT'S OWN INCOME.]

82. How pressed are you financially? Are you having trouble with your [READ EACH CATEGORY AND CHECK ALL THAT APPLY.]
    a. Mortgage or rent payments? Yes ____ No ____
    b. Car payments? Yes ____ No ____
    c. Food expenses? Yes ____ No ____
    d. Insurance (car, other)? Yes ____ No ____
    e. Savings? Yes ____ No ____
    f. Other expenses? Yes ____ No ____

83. If you're having financial problems, how do you think we can help with them? ________________________________

84. In what year were you born? ____________

85. How many years of school have you completed? [READ EACH CATEGORY AND CHECK THE APPROPRIATE RESPONSE.]
    ____ a. Grade school
    ____ b. Some high school
    ____ c. Graduated high school
    ____ d. Some college
    ____ e. Graduated college
    ____ f. Graduate work Degree: ____
    ____ g. Apprenticeship Number of years: ____
    ____ h. Post–high school technical training (but not official apprenticeship program)

86. Are there any problems or issues that we have not discussed that you think may cause problems in your ability to return to work?
    ____
    ____

[IF SOME POTENTIAL PROBLEMS HAVE BEEN INDICATED BY THE CLAIMANT'S RESPONSES, READ THE FOLLOWING INSTRUCTIONS.]

OK, we are finished. I can see from the responses to these questions that you may run into some problems with ________________. [FILL IN THE BLANK WITH THE APPROPRIATE PROBLEM(S). THERE MAY BE PROBLEMS WITH THE FAMILY, JOB, FINANCES, OR PHYSICIAN.] *Let me review your responses more closely and get back to you with some suggestions about how I may be able to help you. Is that okay?* Yes ____ No ____

[IF THE CLAIMANT RESPONDS NO, ASK] What is the problem? [AND TRY AND RESOLVE THE PROBLEM]

[IF THE CLAIMANT RESPONDS YES, SAY] Do you have any other questions?

Thank you very much for your time and your help. I will contact you soon. Goodbye.

[IF NO PROBLEMS ARE INDICATED BY THE CLAIMANT'S RESPONSES, SAY] *Okay, we are finished. I can see from your responses to these questions that you have things under control. However, if you run into any problems, please give me a call and I will try to assist you. Thank you very much for your time and your help. You estimate that you will be back at work by* ___. [FILL IN RETURN TO WORK DATE.] *I will call you at that time to see that everything continues okay.*

Chapter 7
Ensuring Continuity of Disability Management

Once a disability management program is set in place, the real challenge begins—to sustain commitment to program goals beyond the first wave of workers assisted through the program. To do so, the program must be embedded in the organizational system so that it can weather company changes, economic crises, power struggles, and other internal and external forces.

These four strategies help to ensure program continuity:

1. *Program monitoring and evaluation.* Program monitoring tracks program operations to answer questions about how well procedures are being followed, how well staff are performing their tasks, and how well the participants are being served. Program evaluation assesses the extent to which the program is meeting its goals. Evaluation analyzes program cost-effectiveness, impact on productivity, recidivism rate, length of disability, employee morale, job satisfaction, and the like.

2. *Staff training.* Staff training helps implement the disability management program by teaching new tasks and routines and developing new relationships for program staff who require guidance through ongoing training.

3. *Prevention.* Alerting workers to potential problems may help to reduce the incidence of certain disabling conditions. Preventive programs also increase the awareness among workers about disability management, which can result in increased acceptance, trust, and participation should disability occur.

4. *Information dissemination and networking.* Employees and outside organizations should be kept informed about the program. The more workers and others who assist workers know about the program, the more the program becomes an accepted and expected part of the workplace.

Program Monitoring and Evaluation

The role of monitoring and evaluation in ensuring program continuity cannot be overstated. Monitoring and evaluation assess how well the needs of participants are being met, help keep everyone informed about program operations, demonstrate the degree to which program goals are realized, suggest ways the program should be modified to fit organizational and labor force changes best, and provide feedback to program personnel about the quality of their performance.

Monitoring and evaluation require three steps:

1. Data collection
2. Data analysis to answer the questions of interest
3. Review and interpretation of the results of analysis to ensure understanding of program operation or determine if action is required

Data Collection

The quality of the monitoring and evaluation functions depends on the information available to carry them out. It is very important, therefore, to determine what information is needed and set in place a reliable system to record and store this information.

Issues of Confidentiality

It is important to consider the issue of access to information in the data collection effort. Effective program functioning requires access to confidential information, which is protected, to some degree, by:

- Federal and state regulations
- The ethical codes of professional associations
- The workplace policy

Despite existing regulations and policies, however, in disability management the circumstances are not clear-cut about:

- When information about a client may be shared
- With whom the information may be shared
- In what form the information may be shared

Maintaining confidentiality between the worker with a disability and case manager is fundamental to establishing a trusting exchange. Workers will not participate in the program if they perceive that their trust is violated. Employers must, therefore, resolve ambiguity in issues of confidentiality in order to ensure program participation. A guiding principle for employers is that information should be shared, even with employee consent, only on a "need to know" basis. If a person performing a particular task in the disability management program (for example, referral to a community resource, arranging transitional employment) could perform that task better if certain information was available, then sharing that information meets the need-to-know criterion. Conversely, even if an employee has consented to release, let us say, medical data, there would be no reason to provide that information to any supervisor whose responsibilities would not be performed better once privy to that knowledge.

Confidential information is of two types: absolute and relative (Wilson 1978). *Absolute confidentiality* refers to information that is never shared with anyone regardless of the circumstances. This information is protected by law and, therefore, cannot be divulged by the person with whom it is shared unless the worker gives explicit permission for such disclosure. Fully protected information, however, covers only a small part of the relationship between the worker and the disability program.

Relative confidentiality refers to information that is conveyed in confidence or, more usually, when required by law is not revealed to others except under certain circumstances where disclosure is necessary for helping the individual (Reynolds 1976). This latter instance most closely reflects the one faced by the case manager. To explain the need for job accommodation or to refer the worker to the outside service provider best suited to help with the worker's problem, a case manager may need to reveal information about the worker.

Effective disability management should have explicit policies and procedures for determining what information may be shared and how it is to be used without violating the workers' right to privacy and trust. These policies and procedures revolve around the concept of informed consent. *Informed consent* is permission from a worker to disclose the contents of confidential communication (or record thereof) based on the worker's understanding of what is to be disclosed, why, to whom, for what time period, and under the right to revoke such permission.

Akabas, Bellinger et al., in their paper on confidentiality, have summarized the ten conditions outlined by Wilson that, when met, ensure informed consent for the release of information:

1. The client (worker, employee, union member) must know each time there is a request for release of certain data.

2. The client should understand exactly what information is to be disclosed.
3. In order for the client to know what is to be released, provider and client should engage in a thorough discussion of the actual material. If a written report is to be made, the client should read it or have it explained in terms he or she can understand.
4. The client should know exactly to whom the information is to be released—name, position, and affiliation.
5. The client should concur with the reason the information is being requested or released by understanding how it will be used by the receiving party.
6. The client should be sure of the accuracy and completeness of the released information.
7. The provider and client should jointly agree to the release conditions—that is, as to whether or not the receiving party has the right to pass the information on to a third party.
8. The client should be fully aware of any repercussions that might occur should permission for disclosure be granted and any that might result if permission is withheld.
9. Any consent for release of information should be time-limited and revokable.
10. The client's consent for release of information should be in writing on a "Consent for Release of Information" form. A form useful for this purpose is shown in Figure 7-1.

The issues the disability case manager must consider and discuss with the worker before recommending whether or not to disclose information include:

- What information is to be shared, with whom, and for what purpose
- Potential risks and benefits of sharing the information to the client or others
- Whether the worker is able and willing to give consent to the release of the information
- How the request came about and why at this time
- What guarantee is available that the information shared will be used in a responsible manner
- Whether disclosure of the information would violate any laws, established policies, or ethical standards
- Whether disclosure would set any undesirable precedents regarding worker records

The ability to protect confidentiality depends on how records are maintained and accessed. The following are guidelines for keeping infor-

Figure 7-1. Consent form for release of information.

To: Name of facility from which information is requested

From: Name and title of person, and company name, requesting information

Re: Individual's name about whom information is requested

(*Name of employee*) is receiving service through this company. In our effort to serve (*him/her*) we would benefit from information concerning the condition and services received from your facility. (*He/she*) indicates that (*he/she*) was treated by you from ___________ to ___________. Please regard this as a request for information concerning (*name of employee*) during the period identified.

Below, the authorization from the employee is specified.

Date: ___________

This authorization is valid for 30 days from the date appearing above. I hereby authorize the release of information concerning the condition for which you offered me service during the specified period, and the type of service that you provided. I understand that the information to be released is confidential and that in your receipt of that information you will be bound not to disclose it to any other parties except with my express written permission. In agreement with this authorization, I hereby affix my signature.

___________________________	___________________________
(Signature of employee)	(Signature of witness)
___________________________	___________________________
(Print name of employee)	(Print name of witness)

mation confidential. All client records should be stored in locked files to which access is monitored.

• Formal disability management service records should be maintained separately from all other records, such as personnel, medical, or legal records.

• Formal disability management service records should contain only that information necessary to ensure accountability and continuity of care, including dates, service provider, and a brief statement regarding the nature of the problem and the type of service provided. When employees leave the work organization under whose auspices service was provided, their service records should be destroyed.

• In relation to "open" cases, a distinction should be made between formal service records and the "working notes" of the service provider. "Working notes," essential to ensure provision of individualized, appropriate service, are the property of the service provider or case manager and should be maintained by professionals in personal locked files, separate from service records. They should not be available to anyone other than the professional provider. The case manager's use of them should be bound by the tenets of confidentiality, and they should identify the client by number only. These notes should be destroyed as soon as they are no longer required for the professional's ongoing work.

• Information, whether stored as hard copy (paper file) or on the computer, should identify the client by number, and the code should be maintained in a separate locked file. Social Security numbers should not be used as client numbers because they are too easily connected to the individual.

• Protections provided for written records should be extended to all sources of data about clients, including tape recordings, videotapes, and computer files.

• Clients should have access to their formal service records at any time.

• Clients should be able to request that the case manager amend or correct any portion of the record that they think is incorrect.

• The professional's immediate supervisor or the person responsible for ensuring the quality and extent of services provided should have access to the formal service record, and should be bound by the principles of confidentiality detailed above. No other person should have access to the service record except under the circumstances discussed above.

• Aggregate program information should in no way reveal individual program participants. Anytime reports are made, either verbally or in writing, the name of the individual should be excluded. Where information is idiosyncratic to an individual, the information itself should not be disclosed, or the facts should be altered sufficiently to protect the individual. For example, should an employee lose a finger in an accident, and this information become widely known within the workplace, any discussion of the employee's situation should either not include the injury or disguise it (for example, by identifying the injury as a lost toe or a foot injury).

If these seem to be extreme efforts, remember that it is difficult to predict what a particular individual will regard as confidential. The loss of trust that can occur when that boundary is violated can damage the effort not only for the individual involved, but also for the entire disability program. If we remember that a workplace is like a small village, in which reputations, once made, are difficult to overcome, we are likely to understand the importance of gaining a reputation for protecting the privacy of clients.

Finally, in developing policies and procedures for maintaining confidentiality, the decision makers must take into account the need to share information among departments in order to make the program work. The separation of name from record, and the use of coded numbers for which the name/code match is in the hands of only one, high-level supervisor, is a useful device to protect confidentiality and still share information. It is recognized that all information cannot be shared, but the means of releasing information that links the system must be established.

Types of Data Needed for Program Monitoring and Evaluation

The types of data required for program monitoring and evaluation are determined by policy goals and procedures. Thus, the first step in specifying the data to be collected is to formulate an explicit policy and procedures. Policy components are discussed at length in Chapter 5. To summarize, the goals of disability management policy are as follows:

- To promote early intervention
- To maximize return to work and job maintenance
- To contain the costs associated with disability
- To maximize job satisfaction and worker morale
- To minimize lost productivity as a consequence of disability
- To promote prevention and reduce the onset of disability

These goals must be translated into data that can be systematically collected and analyzed.

Figure 7-2 shows a flow chart for disability case management procedures that covers the major data collection issues that must be considered. Program procedures will vary according to the organizational structure, labor force characteristics, and community resources and support unique to the site. In general, however, the procedures must specify:

- How workers are referred to the program
- How intake and assessment are handled
- The intervention components
- How case closing is accomplished
- How follow-up to assess program impact is conducted

Most of the data required for program evaluation can be collected simultaneously with program-monitoring data. In some instances the data are the same but are analyzed differently. Monitoring may involve review of individual cases, while evaluation aggregates the data to focus on overall outcomes. Further, both monitoring and evaluation rely on two types of information: (1) data about program participants and (2) data about how program personnel are functioning. The discussion that follows examines steps in the case management process where such data are obtainable. Each step is shown in the flow chart in Figure 7-2.

Referral to the Program

Program participants are either newly disabled workers out on short-term disability leave or workers having trouble maintaining their jobs because of the onset or worsening of disability or because of reassignment to a job they cannot perform. Workers with disabilities out on short-term disability are identified by the department that administers the short-term disability program, usually the benefits department in the case of non-work-connected accidents, illness, or worsening of condition, and risk management in the case of accident or illness growing out of or in the course of employment. Filing a workers compensation or disability claim form signals that the individual may meet program criteria. Workers who are encountering problems staying on the job because of disability may refer themselves, or they may be referred by their supervisors, managers, the employee assistance program, or the medical department. Thus, the first step is to decide who makes referrals and establish the criteria used to determine who should be referred.

Each department involved in the referral process must assign staff the responsibility for making referrals. For example, all claims officers in the benefits department may be trained to identify workers eligible for assistance through the program, or all supervisors may be trained to recognize such workers. Sometimes a worker with a disability may consult someone

Figure 7-2. Data collection points in the case management process.

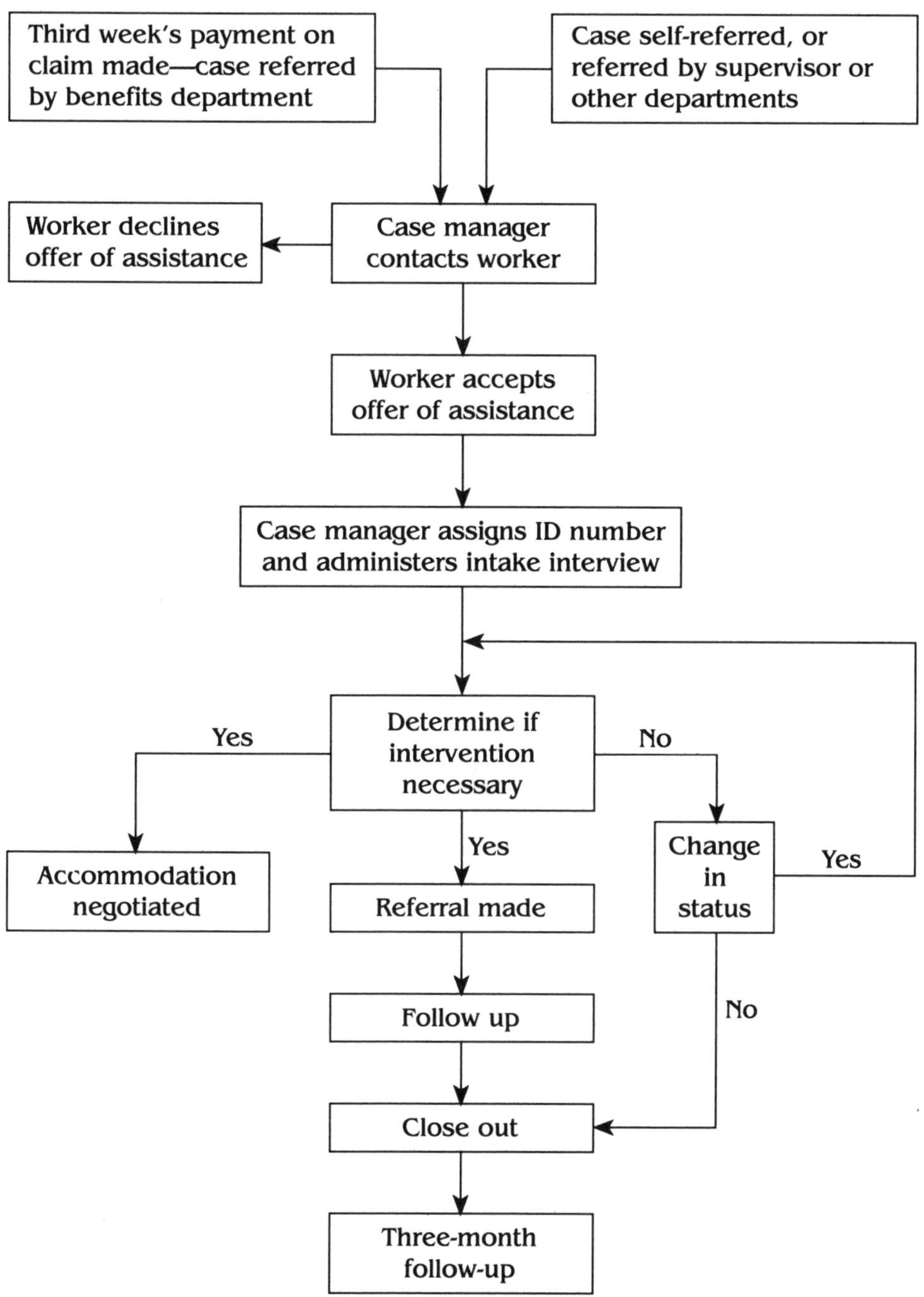

in the organization who is easy to talk with and is concerned with the disability issue, perhaps the affirmative action officer.

The criterion for referral must also be explicit. For example, to meet the objective of early intervention yet avoid contacting people out with a minor illness of short duration, claims officers may be instructed to refer all disabled workers at the time they certify the third week of disability payment. Additionally, certain diagnoses or injuries may also activate a referral despite the length of time out. For example, a worker might have suffered from a first exacerbation of rheumatoid arthritis that only lasted several weeks. Because of the potential for future episodes, however, the worker may benefit from counseling on ways to cope with the disease. Finally, anyone returning to work while still undergoing treatment, whether for a back condition, hypertension, or any other illness or injury, may be referred to the program automatically.

Whatever eligibility criteria are established, they must be reflected in the record-keeping forms. Consider the preceding example. The claims officers must know when the criteria for referral to the disability case manager have been met. Therefore, claim forms must record:

- Date of onset of disability
- Diagnosis
- Prognosis (degree of expected recovery—total, partial recovery, no further progress, deterioration)
- Expected length of treatment
- Expected return-to-work date

The criteria for referring a worker who is maintaining his or her job while dealing with disability may be different from those for someone out on short-term disability. For example, supervisors rely upon behavioral and performance cues to identify referrals. The worker may suddenly start being late for work or absent frequently. He or she may increasingly avoid interacting with the supervisor, co-workers, or supervisees. Or, the person may show trouble completing assigned tasks. Supervisors need a performance checklist to help identify workers in possible need of assistance.

Once a referral is made, the disability program case manager must begin tracking and recording information. The first information to be recorded is:

- Name of employee
- How and where the worker can be contacted
- The source of the referral
- Date of the referral

A form to keep track of this information is shown in Figure 7-3.

Figure 7-3. Workers referred to the program.

Name of Worker	*Phone Number*	*Referral: Source/Date*	*Employee at Work* Yes	*Employee at Work* No
________	home: ______ work: ______	________	___	___
________	home: ______ work: ______	________	___	___
________	home: ______ work: ______	________	___	___
________	home: ______ work: ______	________	___	___
________	home: ______ work: ______	________	___	___
________	home: ______ work: ______	________	___	___
________	home: ______ work: ______	________	___	___
________	home: ______ work: ______	________	___	___
________	home: ______ work: ______	________	___	___
________	home: ______ work: ______	________	___	___

Case Manager's First Contact With the Participant and Assigning an Identification Number

After the referral, the case manager should contact the worker to ask if he or she is interested in receiving assistance through the program and, if so, to schedule a time to administer the intake interview. This step marks the second point where information must be monitored. The case manager needs to record:

- Name of the worker contacted
- Whether or not the worker is going to participate
- The time set to administer the intake interview

Figure 7-4 shows a form for tracking this information.

If the worker would like to participate at this point, the case manager needs to (1) enter the interview date on his or her calendar or diary and (2) assign the worker an ID number. As discussed, the information supplied by the worker must be kept confidential. The procedures for maintaining confidentiality require that the name of the worker not be used on the intake interview form or in any other written information collected by the case manager. The case manager must keep two sets of files. One file contains the names, addresses, Social Security numbers, and other identifying information about program participants and an ID number. The case manager must keep a key list that matches name files and ID numbers. If the list is kept as hard copy (on paper), it should be in a locked file. If the list is maintained on computer, a password should be required to access it, with the password known only to the case manager and his or her supervisor. The list should be kept both alphabetically by name and in numerical order by ID number to ensure access when only the name or ID number is available. For "record" files, which contain all program information, the individual participants are identified only by number.

ID numbers can be any numbers selected by the system planner. They can be consecutive numbers starting with 1, allowing sufficient numbers to cover the expected case volume for a decade. Therefore, if the expectation is 1,000 cases a year, five columns might be assigned ID numbers, the first being 00001 and the last 10000. Alternatively, they can be composed of groups of numbers that carry additional information. For example, the case manager may want an easy way to know at intake whether the participant is out on disability or still on the job. One way to do this is to assign an arbitrary code to each participant that represents this information. The case manager may decide to begin ID numbers with the letter A (or the number 1) for all workers out on disability and the

Figure 7-4. Eligible candidates for program.

Name of Worker	*Phone Number*	*Date of First Contact*	*Participating*		*Schedule for Intake*
			Yes	*No*	

letter B (or the number 2) for all workers still on the job, or, if the worker's sex is an important issue, A (or 1) for all men and B (or 2) for all women. The code selected is then followed by consecutive numbers representing the different participants.

There are several caveats in creating ID numbers that contain additional information:

- They should not be too complicated. The numbers should communicate information quickly and easily; they should not have to be deciphered like code messages from the enemy.
- If data are stored on the computer, the numbers need to conform to the specifications of the program used for analysis.
- The number should not identify so many characteristics of an individual that it could lead to identifying the person. In such a case, the name of the individual might just as well be used.
- The scheme for assigning ID numbers should be set in place before the first participant is referred to the program so that a consistent numbering system is established.

Administering the Intake Interview

At the time of the intake interview, the case manager collects additional information that will assist in both monitoring and evaluation. Characteristics of individual workers help program personnel develop a profile of the workers assisted through the program. Information about insurance coverage helps anticipate demand for benefits and monitor how benefits are used. Important information that needs to be collected at the time of intake includes:

- Characteristics of the worker, such as age, sex, marital status, income, level of education, and language restrictions
- Work history, including length of employment and job title
- Information about the disability, including type of disability, date of onset, expected return-to-work date (if applicable), and date of contact by case manager
- Information about the extent of insurance coverage
- Union membership status, the name of the union, and, if possible, the name and telephone number of the union representative

Figure 7-5 provides a format for recording the kind of information that should be collected during the intake interview to help monitor program utilization.

After completing the Baseline Information Sheet (see Figure 7-5), the

Figure 7-5. Disabled employee baseline information sheet.

Today's date: ______

Client ID number: ______

Disability coverage

Employer/self-insured ______
Collectively bargained health and welfare plan ______
Disability insurance carrier ______
Specify: ______
Workers compensation carrier ______
Specify: ______
None ______

Insurance coverage for physician care

Complete ______
Partial ______
None ______

Insurance coverage for hospitalization

Complete ______
Partial ______
None ______

Client's disability

Trauma ______
Neoplasm ______
Cardiovascular ______
Respiratory ______
Genitourinary ______
Neurological ______
Musculoskeletal/back ______
Musculoskeletal/other ______
Gastrointestinal ______
Infectious disease ______
Mental disorder ______
Multiple diagnoses ______
Other ______
Specify: ______

Date became disabled: ______

Expected return-to-work date: ______

Time between disability onset and assessment interview

Less than one week ______
7 to 15 days ______
16 to 30 days ______
31 to 60 days ______
More than 60 days ______

(*continued*)

Figure 7-5. (continued)

Client's job title classification

White collar
- Professional and technical ______
- Manager and administrator ______
- Salesworker ______
- Clerical worker ______

Blue collar
- Craft and kindred worker ______
- Operative, except transport ______
- Transport equipment operative ______
- Nonfarm laborer ______

Service worker ______

Client's worksite: ______________________________

Date of first employment with this employer: ______________

Union member: No ____ Yes ____ If yes, specify: ______________

Client's date of birth: __________

Sex: Male ____ Female ____

Marital status

Single ______
Married ______
Separated ______
Divorced ______
Widowed ______

Pay last calendar year

Less than $15,000 ______
$15,000–$19,999 ______
$20,000–$24,999 ______
$25,000–$34,999 ______
$35,000–$49,999 ______
$50,000–$74,999 ______
$75,000 and over ______

Level of education

Grade school ______
Some high school ______
High school diploma ______
Some college ______
College diploma ______
Graduate work ____ Degree __________
Apprenticeship ____ Number of years ______
Post-high-school technical training ______

Language restrictions

Yes ____ No ____ Preferred language ____________________

case manager is ready to administer the intake interview. The interview's content (Appendix 6-1) and rationale are thoroughly described in Chapter 6. To review, the intake interview collects data concerning:

- Job requirements in terms of tasks, routines, and relationships
- Physical and emotional consequences of the disability and perceptions of health care
- Limitations in functional capacity given the worker's disability and job requirements
- Financial and personal problems as a consequence of disability

Three aspects of the intake interview are especially important in monitoring program activity:

1. The case manager must always remember to write the ID number on the interview; the name of the disabled employee should not appear on it.

2. The case manager should write the date at the top of the interview. The date of intake allows the length of time between onset of disability (or worsening of the problem) and intervention to be calculated. Effectiveness of the early intervention strategy can be analyzed on the basis of this calculation. It is possible, for example, to *plan* an early intervention program but find, from this calculation, that several months elapse between onset of disability and intake. This would require remediation through a strategy designed to identify workers with disabilities earlier, perhaps through the absentee records or by having supervisors notify the program manager when an employee is out for more than a week.

3. The case manager must always be aware of the need to complete the interview accurately. A response should be recorded for all questions. If the worker refuses to answer part of the interview (a situation that occurs rarely), it should be noted carefully. Case managers must be systematic, accurate, and complete, both to assist the worker effectively and to enable correct summarization of the data. At the end of each interview session the case manager should scan the interview to make sure it is clear and complete.

Determining Necessary Interventions

The next step for the case manager is to determine necessary interventions on the basis of the intake interview. (This step is discussed in detail in Chapter 6.) Information about community resources is of central importance at this step—they are usually the essential determinant of non-workplace-related intervention strategies. The case manager should develop a resource manual of community intervention resources by carrying out two tasks:

1. *Building a file of existing resources.* It should include the organization's name, address, telephone number, contact person, services provided, and eligibility requirements.

2. *Assessing the organization's past performance.* Rating scales should be used to evaluate how well the organization meets the needs of referred workers. An example of what an entry in the resource manual might look like is shown in Figure 7-6.

When the intervention is job-related, the case manager should be able to follow a predetermined procedure that activates appropriate actors at the workplace.

Taking Action

Once the intervention strategy has been formulated, thoroughly discussed with the worker, and the worker's informed consent to continue has been obtained, the case manager takes the proposed action. The record-keeping component of this step involves maintaining a detailed account of contact with the worker, including:

- The problem area where intervention is needed
- The date when the problem was identified
- The date when the action was initiated
- The date when follow-up contact was made
- The date when outcome of the action was determined
- The outcome status, or degree to which the action was implemented
- Case notes or a description of special circumstances that arise, including names and phone numbers of contacts, problems with implementing the intervention, and the like

An intervention checklist (see Figure 7-7) can be used to track this information. The checklist is divided into three categories: (1) workplace interventions, (2) interventions with health care professionals, and (3) interventions with social service agencies or departments. In each category actions are listed. Program staff review the assessment interview (see Chapter 6) to determine which actions might be helpful to program participants. Case managers record the actions that are recommended and the dates when they contacted participants to monitor implementation of the intervention strategy.

(Text continues on page 184.)

Figure 7-6. Resource form.

Name of organization: ____________________

Address: ____________________

____

____

Telephone number: ____________

Service areas: ____________________

____

____

Eligibility requirements: ____________________

____

____

____

Fees: ____________________

Key contact person: ____________________

Rating: ____________________

Additional comments: ____________________

____

____

____

____

Figure 7-7. Intervention checklist.

ID Number ______ Date ______

*Intervention**	*Iden- tified*	*Initi- ated†*	*Followed Up*	*Outcome Deter- mined*	*Outcome Category‡*
Workplace interventions					
Exploration of disclosure	______	______	______	______	______
Job tasks changed	______	______	______	______	______
Job routines changed:					
Number of days worked	______	______	______	______	______
Number of hours worked	______	______	______	______	______
Transportation to/from work	______	______	______	______	______
Exemption from over- time or activities that change routine	______	______	______	______	______
Other (specify) ______	______	______	______	______	______
Negotiate workstation or physical facilities change	______	______	______	______	______
Help to eliminate work- place hazard	______	______	______	______	______
Review technological assistance	______	______	______	______	______
Job retraining for new job	______	______	______	______	______
Education for improved informal workplace responsiveness	______	______	______	______	______
Encourage employer to review formal work- place policy	______	______	______	______	______

*Indicate the primary intervention by placing an asterisk next to the entry.
†Indicate organization initiating the action.
‡Outcome categories: (1) not possible to implement intervention
(2) partial implementation of intervention
(3) implementation of intervention complete

Intervention	*Date* Iden-tified	Initi-ated	Followed Up	Outcome Deter-mined	*Outcome Category*
Protection of legal rights	______	______	______	______	______
Strategic planning for (specify) ______	______	______	______	______	______
General discussion with the employer	______	______	______	______	______
Other (specify) ______	______	______	______	______	______
Interventions with health care professionals					
Discussion with health care professionals about modified work	______	______	______	______	______
Discussion with health care professionals about disability or treatment	______	______	______	______	______
Interventions with social service agencies or departments					
Counseling to help with change in interpersonal workplace relationships with (specify) ______	______	______	______	______	______
Disability-related counseling	______	______	______	______	______
Family or other mental health counseling	______	______	______	______	______
EAP or Human Resources Department	______	______	______	______	______
Benefits Department	______	______	______	______	______
Retirement counseling	______	______	______	______	______
Legal counseling	______	______	______	______	______
Financial assistance	______	______	______	______	______
Job retraining	______	______	______	______	______
Outside placement	______	______	______	______	______
Self-help group	______	______	______	______	______
Home care provider	______	______	______	______	______
Second medical opinion	______	______	______	______	______
Other (specify) ______	______	______	______	______	______

Case Notes (*use additional page or pages*)

To fill out the checklist, the case manager first enters the participant's ID number in the space provided at the top, right-hand corner. Next, the case manager selects the category that best describes the recommended intervention (in some cases, more than one category will be selected). The recommendation is based on review of the worker's intake assessment interview by program staff.

The columns of the checklist are completed as follows:

- *Date identified.* The date of the interview review where the problem and intervention were identified is entered.
- *Date initiated.* The date when action was first taken on the recommendation is entered.
- *Date followed up.* The date when a follow-up phone call was made to the participant to check that he or she was not encountering difficulty with the implementation of the recommended action is entered. This phone call should be made within two *weeks* after the action was initiated.
- *Date outcome determined.* The date of the phone call to the participant to ask about how well the problem was resolved by the recommended action is entered. This call should be made three *months* after the recommended action was initiated.
- *Outcome category.* A 1 is entered if it was not possible to implement the recommended action. A 2 is entered if there was only partial implementation of the recommended action. Finally, a 3 is entered if there was complete implementation of the recommended action. An explanation of why an action was not implemented should be provided in the case notes.

In some cases, one intervention will take precedence over the others. That is, other actions may not be possible until the first is achieved. If there is a primary intervention—one that is highly important or is a precondition for other action—an asterisk is placed next to the intervention category on the checklist. A line can be provided next to the intervention to indicate the specific action or person involved.

The checklist is designed to cover all situations that are likely to require a case manager's attention. Certain categories are likely to be more relevant to an outside case manager (for example, "encourage employer to review formal workplace" or "protection of legal rights").

Bear in mind that *the intervention checklist is not a replacement for a case manager's notes* about implementing the recommended actions. Details about the problems encountered, issues specific to the individual's circumstances, impressions about how the participant is adjusting, and the like should all be recorded in addition to the checklist items.

The following are brief descriptions of the checklist intervention categories:

• *Exploration of disclosure.* If individuals at the workplace do not know about the participant's illness or disability, then the case manager may need to explore the positive or negative implications of disclosing this information.

• *Job task changes, job routine changes, workstation or physical facilities changes, elimination of workplace hazards, review of technological assistance, job retraining for a new job.* Some participants will want assistance negotiating accommodations at the workplace. These interventions are the usual focus of the negotiation.

• *Education for improved informal workplace responsiveness.* In some instances, lack of understanding about the participant's disability or illness and the workplace limitations it causes interferes with successful readjustment to work. Educating supervisors, co-workers, and others at work about the disability improves the effectiveness of the readjustment process.

• *Encourage employer to review formal workplace policy.* Some employers have disability policies, but they can be ambiguous, limited, or poorly communicated. Others do not have an explicit policy despite the fact that they are responsive to the needs of employees with disabilities. Still others do not have disability policies *and* are unresponsive to the needs of disabled workers. In such cases the employer should review existing policy.

• *Protection of legal rights.* If the participant faces discrimination in the workplace as a consequence of disability or illness, then legal recourse may be necessary. Participants in these instances need to be fully informed about their rights.

• *Strategic planning.* This intervention refers to actions taken to address *future* problems. It may be, for example, that someone's disability is not currently affecting the ability to do his/her job but the condition is expected to worsen. In this case, case managers would help to plan for future job accommodation. Another example would be the instance where job maintenance or job return is very unlikely and planning for long term benefits is needed.

• *General discussion with the employer.* The assessment interview provides information about disability policies and practices at an individual's workplace. If an employer is reported as unresponsive to the needs of employees with disabilities, it might be recommended that staff discuss with the employer how to develop more effective disability management.

• *Interventions with health care professionals.* Doctors play a crucial role in determining when, or if, someone returns to work. If a participant has not discussed the ways in which his or her condition might affect job performance, or if the return-to-work date is based on when the individual would be able to perform at 100 percent, then the recommended intervention might be to help the participant discuss with the doctor the possibility of earlier, modified return to work, or, at least, to pursue the implications of the disability for work.

• *Interventions with social service agencies or departments.* Interventions with social service agencies or departments primarily involve referring participants to the organization best equipped to deal with their problem. Referrals may be made to departments within the company, such as the employee assistance program or the benefits department, or to other social service providers in the community.

Closing a Case

In some programs, cases are closed when short-term disability benefits terminate. Other programs, however, continue to serve workers who go on the long-term disability rolls. Specific criteria for case closing, therefore, must be established at each site. Probably the most desirable time to close a file is when the worker's employment situation is resolved on a permanent basis. This includes return to his or her usual work, return to accommodated work, or early retirement. Regardless of when the case is closed, important information needs to be collected at that time, including the following:

- Whether or not the worker returned to work
- If the worker did not return to work, why not
- If the worker did return to work, the date, the number of weeks out, and the return status—to the usual work without accommodation; to the usual work with temporary accommodation; to the usual work with permanent accommodation; to a new job temporarily; or to a new job permanently
- If the worker was accommodated, the exact nature of the accommodation
- If the worker received other types of assistance, the exact types of assistance
- A summary of the cost information, including amount of disability payments, cost of hospitalization, and cost for physician care and other medical expenses

These data provide a basis for cost-benefit analysis as well as help to build a reservoir of effective accommodation solutions.

Follow-Up Survey

An evaluation can be enhanced by follow-up information to monitor program function and outcome. Rehabilitation experts have determined that three months is the average time period needed to determine the stability of readjustment to work. Therefore, three months following the return to work is a good time to survey workers assisted through the program. The survey should ask workers these questions:

- Are you still at work; if not, why not (worsening of disability, new onset of disability, accommodation at the workplace insufficient, problems outside of work)?
- What type of assistance did you receive?
- Was the assistance helpful in returning to work or maintaining job roles?
- How responsive was the case manager in providing assistance? How responsive were referrals in providing expected services?
- What problems did you have in trying to return or readjust to work that the program did not, or could not, address?

Answers to these questions provide the basis for staff accountability and evidence for any needed program changes.

Process Data

Along with the information recorded at each step in documenting specific cases, the activities of program personnel and other affected staff that reflect program operations may also be recorded to allow comprehensive evaluation of the process. These activities generate information in the following forms:

- Minutes of the meetings of the coordinating committee, case managers and their supervisors, management and program personnel, and community resource representatives and program personnel, and minutes of any other meeting that affects disability policy or program operations
- Log books maintained by program personnel that contain copies of all program-related correspondence and notes on process problems and changes

- Monthly status reports of program personnel performance summarizing overall case management activity
- Regular activity reports from these departments: personnel, risk management, benefits, medical, EAP, EEO, or any other department that has information that demontrates the impact of program operations
- Special reports or studies conducted by program personnel that address problems unique to the site

Data Analysis

It should be clear that a significant amount of information can be collected and analyzed to assist in achieving smooth operation, program monitoring, and program evaluation. The function of data analysis is to organize, summarize, and present the information in a useful form.

Organizing the information begins by developing a list of questions the data analysis will answer. There are these categories of questions to consider:

1. Questions to monitor how well program participants are being served.

- Are referrals properly acted upon?
- Are workers referred to the program accepting assistance?
- Are nonwork problems that are identified through the intake interview responded to adequately by available community resources?
- Are the work accommodations offered adequate to assist successful return to work or maintenance of work roles?
- Are program personnel easily accessible and do they provide enough help?

2. Questions to monitor program operations.

- Are referrals made in a timely fashion?
- Is confidentiality properly maintained?
- Does the coordinating committee obtain from case managers and other departments reports and information that allow smooth functioning?
- Do all department personnel and management receive adequate program information?
- Does program activity affect other departmental functions?
- Are adequate networks with community resources maintained?

- Who is not accepting program assistance, not returning to work, staying out too long, or not performing adequately, and why?

3. Questions to evaluate program policy and goals.

- Has the distribution of type of disability experienced by workers changed since program implementation, that is, has prevention taken hold?
- Have the characteristics of workers most frequently affected by disability changed since program implementation?
- Has the number of lost days been reduced?
- Has the number of workers out on long-term disability been reduced?
- Has the number of workers out on short-term disability been reduced?
- Has the length of time on short- and long-term disability been reduced?
- Has the number of workers who stay on the job after program intervention increased?
- Have morale and job satisfaction among workers with disabilities and their co-workers and supervisors increased?
- Have medical care costs decreased?
- Has the amount, or at least the rate of increase, of short-term and long-term disability benefits decreased?
- Has the cost of benefits and number of claims under workers compensation decreased in amount or rate of increase?

The next step in performing a data analysis is to determine which data can help answer the questions of interest. Figure 7-8 summarizes the data that need to be collected and the questions they help answer.

After all relevant data are collected, they must be prepared for analysis. First, they must be coded and entered into the computer. At this point decisions must be made about, for example, how to handle qualitative data or information that is not easily quantifiable. Code books that specify each piece of information, its location on the file, and values it can assume need to be compiled.

Second, a computer program to access the data needs to be written and entered. The program is written in the computer language selected for analysis. Two software packages used frequently for analysis are Statistical Package for the Social Sciences (SPSS) and Statistical Analysis System (SAS). Other software may be better for tracking data and preparing status reports but may not perform the statistical functions adequately. The software options available and their ability to meet analysis needs should be determined at each site. If there is a computer department at the

Figure 7-8. Data contribution to analysis.

Data	*Program Monitoring*	*Program Evaluation*	*Questions Addressed*
Informed consent	*		Is confidentiality maintained?
Criteria for referral	*	*	Are workers in need of assistance being served?
			What is the disability profile of workers in need of help?
Workers referred to the program form	*		Are workers adequately tracked?
Program participants form	*		Are workers contacted and interviewed in a timely fashion?
Interview cover sheet	*	*	What type of assistance may be required?
			What are the characteristics of participants?
Intake interview	*	*	What types of problems are workers experiencing as a consequence of disability?
			What type of intervention may assist return to work or job maintenance?
			What was the time between onset of problem and intervention?
Resource manual	*	*	Are resources available to assist workers?
			Are available resources effective?
Intervention checklist	*	*	Is recommended assistance being provided?
			What types of assistance are needed most frequently?
			What are the relationships between worker characteristics, disability, and type of assistance provided?
Case closing information	*	*	What is the average length of disability?
			What percentage of workers stay on the job or return to work?
			Was the intervention cost-effective?
			Is there follow-up to verify that accommodations have been implemented?

Data	*Program Monitoring*	*Program Evaluation*	*Questions Addressed*
Follow-up survey	*	*	What is the relationship between program participation and staying on the job?
			Was assistance perceived as helpful and effective?
			What are the problems of readjustment to work that the program could not address?
Minutes of meetings, log books, monthly status reports, activity reports, special studies	*		Are program procedures effective?
			Is communication sufficient?
			Is action timely?
			Are conflicts and problems resolved?

worksite, someone from that unit can probably help make these decisions and provide programming expertise.

Third, the data need to be cleaned and thoroughly checked for accuracy and completeness. Discrepant values (for example, a code that is not provided as a response for a particular question) are identified and checked. If possible, missing data are retrieved.

Once the data are entered and cleaned, analysis can begin. Basic analysis requires simple descriptive statistics. Frequency distributions and cross-tabulations summarize the data appropriately and answer the questions of interest. Analysis of the data for evaluation purposes requires comparing current program information with past program performance and performance prior to program implementation. (Chapter 3 discusses the importance of baseline data.) When program evaluation is conducted, the role of baseline data becomes apparent.

More sophisticated statistics are required if the data are to be used for predictive purposes. For example, multivariate regression analysis is one way to estimate what to expect over the next several years on the basis of past program performance. The ability to perform more complicated analyses depends upon the statistical expertise of the program staff, or consultants available to it, and the quality of the data. Data must conform to the specific assumptions underlying the analyses.

Review and Interpretation of the Results

The results of data analysis must be presented in a form that is appropriate for reviewing and interpreting them. To decide the format requires knowing who the report is for, how it is to be used, and what is customary in the company. Case managers, for example, need information on a case-by-case basis. A case manager's supervisor may be interested in a summary of program activity by case manager in order to monitor the work of each. The coordinating committee and upper-level management, however, may only want a report of program activity covering all case managers, or reports may be distributed universally.

Different departments may need only selective data that pertain to their functions. The benefits department may want only detailed information about the referral rates, or the impact of the program on the length of short-term disability. EEO people may be interested in program participants who do not stay on the job or for whom accommodation is problematic. The time period the report needs to cover must also be determined. Is the report a monthly update, a year-end summary, or a comparative study of five years of operation?

Finally, who is responsible for writing the reports? Do case managers produce all reports? Do case managers' supervisors produce summary reports? Are data made available to other departments so that they can produce their own reports? The answers to these questions depend on the size and structure of the company.

Preparation of data analysis reports is of great significance. They provide the basis for discussion of program performance and direction for future actions.

Staff Training

Staff training is fundamental to embedding disability management in the system. Through training, the tasks of disability management become part of everyday operations and not something external or out of the ordinary. Training strengthens the skills and provides the support needed to perform disability management functions and redefines jobs so that disability management becomes a fundamental part of them.

There are many aspects of training to be considered:

- What jobs are redefined and, therefore, need training for?
- Who needs training?
- Who does the training?
- What is the content of the training?
- Who should participate in the training?
- When and where does the training occur?
- How long should the training be?
- How can resistance to training be handled?

What Jobs Are Redefined and, Therefore, Need Training For?

The jobs affected by implementing a disability management program depend on the system set in place and the constraints operating at the worksite. Systems in large corporations may be very elaborate, involving many different departments, a coordinating committee, a number of case managers, many supervisors, and so on. Other systems may be much smaller, reflecting the scale and the needs of a smaller employer. One person may handle all aspects of a disability management system. Unions that administer collectively bargained trust funds have their own unique system.

One of the most important constraints to consider is the union contract. Management at unionized sites should evaluate whether or not changes in job descriptions would violate collective bargaining agreements. Changes may require the approval of the union. Following are the major job description changes needed when a disability management program is implemented. Any particular company needs to consider how the changes apply to its own organizational design.

Program Case Managers

Program case managers are assumed to be trained human services professionals, as discussed in Chapters 3 and 6. The individual must have the basic skills required to do the job, specifically, carry out and analyze the assessment interview, develop appropriate intervention strategies, know how to develop and maintain resource networks, and, most important, develop and maintain a trusting relationship with the disabled worker. However, these professionals still may require training to learn the procedures established at the site. For example, they need to learn how to communicate with the coordinating committee and other departments. If, prior to participating in disability management, case managers did not assist workers with disabilities specifically, they may need training in issues of particular concern to job accommodation. They may also need to learn about the particular jobs at the workplace and the community resources that deal with problems likely to be experienced by disabled workers.

Supervisors

As emphasized repeatedly in this book, *the role of supervisors is central to the success of the disability management effort*. Supervisors may need training to be able to:

- Identify and refer workers to the program. Supervisors need to be able to assess whether or not a worker is an appropriate candidate for the program on the basis of established criteria concerning absence, accidents, or apparent problems in work performance.

• Maintain contact with the worker during the period of disability leave. Contact by the supervisor during the period of disability is one of the primary ways for employers to demonstrate the responsiveness and welcomeness so vital to rehabilitation success.

• Participate in implementing and evaluating work return and accommodated work. Along with the case manager and the coordinating committee, the supervisor helps to determine appropriate accommodated work. He or she understands best what a job involves and, along with the person with disability, can determine how tasks can be assigned to meet the individual's limitations.

• Educate co-workers. Co-workers may need to be educated about the disability and about how jobs need to change during the period of accommodation. Often it is difficult for disabled workers to talk about their disabilities. They may be embarrassed, afraid of others' reactions, or too upset to communicate clearly to co-workers about their condition and the limitations it imposes. Conversely, co-workers may have misconceptions about the disability and the type of impairment it causes that need to be dispelled. For example, Feldman (1976) found in questioning those with a diagnosis of cancer that a significant minority of their co-workers avoided them because they believed cancer to be catching. This is certainly an issue for co-workers of those with AIDS, but is probably a concern with many disabilities. Finally, everyone who worked with a worker prior to onset of disability needs to understand how the worker's job responsibilities will change as a consequence of accommodation and whether or not their own jobs will be affected.

• Monitor performance. Supervisors should monitor performance of workers with disabilities along several dimensions. They need to be able to assess whether accommodated work is appropriate, whether additional training is required, and whether there are changes in performance. Improved performance may indicate that the worker is ready for expanded job tasks. Deteriorating performance may indicate a worsening of disability, problems with the assigned tasks, or other problems in the work environment.

Personnel From Departments Represented on the Coordinating Committee

Personnel from each of the departments involved in the disability management program need to assume the tasks necessary to enable smooth program functioning. Some tasks are the same across departments, while others are unique.

Departments that may be involved in the program include benefits, medical, EAP, risk management, legal, EEO, and personnel. Tasks to be learned include data collection and report preparation, screening, referral, job placement and job identification, resource identification, training, and policy development. In some workplaces a single individual may be responsible for all program tasks, and can be trained by attending a conference or calling in a consultant to help with program development (sometimes insurance companies have personnel available to assist in such training). In others, more than one person, even within a particular department, may share the responsibility. For example, the representative to the coordinating committee may be the department supervisor, while data collection and screening may be the responsibility of department staff.

Who Needs Training?

Anyone involved in the disability management effort requires some training. The content of the training depends on (1) program design and (2) knowledge and skills of the individuals involved and their particular assignment in the program. Most training is task-specific. However, all staff involved in the program and all representatives from outside organizations who sit on the coordinating committee require, at a minimum, a session that provides an overview of the program. *Everyone needs to understand program goals and how he or she fits into the program.*

To determine who requires task-specific training, current job descriptions can be compared to the list of tasks an individual will perform as part of the program. For any job where the current descriptions differ from program tasks, training is needed. For example, claims officers may need to be trained on how to complete a referral form. Supervisors may need to be trained on how to develop accommodated work options. Coordinating committee members may require training on how to facilitate teamwork.

Who Does the Training?

To decide who does the training requires an assessment of both the purpose of the training and the on-site expertise. A training session to provide an orientation to the program may be conducted by management. In this way top management can both explain the process and show commitment to setting it in place. To determine who does task-specific training, management needs to evaluate how training is usually done on-site and whether or not the existing system and expertise can handle it. If on-site resources are not sufficient, outside consultants may be required to offer part or all of the training. University departments of social work or rehabilitation counseling, hospitals with rehabilitation programs, and management consulting firms are among the sources of such consultants.

What Is the Content of the Training?

Training includes the following:

- Contextual orientation, which describes why the task is important and how it fits into the entire program.
- A written description of the task. Staff need a manual to refer to that describes how to do the task, the procedure that needs to be followed, how the recording and reporting need to be done, and who else is involved in the task.
- An opportunity to rehearse the task. This may involve role playing or a supervised first try at completing a form.
- A question-and-answer period to review content.
- Debriefing. After the rehearsal and review, it is necessary to evaluate the effort to correct mistakes and reinforce good performance.

Who Should Participate in the Training?

The training need not be isolated to only those involved in doing the task. Participation by several key personnel will help to convey the importance of the task and the organization's commitment to it. Key representatives include:

- Someone from top management
- The supervisor(s) responsible for overseeing the staff being trained
- A liaison from the coordinating committee
- The program case manager(s)

When and Where Does the Training Occur?

There is no set formula for when or where training should occur. But a specific time and site should be set aside for the training. For example, coordinating committee members may go away on retreat to learn their new roles. Or they may be trained during lunch hour, on overtime, or for an hour at the end of the day. In some instances training is best accomplished on-site. For brief training or situations where on-site resources, such as computer terminals, are needed, training on-site is preferable. Off-site training also has some advantages—in particular, because off-site training takes personnel away from their other responsibilities, it encourages them to give the training their full attention.

How Long Should the Training Be?

The length of the training depends upon several factors. First, it is determined by the content of the training. Discrete, small tasks may take little time to learn. Ongoing, complicated tasks may require several training sessions.

Second, the length of training depends on cost. Lost time at work to attend the training and the expense of the trainers must be taken into account. However, the disability management program works best if personnel know their tasks and how they fit into the program. Training is the up-front investment to accomplish this goal.

How Can Resistance to Training Be Handled?

A final issue to consider is how to handle resistance that may arise in response to changing responsibilities. This resistance is sometimes reflected in the attitude adopted toward training and demonstrated during instruction. Top-management commitment to the program does not guarantee the commitment of lower-level staff. People are uncertain of what is expected of them, how they will be evaluated, what benefits they will gain from the changes, and how existing responsibilities are affected. Some may perceive the program as setting up turf conflicts in cases where tasks overlap between departments. For example, the medical department may not want to refer workers with disabilities to the program.

To handle the resistance, program managers must make certain several issues are taken care of. First, the training must identify and talk about feelings of resistance and conflict explicitly. Second, the opportunity to deal with these issues cannot be limited to one meeting. An ongoing process for evaluating problems and providing support needs to be established. The coordinating committee can serve this function. Personnel should be able to go to the committee to resolve any impasse that is reached between units or to resolve a problem within a department. Third, incentives for participating must be offered. Staff involved in the training and in the program may receive special recognition; for example, their participation may be announced in the company newsletter. Staff may also receive benefits, such as being selected to attend a conference or to represent the company at off-site meetings. Performance appraisals should include participation in the program as an evaluation criterion.

Finally, staff should not feel they are being penalized for participating. For example, new tasks should not be added to someone's job without taking others away unless the former assignment did not demand his or her total working hours. People should not be made to feel that the program is just an added burden to an already overloaded schedule.

Furthermore, management should not debit the budget of supervisors when their units are not as productive as formerly because they are accommodating a worker who is not functioning at 100 percent.

Prevention

Disability management should not be solely reactive to the needs of the work force. To be embedded in company policy, it should also be preventive. The importance of prevention is manifold:

- It can help to reduce the incidence of disability.
- It can demonstrate to the work force that the employer is concerned about employee well-being and, therefore, can affect worker morale and satisfaction.
- It can promote strategies that can help to identify a better way of performing all jobs. (For example, women fire fighters learned to carry heavy equipment on their hips to compensate for a lack of upper body strength. As it turned out, lower back injury was reduced in both men and women when this style of carrying was utilized.)
- It is in line with cost-containment goals. (Preventing disability in the first place reduces the amount of lost time and expenditures on health care and benefits.)

Preventive programs are developed in response to two types of circumstances. First, data collected about disability at the site reveal persistent problems. (For example, data reported on the Employee Report of Accident form [Appendix 7-1] and the Supervisor's Accident Report form [Appendix 7-2] can be analyzed to correlate incidence of disability and location at the worksite.) In response to the identified problems, the coordinating committee or disability manager can develop appropriate interventions. The type of intervention depends on the nature of the problem:

- Preventive responses may be ergonomic. The employer may need to implement physical changes to help avoid certain disabilities. For example, changing stool heights for bank tellers helps to reduce back injury among these workers.
- Intervention may be geared toward developing better strategies to encourage use of safety equipment. For example, the use of seat belts for drivers, hard hats for construction workers, and protective earphones for

steelworkers helps to reduce the incidence of disability among these groups.

• Preventive intervention may entail required training for certain tasks that often lead to injury. For example, nurses aides suffer back injury frequently as a result of incorrectly lifting patients. Training to teach aides how to lift patients may help to reduce the incidence of this type of problem.

• Prevention may involve educational programs. For example, programs to teach employees about nutrition or stress management may help control disabilities affected by diet or exacerbated by stress. Programs may also be developed for physicians to help teach them how to talk with workers about their jobs and the types of modified work that are possible.

• Prevention strategies may be concerned with encouraging employees to participate in activities that maintain health. For example, exercise programs may be offered at the site or the employer may pay for the worker to attend exercise classes at a local fitness club.

Prevention programs are also developed in response to future organizational changes. Proactive prevention strategies can be implemented at the same time that old jobs are phased out and replaced by new ones or when new requirements are added to existing jobs. For example, a company that has decided to begin to train workers for computer operation can include a segment on how to prevent computer-related disabilities as part of the training.

Information Dissemination and Networking

Disability management programs become an integral part of the workplace when they are used. If workers do not know about the services available through the program, if workers are afraid that participation may affect their benefits or job standing, or if workers do not believe that participation will help them, then the program will not become an effective part of the health care system. Providing workers with information about the program overcomes ignorance and mistrust. There are several guidelines for providing information:

• People should know about the program before they become disabled. New hires should receive a description of the program. Workers should be kept informed about the program through the company newsletter, supervisors, departmental meetings, or any other channel of information available to everyone. The program should become part of the corporate culture expressing company philosophy toward its workers with disabilities—to wit, "We expect you to continue at work, despite disability, and we will take care of you. There is no need to undertake adversarial proceedings."

• Disability management program information should be accessible. The information provided should be easy to understand. Everyone should have a clear understanding of what to do if they want to use the program or get more information.

• Program information should be responsive to the concerns of workers. Just describing the program may not be enough. Misconceptions or concerns about program participation should be discussed.

Finally, disability management programs must be embedded in the community as well as in the workplace. Effective disability management depends in part on the participation of community resources that can help with disabled workers. Service delivery is hindered if ties to these resources are not established. Disability managers can take several steps to network into the community:

• They can inventory organizations in their communities to determine what services they offer.

• They can explain the program to service providers and request their participation.

• They can negotiate a referral process with the providers. For example, are there specific people at the organization that workers or case managers should contact? Once a worker is referred, are there procedures that keep the case manager informed of problems or the need to follow up?

• To the extent possible, the referral process should be formalized. This may mean that the agreed-upon procedures are written down. This helps to clarify the role of each organization as well as demonstrate commitment to participating.

• Disability managers should develop ways to encourage service providers to adapt to the needs of the workers when current services are not adequate or develop new services to better meet the needs of the workers.

Appendix 7-1
Employee Report of Accident

Name: ______________________ ID #: ______________________

Year of birth: ______________________

Department/Job: ______________________ Years in present department: ______

Supervisor: ______________________ Today's date: ______________________

Date and time of accident or injury: ______________________

For each of the following questions, please check the answer that best fits conditions at the time you were injured.

The light in the area:
_____ 1. Good
_____ 2. Fair
_____ 3. Poor

The cleanliness of the area:
_____ 1. Clean
_____ 2. Somewhat dirty
_____ 3. Dirty

The floors:
_____ 1. Very slippery
_____ 2. Slightly slippery
_____ 3. Not slippery

In the past two weeks how much overtime have you worked? _____

Were you working overtime at the time of the injury?
_____ 1. Yes
_____ 2. No

Were you smoking at the time of the injury?
_____ 1. Yes
_____ 2. No

How many hours had you worked that day at the time of the injury? _____

Were you feeling well?
_____ 1. Yes
_____ 2. No

Which shift were you working?
_____ 1. Day
_____ 2. Night
_____ 3. Afternoon

Please describe how your accident occurred and the result.

____

____

____

____

____

When did you start working at this job? ______________________
(month/day/year)

The remaining questions are about your usual work.

Do you have any health problems?
____ 1. Yes (please list) ______________________
____ 2. No

What are your average hours worked per week? ______________

Is the lighting adequate in your work area?
____ 1. Yes
____ 2. No

Is cleanliness/housekeeping a problem in your work area?
____ 1. Yes
____ 2. No

If yes, what is the problem? ______________________
____

Do you lift on your job?
____ 1. Yes
____ 2. No

If yes, what do you lift: ______________________
Frequency of your lifting: ______________________
Average weight: ______________________
Maximum lift: ______________________

Do you lift:

From the floor
____ 1. Yes
____ 2. No

From shoulder height
____ 1. Yes
____ 2. No

From overhead
____ 1. Yes
____ 2. No

Do you have to lift in awkward postures that require bent-over or twisting postures?
_____ 1. Yes
_____ 2. No

If yes, what positions (check all that apply):
_____ Kneeling
_____ Squatting
_____ Bending
_____ Sitting
_____ Standing
_____ Reaching

Does your job require walking?
_____ 1. Yes
_____ 2. No

If yes,
How far: ______________________________
How often:
_____ 1. All the time
_____ 2. > ½ the time
_____ 3. 25–50% of the time
_____ 4. < 25% of the time

Do you stand in one position for long periods of time?
_____ 1. Yes
_____ 2. No

If yes,
Floor type: ______________________________
Duration: ______________________________

Do you have to sit for long periods of time?
_____ 1. Yes
_____ 2. No

If yes,
Chair type: ______________________________
Duration: ______________________________

Do you have to carry things on your job?
_____ 1. Yes
_____ 2. No

If yes, usual weight: ______________________________
How often?
_____ 1. All the time
_____ 2. > ½ the time
_____ 3. 25–50% of the time
_____ 4. < 25% of the time
Distance: ______________________________

Do you push on your job?
_____ 1. Yes
_____ 2. No

If yes, usual weight: _____
Distance pushed: _____
How often?
_____ 1. All the time
_____ 2. $>$ ½ the time
_____ 3. 25–50% of the time
_____ 4. $<$ 25% of the time

Do you pull on your job?
_____ 1. Yes
_____ 2. No

If yes, usual weight: _____
What do you pull? _____
How often?
_____ 1. All the time
_____ 2. $>$ ½ the time
_____ 3. 25–50% of the time
_____ 4. $<$ 25% of the time

Do you have to reach on your job?
_____ 1. Yes
_____ 2. No

If yes,
What do you have to reach to? _____
Do you reach overhead?
_____ 1. Yes
_____ 2. No

Do you have to climb on your job?
_____ 1. Yes
_____ 2. No

If yes,
What do you climb? _____
Height of what you climb: _____

How often do you climb?
_____ 1. All the time
_____ 2. $>$ ½ the time
_____ 3. 25–50% of the time
_____ 4. $<$ 25% of the time

Do you have to balance on your job?
_____ 1. Yes
_____ 2. No

If yes,
On what do you balance? ______________________________

Do you perform repetitive motion on your job?
_____ 1. Yes
_____ 2. No

If yes,
What do you do repetitively? ______________________________

Thank you.

Appendix 7-2
Supervisor's Accident Report

Your name: ______________________________

Name of employee incurring accident: ______________________________

Date and time of accident: ______________________________

For each of the following questions, please check the answer that best fits conditions at the time of the accident.

The light in the area:
____ 1. Good
____ 2. Fair
____ 3. Poor

The cleanliness of the area:
____ 1. Clean
____ 2. Somewhat dirty
____ 3. Dirty

The floors:
____ 1. Very slippery
____ 2. Slightly slippery
____ 3. Not slippery

In the past two weeks how much overtime has the employee worked? ____

Was the employee working overtime at the time of the injury?
____ 1. Yes
____ 2. No

How long have you supervised this employee? ____ years ____ months ____ days

How would you evaluate the employee's usual performance?
____ 1. Excellent (top 10%)
____ 2. Good (within top half)
____ 3. Fair (in third quartile)
____ 4. Poor (in lowest quartile)

Were you aware of any special problems the employee was having?
____ 1. Yes (specify) ______________________________
____ 2. No

Were you present at the time of the accident?
____ 1. Yes
____ 2. No

If yes, please describe how the accident occurred and the result.

____

____

____

____

____

Please suggest any changes that you think would help avoid comparable accidents in the future.

____

____

____

____

____

Thank you.

Chapter 8

Profiles of Corporate Disability Management Programs

The earliest descriptions of employer-based disability management programs appeared in the late 1970s and early 1980s and involved companies such as Burlington Industries, AT&T, the 3M Corporation, and the Sears Roebuck Company. The stimulus for establishing these programs, as indicated throughout this book, involved two driving forces:

1. A concern for employee welfare as an extension of a corporate culture that valued employees as individuals (''it's the right thing to do'' theme)
2. Sensitivity to the direct and hidden costs associated with illness, injury, and disability

This dual justification—humanitarian and economic—has served the fields of health care, social services, and rehabilitation well for many years.

This chapter profiles more recent efforts at disability management. It is based on published reports and on the authors' own experiences in conducting disability management case studies and consulting with numerous private and public employers. The selection of programs was difficult due to the number and variety of successful efforts. Significantly more employers of all sizes have implemented various elements of disability management, including prevention, rehabilitation, job accommodations, and return to work than are represented here. The programs selected represent a mix of industries, geographic locations, and sizes, although most are large private employers. Both union and non-union companies are represented. To reflect very recent trends, small employers, a union-based program, and a public employer are included.

The programs illustrate one or more of the key components of disability management programs. No single company incorporates all the characteristics of a model program. Organizations select those approaches and methods that best fit their particular circumstances. The intention here is to illustrate how various employers and unions have responded to the issue of disability in the workplace.

Organizational Profiles

The programs selected are summarized in Figure 8-1. Each corporate profile includes:

- An introduction to the company
- Rationale for the disability management program
- Program philosophy and objectives
- Program components
- Program results and evaluation

These subjects permit us to answer such questions as, Why did the organization adopt disability management? What disability management practices were implemented? What is the evidence of results achieved?

Specific implications or "lessons" demonstrated by the example conclude each profile.

General Motors Corporation* (Buick-Oldsmobile-Cadillac Group) Lansing, Michigan

Introduction to the Buick-Oldsmobile-Cadillac Group

The Buick-Oldsmobile-Cadillac (B-O-C) group in Lansing, Michigan, employing approximately 20,000 hourly and salaried workers, is the largest employer in the mid-Michigan region. Facilities include six major plant sites. The Oldsmobile plant, established in 1897, is the oldest continuous automobile-manufacturing site in the United States. The Oldsmobile Divi-

(Text continues on page 212.)

*Sources for this profile include Butler, John (March 1987) "GM's Approach to Substance Abuse Treatment," *Business and Health;* Butler, John (Fall 1986) "Disability Management and Rehabilitation at the Workplace, A Special Issue," *The Journal of Applied Rehabilitation Counseling;* Frieden, Joyce (October 1989) "Cost Containment Strategies for Workers' Compensation," *Business and Health;* and Tate, Denise, Diane Munrowd, and Rochelle Habeck (July 1987) "Building a Better Rehabilitation Program," *Business and Health.*

Figure 8-1. Summary: organizational profiles.

Employer	*Characteristics*	*Special Features*
General Motors Corporation Buick-Oldsmobile-Cadillac Group Lansing, Michigan	Automotive manufacturing and assembly 20,000 employees Organized work force Multiple sites Back pain, sprains-strains, cumulative trauma disorders Self-insured	Designated rehabilitation case manager Coordinating committee Union involvement in accommodations, light-duty work assignments Training of manager, supervisors, and union representatives Physical therapy at workplace Emphasis on high-quality rehabilitation Competitive selection of preferred rehabilitation providers Investment in ergonomics as prevention strategy Focus on workers compensation claimants EAP and substance abuse services Limited evaluation of impact
Herman Miller, Inc. Zeeland, Michigan	Office furniture manufacturing and sales 5,700 employees Nonorganized work force Multiple sites Strong human resources corporate culture Selected to *100 Best Companies to Work for in America* Back pain, cumulative trauma, mental stress	Emphasis on prevention and health promotion Organizational structure—health and wellness group Designated rehabilitation coordinator (case manager) Transitional work center Physical therapy at worksite EAP and substance abuse services Addresses both on-the-job and non-job injuries Coordinated benefits (disability, workers compensation, social security) Limited evaluation of impact
Long Island Rail Road Long Island, New York	Commuter railroad 7,000 employees 12 union organizations Heavy physical labor/hazardous work Multiple sites Trauma and back, hand, leg, and knee injuries	Devised as part of collective bargaining agreements Coordinating committees, team approach Emphasis on injury prevention and safety Light-duty work assignments and accommodations Contracts with local medical and vocational rehabilitation providers Vocational assessment, job accommodations, back and knee schools, functional capacity evaluation, work hardening Ergonomics and biomedical analysis of jobs Extensive evaluation of impact

Employer	*Characteristics*	*Special Features*
Weyerhaeuser Company Tacoma, Washington	Forestry operations including logging, sawmills, home construction 45,000 employees Multiple sites in 36 states Strong human resources corporate culture Selected to *100 Best Companies to Work for in America* 12 union organizations Heavy physical labor/hazardous work Traumas, back injuries, and alcohol and substance abuse Self-insured	Appointed disability case manager Emphasis on injury prevention and safety Charge workers compensation costs to home departments as incentive Training managers, supervisors, union representatives Competitive selection of preferred rehabilitation providers Focus on workers compensation claimants Light-duty and worksite accommodations via security firm EAP service Evaluation of impact on workers compensation costs
Walbro Corporation Cass City, Michigan	Small-engine manufacturer 900 employees Nonorganized work force Single site Strong human resources culture Hand and lower-back injuries and minor traumas	Extensive analysis of injury experience prior to program implementation Concept of "industrial athlete" Strong emphasis on physical conditioning, health promotion Employs athletic trainers Provides extensive fitness center Fitness and rehabilitation extended to nonwork-related injuries Focus on disability duration, rate of recovery Emphasis on workers compensation claimants Strong physician relations Evaluation of workers compensation costs, disability payments, and "return on investment"
The Will-Burt Company Orville, Ohio	Small industrial job shop 300 employees Employee stock ownership Nonunion 3 sites Third-party-insured Assembly work, welding, grinding, toolmaking Back, hand, foot injuries	Strong "people first" corporate culture Major investment in employee education, development, and preservation Low-cost, home-grown, flexible solutions, including early return to work Role of top management in devising and promoting program Cooperative relations with insurer and Ohio Industrial Commission Commitment to teamwork, interdependence, enlightened self-interest Significant reduction in workers compensation costs, medical costs, and sick days

(*continued*)

Figure 8-1. (continued)

Employer	*Characteristics*	*Special Features*
City of Winnipeg Manitoba, Canada	Public employer 12,000 employees 9 union organizations Multiple sites, 27 departments, 3 hospitals Back injuries Disability pension, jointly managed by city and unions Self-insured	Established written policy and procedures Establishment of rehabilitative employment section Coordinating committee established Union participation in light-duty job assignments Case management services Established relations with health care providers and community agencies Job analysis, job modifications, and return to work Labor-management identification of "rehabilitative positions" Focus on workers compensation claimants Developed evaluation system
Human Resources Development Institute, AFL-CIO Washington, D.C.	Union-based 5 field sites nationwide Access to all unions affiliated with AFL-CIO Partnerships with employers and government	Strong job-training component Provides case management service Involved in research and development Helps represent labor interests to management Helps build trust of labor for disability management effort

sion of General Motors Corporation (GMC) is known for its innovative approach to product engineering and manufacturing. This philosophy is also reflected in its human resources policies and practices.

Rationale for the Disability Management Program

As one of the world's largest manufacturing employers, GMC has confronted intense domestic and international competition, forcing it to focus on enhanced manufacturing efficiencies and cost reduction. Health-related benefits (including mental health, substance abuse, and disability) have been identified as a major cost of doing business. B-O-C realized and was affected by the following factors:

- The development of innovative disability management and rehabilitation efforts at GMC was influenced substantially by the emerging spirit of cooperation between the company and the United Auto Workers (UAW) union. The depressed state of the domestic automobile industry has required management and labor to redefine their relationship at the national and local levels.

• Rising health and benefits costs, compounded by greater benefits consumption by an aging work force, has had a negative effect on the economic position of the corporation and on job security of UAW members.

• Low-back pain syndrome and sprains and strains are the most common cause of work disabilities (the use of pneumatic tools for repetitive motions in product assembly has led to a dramatic increase in cumulative trauma disorders). These injuries can be greatly reduced by prevention programs.

• Changes in the Michigan workers compensation law encourages (but does not mandate) the provision of rehabilitation services and emphasizes return to work. In the early 1980s, the state adjusted the wage replacement benefit for workers compensation recipients from 75 percent to 80 percent of after-tax earnings. These changes prompted B-O-C to take a more aggressive approach to workers compensation. The traditional focus on claims administration was changed to focus on disability management and return to work.

Program Philosophy and Objectives

The disability management program at B-O-C is a comprehensive approach involving prevention, early identification of injured workers, coordinated rehabilitation services, job accommodation, job placement, and follow-up. The objectives of the program are to:

- Provide optimal rehabilitation services to employees.
- Promote rapid recovery and reduce absenteeism.
- Reduce the financial burden of disability on the employee and the employer.
- Improve employee relations.
- Enhance B-O-C's image in the community as a socially responsible employer.

Program Components

In 1985, B-O-C hired a rehabilitation specialist to oversee and coordinate all aspects of the disability management program. The rehabilitation specialist, as case manager, counsels workers, provides vocational assessments, conducts job analysis, assists in negotiating job accommodations, and facilitates job placement and return to work in liaison with supervisory personnel and union representatives.

A coordinating committee including medical, workers compensation, human resources, employee benefits, and union representatives meets every two weeks. It devises individual rehabilitation and return-to-work plans, monitors the progress of each employee through the rehabilitation process, and ensures communication and coordination between all parties involved. Documentation, including monthly case management costs and outcome reports, are provided by the rehabilitation specialist. The specialist also oversees all arrangements with outside vendors.

Prior to the implementation of the disability management program, community-based rehabilitation vendors were rarely utilized. The new policies adopted in 1983 led to an onslaught of private vendors seeking referrals from B-O-C. To manage the situation better and obtain the highest quality services available, B-O-C adopted a request for proposal (RFP) scheme in 1985. Following competitive bids and intense review, the disability management team selects vendors and provides an annual contract subject to renewal, which is based on performance.

The following criteria are used to select rehabilitation vendors:

- Range of services provided
- Area of expertise
- Staff qualifications
- Cost of services
- Timeliness of services and reports
- Performance in returning employees to work
- Well-documented cost reports
- A uniform operating strategy
- Capability to relate to the in-house B-O-C team

Training of supervisors, union representatives, and management is an important feature of the disability management program at B-O-C. Sessions consider such topics as the often negative and suspicious attitudes of co-workers and supervisors toward injured workers, specific activity restrictions and necessary job accommodations, and labor rules regarding job seniority. B-O-C contracts with a private physical therapy group to provide prescribed services to employees—on company time if needed. GMC has also made a major investment in ergonomics as an injury prevention strategy. The rehabilitation specialist incorporates ergonomic requirements in the development of a computerized job bank that assists in placement of all employees with functional limitations.

Program Results and Evaluation

In 1987 a team of researchers at Michigan State University conducted a small-scale evaluation of the B-O-C disability management program.

Twenty disabled employees who returned to work in 1984, prior to establishment of the program, were compared to fifty employees who returned to work in 1985–1986 under the new scheme. The most significant difference between the two groups was the time between the disabling injury and the worker's return to work. The pre–disability management group returned to work on average four years after the disabling injury, while those in the disability management group returned to work within an average of ten months!

The average rehabilitation cost was higher for the disability management group ($765) than the first group ($478). Some of the differences can be accounted for by inflation. Regardless, the significantly reduced time off the job more than offset the increases rehabilitation cost involved.

Lessons From the B-O-C Experience

The B-O-C approach to managing disability in the workplace reflects several of the principles and practices highlighted elsewhere in this book. The most significant lesson to be learned from this example may be that it is possible to implement a progressive disability management program successfully in a traditional "smokestack" industry not noted for its willingness or capacity to accommodate employees with work limitations. The success of the B-O-C program depends most particularly on the following:

- The establishment of a new position (a rehabilitation specialist, who functions as a case manager). The rehabilitation specialist ensures early intervention, coordinates the activities of the several parties involved, maintains frequent personal contact with participating employees, facilitates work accommodations and job modifications, and closely monitors the provision of all services by community resources.
- The UAW made a strong commitment to the return-to-work objective. The union is represented on the coordinating committee, endorses all accommodations and job modifications, and broadly communicates its support of the program to its membership.
- The coordinating committee is vital to linkage, problem solving, communication, and monitoring. Given the size and complexity of the company, several parties and interests are involved in the disability management process. The coordinating committee serves to bring these individuals together around a common purpose.
- B-O-C has invested countless hours in the training of managers, supervisors, and co-workers of employees with disabilities. The company appreciates the fact that the adoption of disability management requires a change in attitudes, responsibilities, and expectations.

• In response to the increasing incidence of cumulative trauma disorder, GMC (along with many other companies) has invested millions in preventive ergonomic work design. Ergonomics, which can make work more cost-efficient and safer, is a powerful disability prevention technique.

Herman Miller, Inc.*
Zeeland, Michigan

Introduction to Herman Miller

Herman Miller specializes in the manufacture and sale of office furniture, products, and services. The company has its headquarters in Zeeland, Michigan, and is an international corporation represented in thirty-five nations. Its U.S. work force numbers 5,700. For several years the company, which is nonunionized, has been listed in *The 100 Best Companies to Work for in America.*

Herman Miller has a rich, unique corporate culture and philosophy. The company readily admits that it has a long, well-established paternalistic relationship with its employees—one it works hard to maintain.

Rationale for the Disability Management Program

In 1982 Herman Miller management noted that a significant number of employees were off the job with work disabilities. Under the Herman Miller compensation system (Scanlon Plan), the company, in effect, was paying these people full pay to stay at home. Herman Miller has a relatively young work force, the average age being 32. When one of these employees incurs a major illness or injury, the company could be obligated to provide disability benefits until the employee reaches age 65, often a period of many years or even decades. Other motivations for starting a management disability program were:

• Top management decided that Herman Miller needed to implement an effective way to keep these employees on the job after accident or illness, or have them return as soon as appropriate. The company became one of the first to establish a transitional work center to facilitate an earlier return to work.

*Sources used for this profile include personal consultations; (Fall 1990) "Disability Management and Rehabilitation in the Workplace, A Special Issue," *The Journal of Applied Rehabilitation Counseling*; Frieden, Joyce (October 1989) "Cost Containment Strategies for Workers' Compensation," *Business and Health*; and Galvin, Donald E. (1986) "Employer-Based Disability Management and Rehabilitation Programs," *Annual Review of Rehabilitation* 5.

• Herman Miller was motivated largely by its concern for its employees' welfare. It is noteworthy that Herman Miller never refers to its employees as "human capital" and rarely cites cost containment as a motivation for its disability management program.

• The office furniture industry has become considerably more competitive in recent years. Established companies such as Herman Miller and Steelcase are competing aggressively for market share, and new competitors, both foreign (Ikea, Scan) and domestic (Westinghouse), have entered the field. To maintain their financial performance, Herman Miller has been forced to review their costs, including health and disability benefits, which are among the most generous in the industry. The company is convinced that it has a responsibility to husband resources for the benefit of its shareholders and employees (all of whom participate in profit sharing).

Program Philosophy and Objectives

The company believes strongly in the mutual commitment of employer and individual employee. Management believes that personal attention, a caring attitude, and support of a "positive mental attitude" make a tremendous difference in whether or not an injured employee returns to work.

Program Components

As recommended by experts, Herman Miller's disability management and rehabilitation effort is closely related to the company's approach to safety, health promotion, and employee wellness. For them, "wellness" includes the physical, occupational, social, emotional, intellectual, and spiritual facets of each employee. The Health and Wellness Group, established under a single director, encompasses these programs:

- Employee health services
- Rehabilitation services
- Employee health promotion
- Substance abuse education
- Employee assistance program

This organizational alignment has substantially enhanced communication, coordination, and service integration. The degree of professionalism and commitment to common purpose demonstrated among this group is a hallmark of the Herman Miller approach.

Transitional Work Center

Herman Miller established its transitional work center (TWC) in 1983 and thus has considerable experience with this disability management intervention. Organizationally, the TWC is assigned to the Health and Wellness Group and is supervised by the director of rehabilitation. Employees injured on or off the job have the opportunity to participate in the TWC. Employees are to report their injuries or disabilities to their supervisor, who then makes an immediate referral to the employee health service for evaluation. The health service, working directly with the employee or in collaboration with the employee's personal physician, establishes work restrictions. If the work restrictions are severe, the health service refers the employee to the TWC. The director of rehabilitation evaluates and counsels all employees with work disabilities and places them in TWC assignments consistent with the restrictions determined by the health service.

Throughout employees' tenure in the TWC, their performance and progress is overseen by the director of rehabilitation, who maintains a close, supportive relationship with every worker. In addition, employees in the TWC are monitored by the health service to ensure that their recovery is not jeopardized by the tasks performed.

The TWC, which originally occupied a single work space (a large office) in the administrative wing, now functions as a "center without walls." Although the original space is still used, TWC workers are now placed in a variety of assignments throughout the facility. The director of rehabilitation reports that this arrangement serves to normalize, integrate, and destigmatize the return-to-work process.

At first, it was difficult to convince supervisors to accept TWC graduates unless they were employees in that department. To correct this situation, a recently adopted policy requires supervisors to accept TWC graduates as long as they are qualified and meet shift and departmental criteria. This policy is a strong endorsement of the objectives of the center and an expression of fairness and equity toward the employees involved.

Other Disability Management Efforts

In addition to the TWC, Herman Miller has adopted a variety of other disability management techniques and methods. For example, the company contracts for physical therapy services from a local private practitioner. The physical therapist, who is provided with space in the medical department, visits the main plant three half-days per week to see employees on referral from the plant physician (also on contract) or the employee's treating physician. With this arrangement vital services are made available to employees at a convenient time and place, and, according to Herman Miller management estimates, at one quarter the cost of such services provided via a hospital or private clinic.

Herman Miller also works closely with the state vocational rehabilitation agency. Injured employees may be referred to the state agency for vocational evaluation, agency confirmation of the return-to-work plan, worksite and home modifications, and prosthesis when not covered by the employee's health insurance. When extensive medical rehabilitation or pain management services are needed, Herman Miller uses a preferred provider arrangement with the Mary Free Bed Rehabilitation Center in nearby Grand Rapids. The company occasionally uses the services of a private case management firm, Conservco, a subsidiary of Travelers Insurance Company.

Herman Miller recently adopted a policy to coordinate disability, workers compensation, and Social Security Disability Insurance benefits. Before the new policy, some employees were receiving as much or more income from benefits by staying home than they would have received from working full time. Obviously this created a significant disincentive to work.

Program Results and Evaluation

The company has engaged in little formal evaluation of the costs and financial benefits associated with its disability management program. Such lack of evaluation is consistent with the prevailing "it's the right thing to do" philosophy of the organization and with management's informal assessment of the success of the TWC and related services in returning hundreds of injured workers to employment. However, the absence of formal evaluation limits the company's ability to identify areas that could be handled more effectively.

Top management at Herman Miller advocates the TWC model enthusiastically and regards it as the cornerstone of their commitment to employees with work disabilities. They are convinced that the TWC and their related health and wellness services permit them to "place anyone for any amount of time he or she can work." This spirit of flexibility, accommodation, and optimism is fundamental to a successful disability management program.

Lessons From the Herman Miller Experience

The challenge to Herman Miller was somewhat the reverse of B-O-C's; that is, they were faced with the question, How does a company with a paternalistic (if not indulgent) tradition adopt an aggressive return-to-work strategy? If Herman Miller were to adopt this new strategy successfully, it had to do so in a way that did not violate their all-important corporate culture.

The company's success in achieving this evolution resulted from a disability strategy responsive to the needs of the employer, to the needs of disabled workers, and to the changes in the workplace required to meet them. In this instance the employer was sensitive to employees' needs and wishes to be integrated with their fellow workers. Here are some of the tactics the company used to implement its strategy:

- In support of its commitment to employees, and to overcome resistance from some supervisors, the company adopted a policy that required supervisors to accept qualified TWC graduates. The policy thus resolved another problem—employees' remaining in a transitional work assignment far longer than medically necessary and thus preventing newly disabled employees from entering the program. To succeed, a transitional work center must "graduate" employees, at the appropriate time, to more traditional, permanent positions in the company. A transitional work center must not become a human warehouse!
- Herman Miller demonstrated a remarkable capacity to blend and connect its internal resources (TWC, physical therapy, EAP, and so forth) with external resources, including the state vocational rehabilitation agency, a comprehensive medical rehabilitation hospital, and a private case management company. This coordination and integration are the responsibility of the director of rehabilitation.
- To deal directly with the issue of work disincentives, Herman Miller made a policy decision to coordinate employees' disability, workers compensation, and Social Security Disability Insurance benefits. Prior to such benefits coordination, some employees received more income from their various benefits than they would have from paid work. Because responsibility for such benefits authorization is often dispersed among two or three departments in a large company, it is not uncommon to find that benefits are not coordinated—and thus misapplied.

Long Island Rail Road*
Long Island, New York

Introduction to the Long Island Rail Road

The Long Island Rail Road (LIRR) is the largest commuter railroad in the United States, operating 740 daily trains carrying 280,000 passengers

*Sources for this profile include Brower, Robert C. (Spring 1990) "The Role of Vocational Rehabilitation in Disability Management on the Long Island Rail Road," *Worklife*; and Cohen, David M., Anthony P. Parrinello, and Thomas D. Kelliher (Spring 1990) "Disability Management on the Long Island Railroad," *Worklife*.

between Long Island and New York City. Forty percent of all railroad commuters in the United States use the LIRR. The LIRR has 7,000 employees, 6,000 of whom are represented by one of twelve unions. The LIRR operates as a publicly owned subsidiary of the Metropolitan Transportation Authority, a state agency that operates rail, subway, and bus transportation in a twelve-county region.

Rationale for the Disability Management Program

In 1985 management discovered that the LIRR had 244 employees who had been off the job for more than one year due to a work disability. While these employees were receiving regular disability benefits, in the form of wage replacement, little or no effort was being devoted to their rehabilitation and return to work. Analysis revealed several obstacles to returning to work, including the following:

- Injury leave was perceived by employees as an entitlement.
- Management did not seek to return employees with work disabilities aggressively because such employees could be replaced by new people with no apparent adverse effect on the departmental budget.
- Much of the work at the LIRR involves heavy physical labor in a hazardous work environment.
- Company policies and collective bargaining agreements made it almost impossible to place employees with disabilities into alternative positions.
- Seniority rights were sacrosanct. Rarely would unions waive the seniority of any employee, effectively denying return-to-work opportunities for many employees with disabilities.
- An adversarial environment often existed between employer and employee, discouraging rehabilitation and return to work.
- Most confounding of all, employees were considered totally disabled if they were not 100 percent able to do their assigned jobs.

The most important impetus for implementing a new approach to work disability at the LIRR was the 1985 collective bargaining contract negotiations. The LIRR made the issue of disability management a major point in its bargaining demands. In settlements reached during 1986 and early 1987, the unions agreed to give the LIRR more latitude in rehabilitation and return-to-work matters.

Program Philosophy and Objectives

The LIRR established a disability management section in late 1984 to reform its approach to disability in the workplace and to achieve savings for riders and taxpayers. The new approach included an emphasis on safety and injury prevention as well as enhanced medical and vocational rehabilitation services. Cohen et al. described the LIRR strategy and program for *Worklife:*

> Each of the new elements is designed to prevent or minimize injuries in the first instance, and to help injured employees return to a productive work life consistent with their disability. While the cost of these new services is high, it has been more than offset by the success in returning injured employees to work and reducing the accident rate.
>
> Specific program objectives include:
>
> - Reduction in accidents and lost time
> - Reduction in long-term disability cases
> - Increased use of restricted-duty placements and transfers
> - Reduction in disability wages paid
> - Reduction in claim dollars paid and medical expenses
> - Increased employee availability and productivity
> - Improved medical care

To achieve these objectives, the LIRR decided it was necessary to develop a team approach to disability management. Coordinating committees representing such departments as disability management, labor relations, medical affairs, and claims management, as well as operating departments, were established. These committees devise the rehabilitation and return-to-work plan for each injured worker. The LIRR established a basic ground rule that all parties had to agree on the course of action for each case. The company thought this was necessary because without it each decision could have resulted in grievance arbitration.

Program Components

Armed with much greater latitude in terms of job assignments, light-duty work, and workplace accommodations, the LIRR decided to replace its in-house medical service with a contract awarded to the Catholic Medical Center (CMC) of Brooklyn. With CMC's assistance, the LIRR added the following services:

- Medical consultation
- Medical rehabilitation of injured employees

- Vocational assessment of employees for placement in new jobs or for outplacement
- Redesign of jobs to accommodate people with disabilities
- Ergonomic/biomedical analysis of jobs
- Back and knee schools to prevent injuries
- Use of work hardening for employees out of work for an extended period
- Functional capacity evaluations

The LIRR also entered into a contract with the Human Resources Center (HRC) in Albertson, New York, for extensive vocational rehabilitation services. Referrals, made to the HRC by the medical department of the LIRR, usually involve individuals who are unable to return to their previous jobs.

Typically HRC case managers:

- Review the medical file.
- Interview the worker at his or her home.
- Interview the treating physician.
- Conduct extensive vocational testing at the HRC.
- Provide written reports outlining skills and possible new job assignments.
- Provide follow-up services after placement within the LIRR.

Since 1985 over 100 LIRR employees have been referred to the HRC for vocational assessment, and more than 75 percent of these returned to work.

Program Results and Evaluation

Cohen et al. report that "through an aggressive, team-oriented approach the LIRR has been able to return hundreds of employees with disabilities to productive work, and simultaneously to reduce costs associated with disabling injuries by more than $6 million a year."

As a result of the disability management program, the LIRR has achieved several dramatic results, including:

- Reduction in the number of accidents and lost time by one third
- Reduction in the number of long-term disability cases from 244 in March 1985 to 8 in December 1988
- Reduction in disability wages paid by 34 percent, from $2.6 million to $1.4 million

- Reduction in the number of injury claims by 40 percent, from 507 in 1985 to 295 in 1989
- Reduction in claim dollars paid by 31.6 percent
- Containment of medical expenses associated with on-duty injuries (such costs had been increasing by 25 percent per year)
- Reduction in disability claims from $24.2 million in 1984 to $21.4 million in 1988

Cohen et al. underscore that disability management is a long-term process. They advise: "An employer contemplating entering into a disability management program must be prepared to commit significant resources for a minimum of three to five years before meaningful results are evident. There are no short-term miracles."

Lessons From the Long Island Rail Road Experience

The management of LIRR, armed with a thorough analysis of their disability problem, made the issue a major bargaining point in contract negotiations with their several unions. The railroad's disability management model is noteworthy in the following respects:

- The highly rational, strategic approach included a thorough analysis of their disability experience, implementation of a comprehensive return-to-work program, and systematic evaluation of results against measurable objectives. Finding that an excessive number of workers were receiving disability benefits, the railroad identified those factors acting as obstacles to rehabilitation and return to work and used this information in contract negotiations.
- Once agreement had been achieved with the unions, the company established a set of measurable objectives and set up a data collection and evaluation scheme to assess the success of the disability management program (see Chapters 3 and 7). This systematic and sophisticated approach to the issue permits the LIRR to be thorough and objective in its evaluation of program results. Unfortunately, few companies have developed this capacity; many, in fact, have only an impression of results achieved.
- It was essential to achieve the cooperation of the unions to transform the return-to-work process. Union concurrence was necessary for the railroad to become more flexible in accommodations and job modifications and in utilization of community resources.
- Contracts negotiated with the Catholic Medical Center and the Human Resources Center substantially enhanced the variety and quality of medical and rehabilitation services available to disabled employees.

Weyerhaeuser Company*
Tacoma, Washington

Introduction to Weyerhaeuser Company

Weyerhaeuser Company, frequently listed among the *100 Best Companies to Work for in America,* is a forest products company headquartered in Tacoma, Washington. The company has 45,000 employees working at 250 facilities in thirty-six states. These facilities include sawmills, logging stations, home-building sites, and other high-injury-risk operations. Twelve unions represent the approximately 30,000 nonsalaried personnel.

Rationale for the Disability Management Program

When the company became self-insured in the late 1950s, each operating unit was directed to handle its own injury claims. In 1973, however, the company decided to establish greater uniformity in claims management by utilizing third-party administrators (TPAs). Under this arrangement, the corporate office worked with the TPAs, and the operating units were no longer involved in claims management.

During this time supervisors had little interaction with employees out on workers compensation. The company contracted with service providers for therapy, but did not monitor such cases closely once employees were referred to the providers. Medical bills were rarely scrutinized, and service providers did not adhere to established fee schedules. Employees who needed specialized treatment often were not given the individual attention they required. Management also suspected that some local managers used disability as a means of ridding themselves of problem employees. Furthermore, managers had little incentive to retain such workers and return them to their jobs.

In the early 1980s Weyerhaeuser was averaging more than 7,000 injuries a year. Workers compensation costs had increased 750 percent, from $3 million paid out in 1971 to over $25 million 1982, and fewer and fewer employees were returning to work after on-the-job injuries.

In 1982, Weyerhaeuser changed its policy and began to administer its own workers compensation program. Ken Gipson, manager of statutory benefits (workers compensation), states, "We realized that the only way we could halt the spiral of losses was to change the way we administered

*Sources for this profile include Hill, Steven, and Ken Gipson (May 1990) "How Weyerhaeuser Improved Its Workers Compensation Program," *Business and Health*; Schwartz, Gail E., Sara D. Watson, Donald E. Galvin, and Elise Lipoff (1989) *The Disability Management Sourcebook,* Washington, D.C.: Washington Business Group on Health.

our claims—from using a third-party service company who really didn't have a vested interest, by administering them internally."

Weyerhaeuser understood that self-administering its workers compensation program would create higher administrative costs. The company realized that the new approach would cost more money at the front end. "But the bottom line," writes Gipson, "is that the company would save money at the other end, where it would see some dramatic improvements in medical, compensation, and disability costs."

Weyerhaeuser also realized that there was no financial accountability for workers compensation because operating units were not charged for these costs. The costs were being charged to the corporation's insurance pool, so there was little "ownership" of the problem by local managers. In 1983, the company made another policy change—it began charging its operating units directly for their workers compensation costs.

Program Philosophy and Objectives

Weyerhaeuser's commitment to "long-term, responsible stewardship of land and timber" is also evident in its human resources strategy; that is, employees are viewed as a vital resource to the company. A caring attitude toward injured or disabled employees is demonstrated through timely delivery of benefits and the utilization of only the most highly qualified service providers. Weyerhaeuser established the following disability management objectives:

- A significant decrease in the number of employees injured on the job
- An increase in return-to-work rate and fewer lost work days
- Improvement in the quality of services provided to injured workers
- A reduction in workers compensation costs

Program Components

To bring its disability claims function in-house, the company created six claims offices across the United States. Each office was professionally staffed and trained to manage—not just pay—disability claims. At each facility, one person, who functions as a disability case manager, is responsible for tracking all workers compensation claims, becoming knowledgeable about the local social service and medical communities, maintaining employee motivation and return to work, and identifying alternative job assignments.

The company also undertook the following initiatives, which substantially intensified its return-to-work program.

Utilization of Rehabilitation Providers

Weyerhaeuser implemented a formal request-for-proposal (RFP) approach in the selection of rehabilitation providers. The company developed a training package and requires every vendor working with its employees to participate in a training session. Weyerhaeuser staff also interview and select each counselor who will be working with company employees. Vendors must adhere to a detailed fee schedule that explains exactly what the company will pay for, and at what rate. Vendors must set specific vocational goals for employees, and submit regular reports describing progress and any deviation from the planned timeline.

Worksite Accommodations

To achieve accommodations for disabled workers, Weyerhaeuser entered into a unique partnership with one of its contractors to create new jobs for disabled workers. Because of a large backlog of disability cases and restrictions on moving employees across local union boundaries, the company entered into a joint venture with Smith Security, which provides Weyerhaeuser with security and janitorial services. The goal was to find productive but less physically strenuous jobs for Weyerhauser employees who suffer disabling injuries on the job.

A number of Weyerhaeuser plants also use modified-duty or light-duty assignments. Employee teams are given responsibility for creating temporary jobs for injured employees to perform while they are recuperating. If employees become disabled, they are expected to accept a modified or restructured job. In this way as many employees as possible remain gainfully employed, and Weyerhaeuser is able to control its disability costs more effectively.

Employee Assistance Program

The company has a firm commitment to its employee assistance program (EAP), which involves information and referral services to a wide range of local providers. A corporate-level consultant provides information and guidance to the company on the latest developments in the field. Alcohol and drug abuse are viewed as conditions that require treatment and rehabilitation, not discipline. Marital, financial, and legal problems are also addressed in this broad-based EAP.

Health and Fitness Promotion

Weyerhaeuser provides fitness and conditioning facilities at its larger facilities. In line with local initiatives, the company sponsors health fairs, fun runs, and other activities to generate interest in wellness and health care issues. To bring attention to those activities that improve health, the company regularly mails a health newsletter to the homes of all employees and retirees.

Program Results and Evaluation

Weyerhaeuser has systematically tracked its health care and workers compensation costs since 1980. They have demonstrated that changes in corporate policies and practices have had significant impact.

• Weyerhaeuser has seen a rise in health care costs of only 5 percent per year since 1982. During the prior decade such costs had increased 16 percent per year.

• Since 1984, Weyerhaeuser's workers compensation costs have decreased 51 percent, and the cost per claim has decreased 18 percent (see table below). While costs increased from 1987 to 1988, reversing the trend, Weyerhaeuser again achieved substantial cost reductions during 1989 and 1990.

Weyerhaeuser Workers Compensation Costs

	Total Workers Compensation Costs (Millions)	*Costs per Claim*
1984	$26.1	$2,640
1985	$24.9	$3,070
1986	$16.4	$2,170
1987	$15.1	$1,950
1988	$16.5	$2,300
1989	$13.5	$2,001
1990	$12.8	$2,161

• The company has achieved a significant decrease in the workers compensation claims rate—from 24 per 100 employees in 1985 to 15 per 100 employees in 1989.

• The company's lost-workday rate also dropped dramatically, from 102 per 100 employees in 1985 to 53 per 100 employees in 1989.

• Incurred cost per claim dropped from $3,500 in 1985 to about $1,500 in 1989.

• The most significant result is reflected in Weyerhaeuser's workers compensation benefits experience when measured against national trends. While benefits payments nationally increased 400 percent from 1976 to

1988, Weyerhaeuser's leveled off in 1985, just after the company reorganized its workers compensation and disability management effort. Significantly, benefits payments have continued to fall since that time.

Lessons From the Weyerhaeuser Experience

Workers compensation costs, rather than disability costs per se, were the principle concern of Weyerhaeuser's top management in adopting disability management. The company recognized that disability management, rehabilitation, and return to work could address many of the problems created by work-related injuries and disabilities. Most important, Weyerhaeuser recognized that to manage the workers compensation situation better, it needed to assume greater control through in-house administration, supervisory accountability, and adoption of the principle that many employees injured on the job can return to work in some capacity. Following extensive policy analysis and administrative study, the company implemented changes. Here are some prominent features of the disability management program:

- A policy of benefits charge-back to the impaired employee's department. This serves as a motivator to supervisors. All too often, workers compensation claims are paid from a pool at corporate headquarters, giving the immediate supervisor no particular incentive to bring the employee back to work. In such circumstances "the problem" is simply shifted to headquarters.
- The Weyerhaeuser approach also illustrates the fact that, in Gipson's words, "The supervisor is the key link between the disabled worker and getting the disability management job done" (see Chapter 5). Weyerhaeuser includes managing disability in the performance review of all front-line supervisors—another powerful motivator!
- Through benefits charge-back and supervisor performance evaluation, the company made it clear that management of disability is a recognized supervisory responsibility. With training, creative accommodations, involvement of case managers, and utilization of community resources, the company supports its front-line supervisors as they seek appropriate solutions.
- Through the request-for-proposal process, requiring high vendor performance standards, and "hands on" monitoring, Weyerhaeuser ensures that employees receive high-quality medical and rehabilitation services at a reasonable cost.
- Weyerhaeuser provides extensive training to all external service providers to ensure that they appreciate the corporate culture and under-

stand the administrative system. All relevant policies, standards, and fee schedules are reviewed during such training sessions.

• The company has established an evaluation system that provides detailed information on costs and results of workers compensation disability management.

Walbro Corporation*
Cass City, Michigan

Introduction to Walbro Corporation

With a staff of 900 employees, Walbro Corporation designs and manufactures system components and small-engine carburetors at three Michigan-based plants. Walbro has demonstrated that a small employer, even one in a relatively rural area, can implement an effective program to manage the costs of disability better.

Rationale for the Disability Management Program

• In the early 1980s Walbro management became concerned by the number of body and hand injuries occurring among employees engaged in light manufacturing operations. In addition, workers at Walbro's foundry were incurring an increasing number of lower-back injuries. These injuries resulted in extended recovery periods well beyond established disability duration guidelines.

• Michigan's workers compensation law encourages employers to provide rehabilitation and return-to-work services. In addition, the Michigan law requires employers to pay injured workers 80 percent of their after-tax wages. These factors constitute incentives to the employer to invest in return to work.

• As a first step in improving its health services and managing disability, Walbro approached Athletic Training Services (ATS), a consulting firm specializing in corporate health promotion and injury prevention programs. To identify employee needs, ATS conducted a survey of the

*Sources for this profile include Tonti, Don G., Tamara Trudeau, and Martin Daniel (September 1987) "Linking Fitness Activities to Rehabilitation," *Business and Health*; "Special Report: Linking Wellness and Rehabilitation" (January 1988) *Employee Health and Fitness* 10 (1); Galvin, Donald E. (September–October 1986) "Health Promotion, Disability Management and Rehabilitation in the Workplace," *Rehabilitation Literature* 47 (9–10): 218–233; and National Institute for Handicapped Research (December 1985) "Fitness and Wellness Among People With Disabilities," *Rehab Brief* 3 (12).

Walbro work force and analyzed two years of workers compensation injury and cost data. The survey results led management to conclude that instituting a disability management and rehabilitation program was both necessary and feasible. Walbro then engaged ATS to set up the program.

Program Philosophy and Objectives

Walbro has instituted a prevention-conscious work environment. Employing an athletic trainer who uses the same rehabilitation techniques found in college and professional sports is key to Walbro's approach to disability management. A corporate mind-set that views all employees—even those in sedentary jobs—as "industrial athletes" is fundamental. The director of human resources observes, "Employees are under more constant physical strain in their daily jobs than in most athletics and suffer the same types of injuries."

The program objectives include:

- Establishing a cost-effective, in-house fitness and rehabilitation program for all employees
- Promoting a rapid rate of disability recovery
- Reducing the associated financial impact of disability on the employee and Walbro
- Enhancing employee relations and strengthening the company's reputation as a responsible employer

Program Components

Walbro extends its fitness and rehabilitation service to those whose injuries are not work related as well as to those whose are. Dependents of employees are also encouraged to use the program. Employees are scheduled for treatment during their usual work hours if the injury occurred at the workplace. In the case of non-work-related injuries, employees receive treatment outside regular working hours.

Three certified athletic trainers hired by Walbro supervise the fitness and rehabilitation program. They provide conditioning and preventive training as well as postinjury and postsurgery rehabilitation treatment and exercise. The company has established a well-equipped health and fitness center, including a whirlpool, paraffin and mineral baths, ultrasound equipment, a jogging track, racquetball courts, and weight-lifting equipment designed to strengthen all muscle groups. Aerobics classes, postural consultation, smoking cessation, and diet control are part of the health promotion program.

Employees enter the program through self-referral, referral by a supervisor, or referral by the Walbro health department. For trauma injuries, treatment starts immediately. If the severity of an injury requires a comprehensive assessment, the employee is first sent to a physician. Once the diagnosis is confirmed, the physician refers the employee back to the health center for an individualized treatment and rehabilitation program. When the trainer is treating a worker with a disability, he or she remains in close contact with the employee's personal physician. The response from area physicians to the program has been very positive; in fact, private physicians have made several referrals to the fitness and rehabilitation center.

Program Results and Evaluation

Athletic Training Services designed a modest evaluation program on behalf of Walbro, which permitted better tracking of the company's costs of its fitness and rehabilitation program, workers compensation, absenteeism, injury recovery time, and success in achieving return to work.

- Between 1985 and 1986, Walbro reduced its workers compensation costs by more than 55 percent at a time when its work force increased by 11 percent.
- Walbro estimated that it would take five years to pay back the original $100,000 investment (assuming a projected 25 percent reduction in workers compensation costs and lower absenteeism). In fact, the initial investment was returned in just ten months!
- In 1986, Walbro achieved a 2.6 percent reduction in sickness and accident payments at a time when such costs increased by 17 percent in the state.
- The average recovery time from injuries was reduced by one third. A Walbro official reports, "Through the ability to restore an individual's functional capacity at an accelerated rate, a positive, get well approach is fostered from the start. The program clearly has demonstrated that just as sports teams keep their athletes in the game, Walbro has found a way to rehabilitate and keep its industrial athletes on the job day after day."

Lessons From the Walbro Experience

Walbro demonstrates that a medium-size employer in a relatively rural community can adopt an effective approach to workplace disability. The company recognized the costs of disability, engaged a consultant to appraise its situation, made a substantial up-front financial investment in response to the assessment, and evaluated the results of that investment.

It did not attempt to implement all components of the disability management program at once. For example, case management and extensive job accommodations were not included in the initial design. Setting all components in place at once is often unrealistic for small and medium-size employers. Nonetheless, Walbro took several impressive steps in managing workplace disability. For example:

- The company conducted a formal needs assessment in devising its program (something often overlooked even by the largest corporations). It assessed its disability experience over a two-year period. This information informed program design and the evaluation scheme, which included follow-up to determine program effectiveness.
- Walbro's disability management strategy is based on primary and secondary prevention, health promotion, and fitness. The company believes that a healthy work force is less likely to experience injury, illness, and disability. It is also committed to an active, early intervention program to ameliorate the impact of injury and disability.
- The concept of the "industrial athlete" is a powerful new paradigm in terms of how employers think about and value their employees. This concept "communicates well" in conveying the values and objectives of the program.
- Since Walbro is located in a small town in a rural area, it was particularly important to secure the confidence and cooperation of the local medical establishment. Considerable effort was devoted to orienting local physicians, arranging for them to visit the fitness center, and accepting physician referrals to the center. This strategy helps to ensure continuity in treatment, reduces concerns regarding treatment competition, and supports good community relations generally.

The Will-Burt Company* Orrville, Ohio

Introduction to The Will-Burt Company

The Will-Burt Company, with approximately 300 nonunionized employees, is located in northeast Ohio and is engaged in a variety of steel fabrication and manufacturing operations. As a typical "Rust Belt job shop," the company is a supplier to the automotive and tractor industry; assembles automatic pin-setting machines for FMC Corporation; provides

*Sources for this profile include personal communications with the authors.

telescoping towers for minicams used by television news organizations; and manufactures storage devices for hazardous material. The tasks engaged in by employees range from unskilled work, such as materials handling and sweeping, to skilled work involving welding, grinding, hand assembly of precision equipment, and toolmaking. The company has an employee stock ownership program (ESOP). The employees purchased Will-Burt from the founding family in 1985 at a time when it was a takeover target. Harry Featherstone, a former Ford Motor Company executive, became president and CEO at the time of the buyout.

Rationale for the Disability Management Program

Following the leveraged buyout, the company found that it was in debt for over $1 million and desperately needed to reduce costs and enhance the skills and performance of its work force. Costs associated with worker injury and workers compensation (which were averaging $200,000 per year) became an immediate target for cost reduction.

The management of Will-Burt determined that safety and injury prevention were essential functions that needed to be supported as a critical component of a newly devised corporate culture, which had as its objective the "humanization of the workplace."

Program Philosophy and Objectives

To effect the new corporate culture and enhance employee skills, the company made a strategic decision to emphasize employee education, development, and preservation. This decision was consistent with the belief that more skilled workers would produce better products and that more knowledgeable employees would understand company objectives better. Most important, the investment in education was interpreted in terms of a critical message, namely, that the firm was an interdependent enterprise, that all workers were important to the success of the firm, and that teamwork and personal regard for each other were vital to eventual success.

Program Components

In collaboration with the University of Akron, Will-Burt enrolled employees in such classes as mathematics, advanced blueprint reading, industrial engineering, and geometry. Later a "mini-MBA" program was established. All employees, regardless of present job assignment, are eligible to participate in the education program (on company time). The employer pays all fees after successful completion of two years of study. In 1988–

1989, for example, 60 employees (20 percent of the work force) completed the two-year course of study.

This educational investment demonstrates Will-Burt's commitment to its employees, reinforces the team-building objective, and fosters enlightened self-interest and a "we're in this together" attitude. Employees have become more sensitive to cost factors and more aware of the contributions made by all employees to the company.

The prevailing value of concern for every employee was apparent when, in 1990, three assembly workers had to undergo back operations. Rather than simply paying benefits, the company brought the three workers back to work as soon as it was approved by their treating physicians. Because it was not advisable to return the workers to their original jobs, they were placed in office and sales positions. Somewhat later an assembly worker with a chronic illness was brought back to work on a limited basis of two hours per day. His time on the job was gradually increased until, after eight months, he was again working full time as the company's communications specialist.

Management believes that anyone with a disability, for any reason (work or non–work related), can be returned to work in some capacity. Managers make it clear that injured workers may try a variety of transitional work assignments. If the first one does not work out, the employee may try something else. Team leaders (as first-line supervisors are known) are expected to provide supportive counseling, encourage the employee, and extend every opportunity for a successful return to work.

Here are some highlights of the program:

- An unexpected result of these accommodated assignments was the high level of motivation and knowledge of the company and industrial operations that these "blue collar" workers brought with them to their new safety and sales assignments.

- In embarking on this new approach, Will-Burt conferred with its insurance company and the Ohio Industrial Commission (the state workers compensation agency). The commission has provided outstanding medical and vocational rehabilitation services to several Will-Burt employees.

- Management acknowledges that not all of its efforts have been successful. For example, the company hired an eighteen-year-old deaf man, but this endeavor was not successful because of an overprotective attitude on the part of team leaders. The team leaders felt uncomfortable with this individual and feared he would injure himself. Two factors are noteworthy in this example: First, the company found the young man another job with a local employer; second, the company added sign language as a course in the mini-MBA program.

• The Will-Burt approach also provides work hardening, job sharing, and job analysis in addition to informal transitional job placement. Job modification, including ergonomic design to accommodate individuals with functional limitations, is a standard procedure.

• The Will-Burt approach is based on resourceful and creative problem solving. For example, the stockholders of this small company would not likely approve the expenditure of capital on elaborate, expensive rehabilitation techniques such as physical therapy or a plant medical service. Rather, the company engages in innovative, team-oriented, low-cost solutions.

Program Results and Evaluation

Although the Will-Burt Company has not conducted an elaborate assessment of all the costs and benefits associated with its disability management efforts, it does report some impressive results:

• In 1985 workers compensation costs were $200,000. In 1990 they were $9,000. The prediction is that in 1991 they will be no more than $4,000!

• During the same time, medical costs declined significantly. In 1985 the company paid out $1,961 per employee for health benefits. By 1990 it paid out $1,993 for such benefits, although the medical costs price index increased by 83 percent during this time.

• During the same five-year period, sick-day usage fell by half.

This record seems a straightforward and powerful affirmation that the Will-Burt Company is doing something right in managing the cost of work force disability.

Lessons From the Will-Burt Experience

The Will-Burt Company proves the point that the small employer need not be defenseless in the face of disability costs. A company of this size can take strategic, meaningful action within the limits of its resources to manage the financial and human costs of disability. Other lessons provided by the company's experience include these:

• Buttressed by a corporate culture that values employees and a positive attitude of self-reliance, an employer can achieve significant results.

• The role played by top management is critical in adopting effective disability management practices. Management must take a direct, hands-on, committed role in all aspects of the program. It should adopt a "people first" value system, emphasizing education and enlightenment as the keys to a successful work environment. The dual factors of human concern and cost reduction are powerful motivators and can be used effectively to convince managers and employees of the value of disability management.

City of Winnipeg*
Manitoba, Canada

Introduction to the City of Winnipeg

Winnipeg is the capital of the province of Manitoba, Canada. With a population of approximately 618,000, Winnipeg is a major transportation, commercial, governmental, and agricultural center.

Approximately 12,000 employees work for the city of Winnipeg, 10,000 full time and 2,000 part time. The majority belong to one of nine unions or employee associations. The Canadian Union of Public Employees is the largest, with over 6,000 members. The city government is composed of twenty-seven different departments, encompassing police, fire, ambulance, street and sewer construction, waterworks, refuse collection, and hydro, park, and recreation services. The city also operates three hospitals.

Winnipeg is unique in Canada in that it administers its own self-insured and -managed disability program as part of the employee pension scheme. The pension plan is jointly "trusteed" by management and union personnel and jointly funded by the employees and the city.

Rationale for the Disability Management Program

In 1977 a Winnipeg employment officer was assigned to place disabled city employees capable of performing light-duty work in suitable positions as vacancies occurred. This was a limited effort because the employment officer could only devote approximately 30 percent of his time to the task. In 1980 and 1981 the Employee Benefits Board, which administers the city's retirement and disability fund, reported that many city employees receiving disability benefits were capable of working in light-duty jobs. This finding indicated that substantial savings in disability payments could

*Sources for this profile include personal communications; and Irvine, John D., and Steve Kraichy (1990) "Cost Effective or Not," *Rehabilitative Employment*. Winnipeg, Canada: City of Winnipeg.

be obtained by finding some type of "rehabilitative employment" for these employees.

In May 1984 the board of commissioners of the city approved a policy of alternative or light-duty work for employees receiving workers compensation benefits. The board also created the Rehabilitative Employment Section, which was made a permanent department in 1990, demonstrating top-management commitment to a rehabilitation and return-to-work approach to employees with disabilities. The Canadian Union of Public Employees participated actively in all facets of the program's development and implementation.

Program Philosophy and Objectives

Return-to-work programs can be incorporated into an organization that values its employees and treats them as an appreciating asset. Winnipeg management recognizes that the employee and his or her supervisor are the two most important players in the return-to-work program, while the union must be a party to all negotiations and decisions.

The objectives of the program include:

- Minimizing the financial impact of disability on the city, the employee, and his or her family
- Providing productive work for the organization and allowing an employee with valuable experience to continue making a contribution to the city
- Bringing all parties into the return-to-work process sooner
- Enhancing employee self-esteem and self-worth
- Preventing the employee from "settling into a sick role"

As stated by Irvine and Kraichy (1990), "Rehabilitative Employment Programs must reflect the employer's unique situation. Programs must be home grown to coexist with the employer's corporate culture, history and value system, business and human resource philosophy, organizational structure, benefit packages and most importantly, the Management and Union relationship."

Program Components

In establishing their rehabilitative employment program, the city of Winnipeg:

- Formulated an official policy statement.
- Offered training to departmental supervisors, employees, and union representatives.

- Clarified the roles and responsibilities of all involved parties.
- Established comprehensive and systematic rehabilitation services with health care providers and other community agencies serving employees.
- Developed a systematic approach to the return-to-work plan, including a formal cooperative agreement between all parties, job analysis, job modifications, and other placement services.
- Developed an evaluation system, including statistical and financial data collection and analysis, to assess the economic viability of the program.

The city's rehabilitative employment strategy is founded on four basic principles:

1. Early identification and intervention
2. Alternative or light-duty work assignments
3. Case management to provide a team approach in the rehabilitative employment process and to provide the employee with the ability to participate in his or her rehabilitation program
4. Monthly meetings of administrative and supervisory personnel to review individual employee progress, develop plans of action, as well as attend to administrative matters

The letter of understanding between the city and the Canadian Union of Public Employees calls for the following:

- Rehabilitation is a mutual responsibility of the city and the employee as well as management and the union.
- All parties will work cooperatively to foster an atmosphere conducive to rehabilitation and return to work.
- The city will identify positions which, subject to the approval of the union, shall be utilized as rehabilitative positions.
- Those employees who have been accepted by the city as permanently partially disabled (that is, they will probably never be able to return to their former jobs) are eligible for rehabilitative positions.
- A list of eligible employees will be developed and maintained on the basis of seniority status.
- Employees who have been denied positions shall have the right to grieve in accordance with the provisions of the collective bargaining agreement.
- In the event of a dispute on medical grounds, the matter will be referred to an independent physician agreed to by the parties.
- Upon placement in a rehabilitative position, employees will con-

tinue to hold seniority within their previous department and, as well, within the new department commencing with their rehabilitative assignment.

Program Results and Evaluation

Irvine and Kraichy report that from 1988 to 1989, 410 city employees were placed in rehabilitative employment. These efforts resulted in a $2.7 million cost savings to the workers compensation account and the Civic Employees Pension Plan Disability Program.

Lessons From the City of Winnipeg Experience

Public employers face the same dynamics and demographics as their counterparts in the private sector; for example, high benefits costs, shrinking revenues and resources, an aging work force, labor-management negotiations, and limited experience with disability management and return to work on the part of employees with functional limitations. Winnipeg, however, has demonstrated that through awareness of innovative disability management developments, labor-management leadership, and cooperative problem solving the public sector can implement programs that are responsive to the needs of employers and their disabled employees. After analyzing data spanning a ten-year period, the city took the following initiatives:

- Wrote a formal disability management policy establishing rights and responsibilities; put in place an organizational structure (the Rehabilitative Employment Section); addressed grievance, dispute resolution, and seniority concerns; and founded the policy on a "letter of understanding" between the city and the Canadian Union of Public Employees. The thoughtful development of this policy statement was absolutely essential to the successful implementation of the new program.
- Distributed the letter of understanding to ensure that all parties (departments, unions, employees) were informed of the new program. The city was aware that potential participants in disability management programs needed to know of such opportunities *before* the injury or disability occurred.
- Built a program sensitive to the psychosocial needs of the employee with emphasis on employee participation in the case management process and sensitivity to the psychological problems that can interfere with successful return to work.

Human Resources Development Institute American Federation of Labor-Congress of Industrial Organizations* Washington, D.C.

Introduction to the Human Resources Development Institute

The Human Resources Development Institute (HRDI) was established by the American Federation of Labor-Congress of Industrial Organizations (AFL-CIO) in 1968 to serve as a mechanism for the labor movement to participate in the nation's employment and training system.

The HRDI works at the national, state, and local levels. Through the national headquarters, HRDI staff have access to the AFL-CIO's 12 regional offices, 50 state federations, and over 700 local central labor bodies. The HRDI also works through the leadership of more than 90 national and international unions affiliated with the AFL-CIO. The central office, located in Washington, D.C., develops and oversees initiatives to assist job training and employment opportunities for dislocated, disadvantaged, disabled, and unemployed workers. Specifically, HRDI national staff have responsibility for providing administrative services and technical assistance to advance labor's involvement in training; developing technical materials; serving as a national clearinghouse for information on labor's involvement in employment and training programs; and providing administrative and fiscal oversight to HRDI-operated programs. To carry out program initiatives, HRDI operates five field offices nationwide.

Rationale for the Disability Management Initiatives

These are the factors that stimulated the HRDI's involvement in disability management:

- The HRDI was developed because of organized labor's recognized need to respond to the increasing rates of unemployment among America's unskilled, economically disadvantaged, and disabled workers and to the

*Sources used for this profile include Akabas, Sheila H., and Lauren B. Gates (1991) *Disability Management and Labor Management Initiatives in Early Intervention, Final Report*. New York: Center for Social Policy and Practice in the Workplace, Columbia University School of Social Work; Akabas, Sheila H., and Lauren B. Gates (Autumn 1990) "Organizational Commitment: The Key to Successful Implementation of Disability Management," *American Rehabilitation* 16(3): 9–13; and Gates, Lauren B., Yecheskel Taler, and Sheila H. Akabas (1989) "Optimizing Return to Work Among Newly Disabled Workers: A New Approach Toward Cost Containment," *Benefits Quarterly*, 5(2): 19–27.

prospect of millions of workers facing permanent dislocation as plants close and industries downsize.

• The passage of the Job Training Partnership Act of 1982 (JTPA) provided a new avenue for labor to become involved actively in the development and operation of job training programs. The HRDI helps ensure that JTPA programs meet the needs of jobless workers, protects those still employed, and offers services to help labor organizations plan and conduct JTPA programs.

Program Philosophy and Objectives

The HRDI recognizes that the key to better jobs for disabled workers lies in close working partnerships among organized labor, employers, government, and the rehabilitation community. In cooperation with government initiatives, it provides a variety of services to unions and employers that attempt to develop these partnerships.

The program aims to:

- Assist disabled people to enter the work force, done by collaborating with vocational rehabilitation, community and government agencies, and unions and employers to help disabled people prepare for employment.
- Assist return to work for those out on disability, carried out through provision of early intervention services to help workers return to their former jobs or other positions with the same employer.
- Help disabled workers take charge of their job search in order to secure productive employment.
- Help disabled workers manage their disabilities, done by providing information about illness or injury, promoting awareness of available benefits and services, providing information about recovery and return-to-work opportunities, and referring workers to local service providers.
- Help resolve problems in return to work that develop out of conflicts with labor-management agreements.
- Develop return-to-work assistance as a union service to its members.
- Help contain the cost of labor-management health and welfare programs.
- Help coordinate the activities of organized labor, employers, insurers, government, and others involved in providing assistance to disabled workers.

Program Components

The five HRDI field offices carry out program objectives under the supervision of the national headquarters. Disability specialists at these offices are involved in the following activities:

- Counseling disabled workers about available employment and training opportunities and assessment of the need for pre-employment services to become ready for jobs or training
- Placing disabled persons in jobs or training
- Providing case management services for disabled workers, such as job referral, job counseling, help with obtaining technological assistance, help with modifying workplace facilities or equipment, and assistance with transportation to and from work
- Developing working relationships with major unions and companies employing large work forces, done in order to expand job opportunities for disabled people, including providing policy guidance and working with employer-union teams
- Participating in educational and technical conferences to explore issues involved in employment of disabled people
- Providing technical assistance to organized labor, employers, vocational rehabilitation agencies, JTPA agencies, and others to enhance employment and training opportunities for disabled people, including participation on coordinating committees and the training of union representatives to provide such assistance
- Participating in research efforts that explore ways to help disabled workers return to work and maintain work roles and document their experiences; specifically, collaborating with the Workplace Center at the Columbia University School of Social Work in an early intervention program funded by the National Institute on Disability and Rehabilitation Research (NIDRR)

Program Results and Evaluation

The HRDI has met with success. Through the Institute over 300 disabled workers have been reached as part of the early intervention program. Many of these workers received counseling and referrals that enabled them to return to work.

From October 1986 to March 1988 job development and placement services were provided to over 1,000 disabled people. These services included job development, vocational evaluation, employability training, occupational skills training, job modification, job placement, and assistance to employers.

The extent of partnerships formed with employers and other organizations that assist disabled people is difficult to quantify. All five field offices, however, report that they are active in this area.

Lessons From the HRDI Experience

HRDI activity demonstrates the significance of unions to disability management. They are important in this area for several reasons:

- Unions help to represent the interests of disabled workers to management.
- At organized workplaces, unions are part of the team that negotiates accommodated return.
- They can provide services not offered by the employer.
- Unions help to establish the trust of disabled workers, which is needed to secure their participation in the disability management effort.
- They can take a proactive role in disability management by developing and testing new initiatives in providing services to disabled workers.

Clearly, the workplace is the front line, where successful accommodation occurs. The HRDI shows how the union can assist this process in a constructive way.

Conclusion

Disability management is a relatively new expression of the corporate concern for human capital and cost containment. To a large extent it is driven by the extensive health and welfare role that has been assumed by American employers over the last fifty years and likely will continue to be propelled by them. In America today, employers are expected to provide much more than a simple paycheck to their employees. We are reminded of Peter Drucker's admonition to managers that there are "no quick fixes" to significant, complex organizational problems. To underscore the comment by Cohen et al. (1990) in the Long Island Rail Road study regarding disability management: "An employer . . . must be prepared to commit significant resources for a minimum of three to five years before meaningful results are evident." If the company also needs to change its corporate culture, the process may take even longer to achieve intended results.

The good news, of course, is that research is beginning to confirm that it is within the power of the employer to enact policies and practices that will reduce the number of injuries significantly, increase the number of injured employees who return to work, and at the same time lower disability costs (Hunt et al. 1989).

Evidence also indicates that while disability management initiatives may not be "cheap," they are more than justified by their return on investment. As Eckenhoff (1984) states:

> The conclusion is really quite clear: the sooner a chronically ill, impaired or disabled person recovers and returns to a productive work role, the more it will benefit the worker, the employer and the insurer. The choice seems relatively straightforward. The firm may choose to bear the ongoing costs of sustaining injured and disabled employees in dependency, or it may choose to underwrite disability management, thus minimizing its ultimate outlay or, when the employee returns to work, eliminating it entirely.

Lessons From the Profiles

No single profile examined here includes all possible features of a disability management program. The more established and successful programs, however, appear to share many techniques and approaches:

- As demonstrated by B-O-C, 3M, Herman Miller, and the Long Island Rail Road, the employer must clearly designate responsibility and accountability when implementing a disability management program. These companies charged one person (disability manager, rehabilitation coordinator, or case manager) with monitoring and managing the process and ensuring communication, coordination, and integration among the individuals and departments involved.
- In addition, the disability (or case) manager commonly provides direct services to injured or disabled employees, captains a team approach to disability in the workplace, oversees and coordinates services provided by external resources, and documents results by collecting, analyzing, and regularly reporting relevant data.
- 3M and Weyerhaeuser demonstrate that the practice of assigning responsibility for disability management to local facilities, units, and departments—including the charging of disability and workers compensation costs to such local operations—is a powerful and effective incentive. The companies noted that local managers were much more likely to "take ownership of their disability problems" if they had a vested economic interest.

• The city of Winnipeg, B-O-C, the LIRR, and Weyerhaeuser demonstrate that an effective disability management effort can, and must, be developed in cooperation with union or employee representatives. Union officials have been effective participants in supporting such programs, educating and encouraging employees to participate, identifying and referring employees in need, and supporting job accommodation efforts.

• Herman Miller, Walbro, 3M, and others have adopted a policy of providing services to individuals across the disability spectrum—those on short-term disability, long-term disability, or workers compensation—and also to those whose injury or disability is not work related.

• Successful programs must include an educational and training effort directed toward managers, supervisors, and the general work force. Preconceived notions and attitudes about people with disabilities are detrimental to the success of disability prevention, rehabilitation, and return-to-work programs and must be addressed and resolved through education. In addition, many employees must adopt new tasks as part of the disability management function; they can do so most effectively with a good training program.

• All the companies cited have adopted the practice of easing injured and disabled workers back to work. Whether they adopt a transitional work center (TWC), light-duty assignments, adjusted hours, modified work tasks, job accommodations, or some combination of these or other approaches, the principle must be to permit the worker to reestablish job readiness and work stamina gradually.

• Employer contracts with medical and vocational rehabilitation providers are becoming a more common practice. Significantly, all programs profiled have established systematic relations with a variety of community-based providers. A few of the firms have developed formal procedures to select such providers and closely monitor costs and performance, but all acknowledge that disability management takes place within a community environment.

• Disability management is but one dimension, though an important one, of establishing a workplace culture marked by individual responsibility, teamwork, high regard for human resources, and high productivity.

Chapter 9
How Do We Know Disability Management Will Work?

Preventing workplace injuries and providing assistance to workers who do become disabled are not new ideas. Federal regulations have long been instrumental in preventing disability through stipulation of safety guidelines. Workers compensation, Social Security Disability Insurance, and other government-funded programs to provide income support to workers who become disabled have also been around for some time. Employer-supported early intervention and accommodated return to work are other sources of assistance offered to workers with disabilities by some employers. Thus far, however, these efforts have had a limited effect on the high costs associated with disability because their implementation tends to be partial and unsystematic. The conditions outlined in this book are not typically taken into account to develop a coordinated, comprehensive disability management program. Consequently, the chances that a worker with a disability will become unemployed or underemployed still remain high.

The disability management approach offered in this book presents an alternative, comprehensive approach to management of disability in the workplace. A fair question to ask the authors is, How do you know what you recommend works? The approach is based on findings from studies that evaluate existing strategies. This chapter reviews what we have learned from these studies—how we know what we know.

Overall, disability management research tells us the following:

- Unemployment and underemployment rates among workers who experience disability are high. They are partially explained by the disincentives in the structure of the benefits programs and the attitudes of employers.
- Return to work and job maintenance are affected by more than the physical problems caused by a disability. Psychological and social

issues related to disability also affect the ability to sustain employment.

- Return to work and job maintenance are also affected by workers' perceptions of the workplace.
- Employer responsiveness to the range of problems experienced by workers with disabilities determines disability program effectiveness.
- The size and structure of the organization also have a significant influence on the effectiveness of disability management.
- The cost of accommodation is minimal.
- Disability management improves productivity.
- New programs at the workplace suggest that employers recognize that prevention programs reduce the incidence and costs of disability.

The discussion that follows presents evidence supporting each of these observations.

Structural Disincentives in the Benefits Program

High unemployment and underemployment rates among the working-age disabled population are partially explained by the disincentives in the structure of benefits programs and by the attitudes of employers. Persons with a work disability are more than three times as likely as those without one to be unemployed (Kraus 1989). The 1988 *Current Population Survey* shows that this difference in rate of full-time employment persists even when controlling for sex, race, or ethnicity. The traditional interpretation of these data assumes that unemployment and underemployment among workers with disabilities is high because their preference is to receive benefits and stay home rather than return to work. This assumption is not supported by research findings:

1. There is evidence that workers with disabilities prefer to work and that work is a very important part of their lives. A 1986 Harris Poll of people with disabilities found that two thirds of those who were unemployed working-age adults did, in fact, want to work. A study by Akabas and Gates (1991) of the factors that affect return to work among newly disabled workers also found that most people (95 percent) wanted to return to work. Work is a very important part of people's lives for both the financial rewards and the sense of self-esteem and well-being it provides.

In the Akabas and Gates study, 258 workers with disabilities were asked to rate the importance of various benefits of work on a three-point scale ranging from "very important" to "not at all important." Not surprisingly, 90 percent rated financial rewards as very important. A significant 70 percent, however, rated "a way to feel good about oneself" as very important, 59 percent rated "a way to learn new things" as very important, 47 percent rated "a way to organize the day" and "something to think about" as very important, 46 percent rated "a way to gain respect" as very important, and 32 percent rated "a way to socialize" as very important. Work is a many-splendored activity and people with disabilities want, like the rest of us, to participate in it for a variety of substantial reasons.

2. Researchers find that the rationale for the benefits system, which equates disability with inability to work, poses a major disincentive to return to work or job maintenance (Berkowitz and Hill 1986; Yelin 1986). The programmatic translation of this perspective is to pay workers to stay home. Federally funded Social Security Disability Insurance and workers compensation are available only to those who are not working. A further disincentive for some, especially those with a large number of dependents, is that their nontaxable SSDI benefits may exceed predisability take-home pay (Sullivan and Bagby 1989).

A study by Meyer, Viscusi, and Durbin (1990) illustrates how provision of benefits affects the likelihood of return to work. These researchers found that increasing benefits payments by 10 percent was associated with a 3 to 4 percent increase in the length of time out on short-term disability. During the 1980s Kentucky raised its maximum workers compensation benefits by 66 percent, and Michigan raised its maximum benefits by 70 percent. The researchers measured changes in time out on short-term disability before and after the changes in maximum benefits. Controlling for severity of injury, age, gender, marital status, and industry, they found that duration of time out increased significantly for those who received the higher maximum benefits, whereas length of time out was unaffected for those whose benefits did not increase significantly.

3. The attitude of employers often interferes with bringing workers with disabilities back to the workplace. Employers tend to believe that workers with disabilities do not want to return and that there are too many barriers to accommodation. In a study by the Menninger Foundation, 315 employers responded to questions in a mail survey about their attitudes toward workers with disabilities and return to work (Hester et al. 1988).

Respondents were asked if they agreed or disagreed with the statement that almost every employee who becomes disabled wants to return to work if possible. Thirty-five percent of the respondents did not agree with this statement. Employers were also asked about what they perceived as barriers to return to work. Fifty-three percent agreed that most union contracts make it impossible to shift job assignments for employees with disabilities. Thirty-four percent felt it is impractical to revise work techniques in their firms to accommodate employees with disabilities. Finally, 27 percent agreed that it is too expensive in their companies to modify equipment to accommodate employees who become disabled. Although not strictly representative of all employers in the United States, employers responding to the survey did come from a range of industry types and company sizes.

A Bio-Psycho-Social Approach to Disability Management

Return to work and job maintenance are affected by more than the physical problems caused by a disability. Psychological and social issues related to disability also affect the ability to sustain employment.

Onset of illness or disability affects not only physical health, but all aspects of a worker's life, including psychological well-being and social support. Problems in all three of these realms can affect the ability to sustain employment. Ensuring return to work and job maintenance, therefore, is more than a matter of addressing the physical symptoms of the disability. Disability management is most effective in overcoming the barriers to return to work or job maintenance by taking a bio-psycho-social approach that is concerned with all problems that interfere with successful employment.

A study of the workers compensation system in the state of Washington demonstrates the psychological impact associated with longer periods of disability (Ray 1986). Two samples of injured workers in Washington were compared: injured workers with compensable claims open for over 120 days and a control group of injured workers with noncompensable claims open for less than 120 days. Workers were mailed a questionnaire that asked about how their injury affected their physical condition, employment status, financial stability, psychological well-being, and family and social life. The total final sample size was 2,540, a response rate of 62 percent. Results showed that workers with compensable claims open more than 120 days reported more frequently than the comparison group that they felt depressed, felt they had less control over their lives, including their health, saw themselves as victims and at the mercy of external forces, and expressed lower self-esteem. Loss of self-esteem, depression, loss of perceived control over one's life, anxiety, fear and uncertainty of the future, or a sense of isolation may result from the onset of disability. Research shows that the probability of return to work decreases, the length of time out of work increases, and the cost of disability skyrockets when a worker experiences the negative psychological consequences of disability.

The psychological effect may result, in part, from how the worker copes with the disability itself. It is not hard to understand how the sudden onset of disease in a healthy individual might cause depression. However, the response of the employer and co-workers to the disability also affects the employee's level of psychological well-being and thus return to work. When the employee perceives that the employer does not care whether or not he or she returns to work, or when the worker is dissatisfied with his or her job, then the likelihood of return to work decreases (Akabas and Gates 1991; Mitchell and Leclair 1988).

The social consequences of disability can be just as debilitating. Disability can affect relationships with family, friends, relatives, neighbors, and co-workers. Some relationships may be strengthened, while others are weakened. For example, restrictions imposed by the disability may require someone to seek help with the activities of daily living (ADL), such as bathing, eating, dressing, shopping, and transportation. Some may turn to family members to provide help. Others may need to count on friends, neighbors, church groups, or community service agencies. The ability to rally these social networks to solve the problems caused by the disability is important to resuming work roles. Research finds that family support can enhance the likelihood of return to work (Greenwood 1988; Ray 1986). However, when disability negatively affects relationships, return to work can be hindered. In particular, when family stability is disrupted, return to work is less likely (Hood and Downs 1985; Ray 1986; Akabas and Gates 1991).

The Workers' Disability Syndrome

Return to work and job maintenance are also affected by workers' perceptions of the workplace. If workers perceive that the employer does not care what happens to them, or prefers that they not return, then they are less likely to return. Research shows that motivation to return to work is greatly diminished when the employer has no contact with the employee following the onset of disability and there is no process in place to assist return and assure the worker that there is a place for him or her at the workplace. In response to the perceived attitudes of employers toward return to work, workers with disabilities become "disability dependent" or caught in the "workers' disability syndrome" (Hood and Downs 1985). They are discouraged workers. They come to believe that they cannot return to work and lose the motivation to try.

On the other hand, support from supervisors and co-workers enhances well-being. In turn, those with higher levels of well-being are more likely to return to work. In a study of the effect of well-being and social support on return to work following short-term disability, El-Bassel (1989) interviewed 185 female New York City workers who suffered either physical or mental disability. She reports that workers with disabilities who return to work have larger support networks and are more satisfied with the quality of support than those who do not return. Further, well-being increases when the size and quality of the work support network increase. Finally, she found well-being to be a significant predictor of return to work.

The study by Akabas and Gates (1991) demonstrates how the disability management program plays a direct part in affecting worker perceptions of the workplace. Participants in a study of early intervention reported that the intervention did not affect return to work as much as the fact that the case manager took an interest in their cases and showed caring on the part of the employer and co-workers. The contact and the expression of caring provided the motivation to return. In a subsequent early intervention project, a strong relationship was found between an employee's perceived probability of returning to work and whether or not the employer wanted the worker back. Perceived probability of return decreases when the employer does not care if the worker returns or does not want the worker back, a rich example of a self-fulfilling prophecy in which believing makes it so. The lesson is to help the employee believe he or she is valued and return is desired.

The Effect of Employer Responsiveness

Employer responsiveness to the range of problems experienced by workers with disabilities determines disability management effectiveness. Employer responsiveness is the extent to which the company supports worker well-being and offers assistance to minimize the impact of the array of problems that interfere with return to work or job maintenance. Responsiveness is directly expressed through disability prevention and management practices and indirectly through the corporate culture. Employee well-being is enhanced in companies where the workers are informed about company policies and operations and participate in decision making.

Specific components of disability management and prevention practices that indicate employer responsiveness were identified by Akabas and

Krauskopf (1989) in their study of employee assistance programs (EAPs). Although this list is not all-inclusive, it provides a range of possible factors:

- There is an EAP in the workplace.
- There is a formal employment maintenance policy at the workplace.
- The employer will modify equipment.
- The employer will negotiate changes in routines.
- The employer will negotiate changes in job design.
- The employer offers transitional work.
- Supervisors are encouraged to accommodate.
- The employer provides transfers.
- The employer offers retraining.
- The employer offers comprehensive health insurance.
- The employer provides access ramps.
- The doors are widened for wheelchairs.
- Restrooms are accessible to people with disabilities.
- The employer actively recruits workers with disabilities.
- TDD (telecommunications device for the deaf) and TTY (teletypewriter) or phone amplification are available.
- Braille or audio cues are in the elevators.

Habeck and her colleagues (1991) studied the relationship between these types of factors and the incidence of workers compensation claims. Michigan employers with fifty or more employees that closed workers compensation cases during 1986 were selected for study. The researchers sorted the companies by industry and selected food production, fabricated metals, transportation equipment and manufacturing, and health care services for in-depth analysis. These industries were selected on the basis of diversity in size and product and variability among number of claims closed. A further subset within each industry was then selected. The 15 percent with the most claims (high-claims employers) and the 15 percent with the least claims (low-claims employers) became the final study sample. A self-administered survey was sent to these companies asking what organizational and disability management factors they thought contributed to differences in the number of claims. Of 284 companies in the sample, 124 responded.

Significantly, study results showed that the number of workers compensation claims varied considerably within industries, and thus appeared to be influenced by internal factors, which are under the control of the individual companies. The factors found to exist significantly more often among low-claims employers include:

- Larger number of employees
- Higher proportion working overtime
- Systematic monitoring and correction of unsafe behavior
- Safety training for new or transferred employees at the time they start their new assignments
- Active participation of management in safety issues
- Wellness programs or fitness resources for employees
- Use of modified work assignments for returning disabled workers
- Active participation of supervisors in the return-to-work process
- Employee assistance programs
- Regular screening of employees for health risk factors
- Corporate culture that promotes work incentives such as profit sharing and employee involvement in company decision making and information exchange

High-claims employers differed from low-claims companies along several dimensions. They tended to be unionized and they had had a greater proportion of workers who were minorities, had less than two years of tenure, or had sustained injuries resulting in lost work time. These employers also experienced a higher turnover rate.

Habeck et al. (1991) suggest that these results indicate that the number of claims is higher in companies with poor working conditions and problematic labor relations. Collective bargaining tends to arise in response to negative working conditions. Further, the higher incidence of injury and lost time and the shorter time on the job indicate that high-claims companies are less attractive places to work. In other words, high-claims companies appear to be unresponsive to the specific needs of their employees, including those with disabilities. Conversely, low-claims companies tend to be responsive to the specific needs of workers with disabilities as well as support a corporate culture that demonstrates caring about worker well-being and involvement.

The early intervention project referred to earlier further demonstrates the importance of workplace responsiveness to return to work (Akabas and Gates 1991). The project investigated the factors affecting return to work of workers with disabilities and through a demonstration program showed how program components help or hinder return. An interview administered to newly disabled workers identified potential barriers to return to work in four areas—workplace problems, health-related problems, family and personal problems, and financial problems. According to the outcome of the interview, the case manager suggested possible interventions that might help to solve the problems. Case managers monitored each worker, and three months after initial intake administered a follow-up survey to evaluate intervention effectiveness. A total of 258 disabled workers participated in the project, representing fourteen unions.

From responses to the intake assessment interview, an exploratory model of the factors that affect length of time out on short-term disability was developed. The model in Figure 9-1 shows that the number of weeks out on disability increases as the perceived probability of return to work decreases. Length of time out and perceived probability of return to work, on the one hand, are determined by how severe the worker perceives his or her disability. Furthermore, the perceived flexibility of the supervisor and the employee's perception of whether or not the supervisor wants him or her back determine length of time out and perceived probability of return to work.

It is the perception of the supervisor's flexibility and interest that are indicators of workplace responsiveness. From the perspective of the worker, the supervisor is the key person conveying workplace policy and controlling the probability of return to work. For example, without an explicit policy, accommodation becomes an informal process that is left to the discretion of the supervisor. If the relationship between the worker and the supervisor prior to the disability was troubled (as measured by job dissatisfaction), or the worker believes that the disability is too severe and the supervisor determines the opportunity for accommodated return, then the worker perceives return as less likely. Again, this confirms that the outcome of return to work is influenced by the behavior of the employer rather than the disability of the employee.

Figure 9-1. Model predicting length of time out on disability.

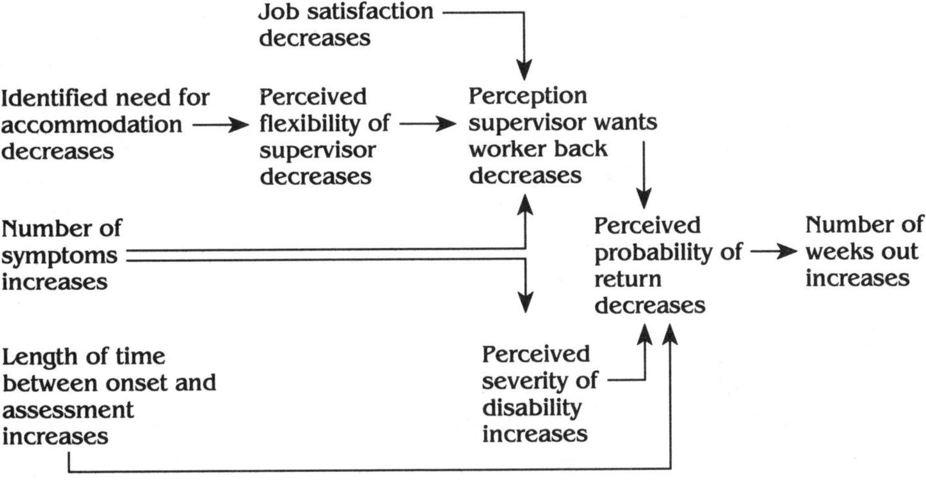

The Influence of Organization Characteristics

The size and structure of the organization also have a significant influence on the effectiveness of disability management. Research has identified characteristics of organizations that affect implementation of effective disability management programs. Hester and Decelles (1990) investigated disability management practices in 309 small (less than 250 employees), medium (250 to 999 employees), large (1,000 to 4,999 employees), and extra large (more than 5,000 employees) companies. They determined that company size did not affect the perceived importance of return to work and the potential impact of return to work on cost containment. There were differences among companies, however, in how disability management practices were carried out. These include the following:

- Larger companies are more concerned with containing workers compensation costs than smaller ones.
- Larger organizations are more likely to store long-term disability and workers compensation data.
- Larger companies are more likely to be self-insured, and self-insured companies overall were found to have a greater interest in return to work and in preventing long-term disability.
- Larger companies are more likely to have formalized programs such as written procedures and methods of communication with workers.
- Larger enterprises are more likely to place importance on prevention, especially employee assistance programs and wellness programs.
- The availability of return-to-work programs is directly proportional to the size of the employer—the larger the firm, the more likely the services are available.

The differences in disability management practices arise because larger employers are more likely to be self-insured, and therefore more likely to see immediate savings from disability management efforts; they have a greater need for formalized programs to assist employees, and they have more staff and job diversity.

The challenge of implementing effective disability management in larger companies is significant, nonetheless, because of the need to coordinate the potential number of departments and people involved in the disability management process. Departments both within and outside an organization influence the effectiveness of the process. A 1986 national survey of 400 employers identified the different departments that play a role in disability management (Schwartz 1986). These include:

• *Benefits departments.* It was found that benefits departments most often have responsibility for disability management within the firm. Department staff responsibilities may include evaluating claims, ensuring proper compensation, working with health care professionals to determine if compensation is warranted, counseling employees about benefits, monitoring benefits payments and return to work, and working with insurance companies.

• *EAPs.* EAPs, available to disabled and nondisabled employees, provide confidential support services for personal problems of employees and their families. They may also serve a case management function, provide training, and offer liaison with community social resources. Sometimes EAPs are assigned responsibility for coordinating the disability management policy, and they may direct the coordinating committee, which includes representatives of all the other departments.

• *Finance departments.* Finance departments play a central role in disability management through their involvement in budgetary decisions and evaluation of incentive policies. In some organizations the finance department actually administers workers compensation and other benefits plans.

• *Health promotion departments.* These departments are responsible for developing educational prevention initiatives in response to data uncovered by the disability management effort.

• *Labor relations departments.* Labor relations are involved in contract negotiations that affect benefits coverage and in defining jobs appropriate for modified or accommodated work return. They are also involved in disciplinary or grievance proceedings that arise in some cases where disability issues are the underlying cause of the problem.

• *Legal departments.* Legal departments litigate contested cases, participate in workers compensation hearings, and interpret disability legislation and review disability policies for their legal implications.

• *Medical departments.* Medical departments conduct medical evaluations and provide physical examinations at company-based health facilities, develop prevention and wellness programs, provide clearance for return to work for workers with disabilities, help develop return-to-work accommodations, review workers compensation reports, and review short-term and long-term disability cases. Department staff may also establish contact wth local providers of health care or actually provide direct care to employees.

• *Risk management departments.* Risk management departments usually have responsibility for administration of the workers compensation plan.

• *Safety/industrial hygiene departments.* Safety departments are primarily involved in disability prevention through education and, to some extent, counseling on accommodation. They may also be involved in reviewing accident reports to identify gaps in safety procedures.

• *Tax departments.* Tax departments may be involved in providing counseling related to the tax implications of benefits program design and incentives around taxes associated with disability income replacement. For example, if the employer requires contributory payments from employees for benefits coverage, it may be best for the employee's contribution to be targeted to cover disability benefits costs because when the employee pays the premium for long-term disability benefits, then the benefits income is not taxable. However, when the employer pays the premium, the benefits would be taxable income to the employee. Finally, when employer and employee share premium payments, the employee pays taxes only on the portion contributed by the employer.

The list of departments identified by the Schwartz survey is not all-inclusive. Others include engineering departments, which may be involved in design and construction of physical accommodations, and management information systems (MIS) departments, which may have responsibility for data collection and analysis.

The most unique potential contribution is reserved for EAPs. There is growing awareness of the potential role of EAPs in disability management. Traditionally, benefits departments have had the primary responsibility for disability management. They lack experience, however, in problem assessment and implementation of effective intervention strategies. Generally, benefits personnel are not equipped to deal with the multifaceted problems workers with disabilities face beyond those involving their benefits (Akabas and Gates 1991). EAP staff have the necessary qualifications. Their professional commitment requires confidentiality. Further, they have connections to the wide range of community resources required to provide assistance for the varied problems encountered by persons with disabilities.

The Workplace Center of Columbia University surveyed 1,000 EAPs to determine their practice in relation to disability management (Akabas and Krauskopf 1989). Organizations from thirty-three states and the District of Columbia responded to the questionnaire. Results showed a missed opportunity. Despite their potential to play a significant role, most EAPs do not consider physical disability part of their purview. Only 5 percent of the organizations' clients went to the EAP with a physical disability as the problem. Yet, those EAPs that were already involved in disability management were significantly more likely than all other EAPs to plan expansion of their disability management function, suggesting that once involved, EAPs view disability management as a rewarding function.

The ability of the employer or collectively bargained trust fund to coordinate people and organizations outside the work organization also influences the effectiveness of the disability management effort. Insurance providers, community service agencies, union representatives, and the disabled worker's family, friends, and relatives can all affect the return-to-work process. The relationship among the disabled worker, the health care professional, and the employer is of particular importance. The disabled worker's physician plays a central role in the decision to remain on the job or return to work (Gates et al. 1989; Akabas and Gates 1991; Mitchell and Leclair 1988; Wolfhagen 1989; Beaudway 1986; Greenwood, 1988).

The Gates et al. study (1989) of the factors influencing return to work among newly disabled workers showed that the return-to-work date set by the physician in almost all cases determines when a worker resumes his or her job. Too often, this date is based on the diagnosis and does not take into account the requirements of someone's job or the policies of the employer. As a consequence, the return-to-work date is not always the most appropriate time to resume work. Consider the occurrence of a back injury. If the date is set by diagnosis rather than by occupation and organizational policy, an itinerant construction laborer is treated similarly to a computer programmer. The physically demanding requirements of the first job obviously would indicate the need for a longer recovery period than the second. Further, in instances when no return to work is set, the chances of continuing on long-term disability greatly increase.

Finally, research evidence confirms that a systematic, coordinated process is needed to deal with disability management because there are so many variables both within and outside the workplace. A process in place that allows communication and coordination and streamlines procedures—before workers suffer injury—is a major determinant of disability management effectiveness.

Disability has ramifications throughout an organization, and no one within an organization acts in isolation. Process research that provides an understanding of how the structure and operation of an organization are affected by the interdependencies among its components helps guide organizational response. This builds on ecosystems theory.

Initially described by Darwin, the ecosystem is the process whereby plant and animal communities reach a state of equilibrium that allows for coexistence and growth. Sociologists later applied this concept to human communities (Berry and Kasarda 1977). In so doing, they shifted the emphasis from the classical Darwinian concepts of competition dominance, succession, and segregation to that of functional dependencies.

The view became established that successful adaptation to a changing, yet restrictive, environment is dependent on the total pattern of relationships among the individuals and organizations. In other words, an organization improves its chances for survival by developing an effective system of interdependencies.

The steps involved in this approach are:

1. Identify all the people and departments within the organization that might be involved in disability management.
2. Identify all the people or organizations outside the workplace that might affect return to work or job maintenance.
3. Coordinate the activities of the system—that is, the different people, departments, and organizations that have been identified.
4. Identify the individual needs of the workers with disabilities and coordinate those needs with the system's behavior.

It is important to remember that systems change. The analysis of the workplace from a systems perspective is not a one-shot deal. The values or goals of the organization will change over time. The workplace may reorganize as the company grows or experiences downsizing or a merger. Change will affect the operation of the disability management program. Thus, constant program monitoring and evaluation are necessary. Finally, without adequate data the monitoring and evaluation functions are impossible to carry out.

Minimal Costs of Accommodation

Employers who resist accommodation argue that accommodating workers with disabilities increases costs with no compensation in production or revenues. Conversely, employers who provide accommodation report that productivity is enhanced. For example, flexible work hours assist workers with disabilities but also increase satisfaction and productivity of all workers. Barrier-free workplace design improves communication and movement for all employees. In fact, ergonomics grew out of the effort to accommodate physical needs and limitations.

Research confirms that accommodation rarely involves significant costs. The Harris study for the International Center for the Disabled (Taylor et al. 1987) found that 75 percent of the managers surveyed reported that the average cost of employing workers with disabilities and workers without disabilities was about the same. Managers representing large companies reported that the costs associated with accommodation tended not to be high and that these costs rarely increased the cost of employment of workers with disabilities above the average cost for all employees.

The same findings resulted from a 1982 study by Berkeley Planning Associates (Collignon 1986). The study collected information about accommodation from four sources: (1) a survey of federal contractors who provided accommodations in companies that employed over 19,000 workers with disabilities, (2) in-depth telephone interviews with 85 organizations that implemented accommodations, (3) 10 companies that were found to have successfully provided accommodations to their disabled employees, and (4) workers with disabilities. Results showed that 51 percent of the reported accommodations cost nothing (usually measured as direct costs), 30 percent cost less than $500, and only 8 percent cost more than $2,000.

Other major findings from the Berkeley study include these:

- Larger companies are more likely to recruit and accommodate workers with disabilities. Access to resources and job diversity seem to give these firms an edge in being able to provide accommodations.
- Accommodation seems to be an important job retention strategy. Once a worker is hired, he or she is more likely to be accommodated regardless of occupation or skill level. Further, the more skilled the worker, the more likely the worker will receive more expensive and extensive accommodation. More-skilled workers are more likely to receive physical adaptation of the workplace or special equipment. Less-skilled workers tend to be accommodated through job retraining, job redesign, or selective placement.
- Accommodation does not affect standing in the firm. The probability of promotion is not helped or hindered by accommodation. Rather, accommodation is seen as an aid to doing the current job better.
- A range of accommodations was implemented by the companies studied. No type was predominant. Accommodations varied by occupation and type of disability and included removing physical barriers, adjusting the work environment, relocating the worksite, providing special equipment, providing job transportation, reassigning tasks, modifying work hours or other routines, providing such help as aides or readers, providing additional job training, educating co-workers and supervisors, and allowing job transfer. The most expensive of these accommodations were those provided to wheelchair-bound or blind employees.

Results from the study confirmed that employers perceived accommodation as having a significant positive effect on productivity and morale and that costs were not a limiting factor. Fifty percent of the firms surveyed indicated that accommodation had increased workers' productivity compared to 5 percent who reported it did not. In relation to costs, 39 percent reported that the benefits from accommodation exceeded actual costs. Only 7 percent reported the opposite.

The work of the Job Accommodation Network (JAN) is another testimonial to the tremendous range and affordability of accommodation offered at the workplace. Established in 1983, JAN is a computerized database developed both to provide information about the types of accommodations that employers have used and to offer an assessment of how well they have worked. There are on file over 4,000 workplace modifications and types of technological assistance that have been used to accommodate workers with disabilities. JAN is available to advise any person needing information or accommodation; the telephone number 1-800-526-7234. Calls are answered twenty-four hours a day and responses are swift and extensive.

Disability Management and Productivity Improvement

Taking workers back after the onset of disability may be a highly profitable strategy. Louis Harris and Associates (in cooperation with the National Council on the Handicapped and the President's Committee on Employment of People with Disabilities) conducted a national survey of managers for the International Center for the Disabled (Taylor et al. 1987). The purpose of the study was to gain an understanding of employer experiences with people with disabilities. Interviews were conducted with 210 top managers (corporate executives with at least the rank of senior vice-president), 301 equal employment opportunity (EEO) managers, 210 department heads and line managers, and 200 top managers in very small companies (employing between 10 and 49 people). Results of the survey showed overwhelmingly that managers find the performance of workers with disabilities comparable to or better than that of workers without disabilities. Specifically, results showed:

- Overall job performance of employees with disabilities tended to be rated good to excellent. Ratings of good to excellent were provided by 88 percent of the top managers, 91 percent of the EEO managers, and 91 percent of the department heads or line managers.
- Managers rated the quality of work by employees with disabilities comparable to or better than that by nondisabled employees. Measures of quality of work included willingness to work hard, reliability, attendance and punctuality, productivity, desire for promotion, and leadership ability.

• Eighty percent of department heads and line managers thought that employees with disabilities were no more difficult to supervise than all other workers.

The Need for Prevention

New programs at the workplace suggest that employers recognize that prevention programs reduce the incidence and costs of disability. OSHA regulations, workers compensation laws, and the decline of the more hazardous manufacturing industries have helped to reduce the incidence of injury at the workplace. It has been estimated that over the past decade the risk of injury declined from 11.0 to 7.6 injuries per 100 workers (Victor 1985). However, chronic disease and injury continue to be prevalent, and the costs associated with these disabilities continue to soar. In response, many employers have invested in health promotion and disability prevention programs. One survey reports that over 50 percent of all employers sponsor formal health promotion activities (Kelly 1986). Further, program evaluation provides evidence that these programs are effective in lowering costs and increasing productivity (Polakoff and Rourke 1990).

Schwartz and Rollins (1985) quantified the costs accompanying chronic illness among employees at the Atlantic Richfield Company (ARCO). They found cardiovascular disease, stroke, cancer, and mental health problems to be the most costly in terms of medical care and disability expenditures. For example, smoking-related cancers, cardiovascular disease, emphysema, and other chronic obstructive pulmonary diseases cost ARCO $48.2 million annually. These costs include medical care, short- and long-term disability payments, permanent replacement costs, absenteeism costs, and loss of productivity. Schwartz and Rollins estimated that if all at-risk employees were active participants in the hypertension screening, smoking cessation, breast self-examination, and colorectal cancer education programs, ARCO could realize a potential savings of $55 million per year.

The most frequent workplace injuries are strains and sprains, cuts, contusions, and fractures. One of the most expensive—and the leading cause of hospitalization—is back injury. One third of all hospitalizations are for back injury (Victor 1985), and the National Council on Compensation Insurance has estimated that, in 1982, lower-back injury cost over $5 billion in workers compensation cases (Sparrell and McKeon 1985).

Other studies have shown that the employer's costs for nonwork-related back injuries are even greater. They have been estimated at $14 billion annually. Liberty Mutual Insurance Company has responded to these costs with a list of three recommendations designed to help control the incidence of back injury:

1. Medical screening after an offer of employment is important to determine if medical history and physical examination suggest that the individual may be unable to perform the demands of the job.
2. Training programs are necessary for workers, supervisors, and management. Workers need to learn safe techniques to prevent injury. Supervisors and management can be trained to ensure compliance and reinforce safety.
3. Jobs can be analyzed in relation to the tasks that contribute to back problems. The jobs may then be changed to reduce the risk of injury. For example, raising a workbench or rearranging a workstation to eliminate twisting while performing a repetitive task helps to avoid back problems.

Prevention programs take many forms. Some are provided in-house while others are offered through outside vendors. Some are comprehensive while others focus on the most prevalent problems of the particular work force. Regardless of the strategy, most successful programs share several components (Kelly 1986):

- Clear organizational commitment to a healthy work force as expressed through explicit goals and objectives, as well as the visible support of top management
- A well-conceived strategic plan
- Baseline data to inform program planning and enable evaluation
- Uniformity and consistency in implementing the program
- Flexibility in order to allow for differences among employee needs
- Knowledgeable, experienced, and enthusiastic providers
- Formal program evaluation to assess how well the program is meeting its objectives and how best to modify the program for the future

An example of a program that incorporates many of these components is the Ford Motor Company and the United Auto Workers (UAW) wellness program provided through their employee assistance program. This program is noteworthy for several reasons: It is a collaboration between employer and union to solve problems of importance to both; it utilizes the EAP; it provides comprehensive services; and it involves 85 to 95 percent of the available work force (Erfurt and Foote 1990). Program activities include:

- Wellness screening or "health risk appraisal"
- Wellness or health promotion classes
- Follow-up every six months with employees at risk for cardiovas-

cular disease (especially those with high blood pressure or high cholesterol)

Specific services include blood pressure screening and control, cholesterol screening and control, weight control, smoking cessation, physical fitness, general nutritional counseling, and stress education. When evaluated, such programs provide research evidence of the gains from prevention initiatives.

Research commends a shift in approach toward disability management—from paying workers to stay home to bringing them back into the work force at the optimal time as determined by their condition, their prognosis, and the available accommodations and transitional jobs. Research confirms the disincentives embedded in the traditional approach toward disability management. Overcoming these disincentives requires a coordinated, systematic approach. This approach involves identifying the interdependencies among people, departments, or other organizations and determining their effect on the biological, psychological, and social well-being of the worker. Effective disability management depends on developing a program within the organization that coordinates the process and is responsive to the wide range of problems disabled workers confront when trying to return to work or maintain work in the face of disability. The gains in productivity and reduced costs can be enormous.

References

Akabas, Sheila H., and Lauren B. Gates (1991) *Disability Management: Labor Management Initiatives in Early Intervention, Final Report.* New York: Center for Social Policy and Practice in the Workplace, Columbia University School of Social Work.

Akabas, Sheila H., and Lauren B. Gates (Autumn 1990) "Organizational Commitment: The Key to Successful Implementation of Disability Management," *American Rehabilitation* 16 (3): 9–13.

Akabas, Sheila H., and Marian S. Krauskopf (1989) *Managing Disability Costs at the Worksite: The Role of Employee Assistance Programs in Disability Management.* New York: The Center for Social Policy and Practice in the Workplace, Columbia University School of Social Work.

Akabas, Sheila H., Susan Bellinger, Michelle Fine, and Richard Woodrow (undated) "Confidentiality Issues in Workplace Settings: A Working Paper." New York: Industrial Social Welfare Center, Columbia University School of Social Work.

Austin, C. D. (1983) "Case Management in Long-Term Care: Options and Opportunities," *Health and Social Work* no. 8: 16–30.

Austin, D. M., and Paul Caragonne (1981) *A Comparative Analysis of Twenty-Two Settings Using Case Management Components.* Austin, Tex.: School of Social Work, University of Texas.

Beaudway, Deborah L. (1986) "3M: A Disability Management Approach," *Journal of Applied Rehabilitation Counseling* 17 (3): 20–22.

Berkeley Planning Associates (1989) *The Disabled Workforce and Job Retention in Small and Large Firms.* Oakland, Calif.

Berkeley Planning Associates (1982) "Study of Accommodations Provided to Handicapped Employees by Federal Contractors." Berkeley, Calif.

Berkowitz, Edward (1987) *Disabled Policy,* 3. Cambridge, Mass.: Cambridge University Press.

Berkowitz, M. (1990) "Overview." In *Forging Linkages,* ed. M. Berkowitz, 9. New York: Rehabilitation International.

Berkowitz, Monroe, and M. Anne Hill (1986) "Disability and the Labor Market: An Overview." In *Disability and the Labor Market,* ed. Monroe Berkowitz and M. Anne Hill, 1–28. Ithaca, N.Y.: ILR Press.

Berry, Brian J. L., and John D. Kasarda (1977) *Contemporary Urban Ecology,* 497. New York: Macmillan.

Bey, Jean M., Anne Keenan Widtfeldt, and John M. Burns (October 1990) "The Nurse As Health Manager," *Business and Health* 8 (10): 24–31.

Bowe, F. (1980) *Rehabilitating America*. New York: Harper & Row.

Broskowski, Anthony (1990) "Current Mental Health Care Environments: Why Managed Care is Necessary," *Professional Psychology: Research and Practice* 22 (1): 1–9.

Bush, Gerald W. (1989) "Catastrophic Case Management: Thoughts From a Teacher/Consumer/Advocate," *Brain Injury* 3 (1): 9–100.

Carbine, Michael E., Gail E. Schwartz, and Sara Watson (July 1989) "Disability Intervention and Cost Management Strategies for the 1990's." A report from the Second Annual National Disability Management Conference of the Washington Business Group on Health.

Collignon, Frederick C. (1986) "The Role of Reasonable Accommodation in Employing Disabled Persons in Private Industry." In *Disability and the Labor Market,* ed. Monroe Berkowitz and M. Anne Hill, 196–241. Ithaca, N.Y.: ILR Press.

Debusk, R. F., C. A. Dennis, and S. Sidney (July 1988) "New Inroads in Return to Work," *Business and Health* 5 (9): 32.

Eckenhoff, Edward A. (May 1984) "Medical Rehabilitation and Disabled Employees," *Business and Health* 1 (6): 31.

El-Bassel Nabila (1989) "Factors Affecting Return to Work Following Short-Term Disability Among Female City Workers and the Role of Social Support System," 189. Ph.D. diss. Columbia University.

Erfurt, John C., and Andrea Foote (January 1990) "A Healthy Alliance," *Employee Assistance,* 41–44.

Feldman, Frances (1976) *Work and Cancer Health History: The Experiences of Recovered Patients*. Oakland, Calif.: American Cancer Society, California Division.

Flynn, Theresa J., and Sean Sullivan (1987) *Providing Mental Health Benefits: Alternatives for Employers*. Washington, D.C.: American Enterprise Institute.

Follman, Joseph F., Jr. (1978) *Helping the Troubled Employee*. New York: AMACOM.

Friedin, Joyce (October 1989) "Cost Containment Strategies For Workers Compensation," *Business and Health* 7 (10): 48–53.

Galvin, D. E., E. Lipoff, and M. E. Carbine (1990) A report from the Third Annual National Disability Management Conference of the Washington Business Group on Health.

Galvin, Donald E., Denise Tate, and Gail Schwartz (1986) "Disability Management Research: Current Status, Need and Implications for Study," *Journal of Applied Rehabilitation Counseling* 17 (3): 43–48.

Gates, Lauren B., Yecheskel Taler, and Sheila H. Akabas (1989) "Optimizing Return to Work Among Newly Disabled Workers: A New Approach Toward Cost Containment," *Benefits Quarterly* 5 (2): 19–27.

Greenwood, Judith (1988) "Very Early Intervention Project Final Management Report." West Virginia Workers' Compensation Fund.

Habeck, V. Rochelle, Michael J. Leahy, Fong Chang, and Edward M. Welch

(March 1991) "Employer Factors Related to Workers' Compensation Claims and Disability Management," *Rehabilitation Counseling Bulletin,* 34 (3): 210–226.

Hahn, Harlan (1984) *The Issue of Equality: European Perceptions of Employment for Disabled Persons,* 10. New York: World Rehabilitation Fund.

Harris, Louis, and Associates, Inc. (1986) *The ICD Survey of Disabled Americans: Bringing Disabled Americans Into the Mainstream.* New York: Louis Harris and Associates, Inc.

Hatherley, James A. (October 1991) Speech at the annual meeting of the Washington Business Group on Health. Washington, D.C.

Hembree, William E. (July/August 1985) "Getting Involved: Employers as Case Managers," *Business and Health* 2 (8): 11–14.

Henderson, Mary G. (February 1988) "Measuring Quality in Medical Case Management," *Quality Review Bulletin,* 33–39.

Henderson, Mary G., and Stanley S. Wallack (January 1987) "Evaluating Case Management for Catastrophic Illness," *Business and Health* 4 (3): 7–11.

Henderson, Mary G., Andrew Bergman, and John M. Burns (March 1989) "A Guide to Setting Up a Case Management Program," *Business and Health* 7 (3): 26–30.

Hester, E. J. (1989) *Preliminary Results of the Ideal Employer Based Disability Management Practices Survey.* Topeka, Kans.: Menninger Foundation.

Hester, E. J., and Paul G. Decelles (1990) *The Effect of Employer Size on Disability Benefits and Cost Containment Practices.* Topeka, Kans.: Menninger Foundation.

Hester, E. J., and P. G. Decelles (1985) *The Worker Who Becomes Disabled: A Handbook of Incidence and Outcomes.* Topeka, Kans.: Menninger Foundation.

Hester, E. J., Paul Decelles, and Thomas Planek (1988) *Attitudes of Employers and Rehabilitation Professionals Toward Employees Who Become Disabled.* Topeka, Kans.: Menninger Foundation.

Hill, S., and K. Gipson (May 1990) "How Weyerhaeuser Improved Its Worker's Compensation Program," *Business and Health* 8 (5): 38–44.

Hoeffel, Joan Z. (1987) "In-House Rehabilitation," *Rehabilitation Education* no. 1: 111–114.

Hood, Layne E., and John D. Downs (1985) *Return to Work: A Literature Review.* Topeka, Kans.: Menninger Foundation.

Hunt, H. Allan, Rochelle V. Habeck, Michael J. Leahy, and Edward M. Welch (Winter, 1989) "Employer Control of Workers' Compensation Costs," *Business Outlook* 5 (2).

Johnston, W. B. (1987) *Workforce 2000: Work and Workers for the Twenty-First Century.* Indianapolis: Hudson Institute.

Kahn, R. L. (1981) *Work and Health,* 10. New York: John Wiley & Sons.

Kaplan, Karen O. (1990) "Recent Trends in Case Management," *Encyclopedia of Social Work,* 18th ed. Supplement. Silver Spring, Md.: National Association of Social Workers.

Kelly, Kathryn E. (March 1986) "Building a Successful Health Promotion Program," *Business and Health* 44–45.

Kertesz, Louise (1991) "Firms Tout Wellness Savings," *Spotlight on Health Cost Management,* 10–14. National Association of Manufacturers.

Kraus, Lewis E. (Fall 1989) "Disability and Work," *Worklife* 2 (3): 37–39.

La Plante, M. P. (1988) *Data on Disability for the National Health Interview Survey, 1983–85,* 7. Washington, D.C.: National Institute on Disability and Rehabilitation Research.

Lesher, Cynthia L. (July/August 1985) "Rehabilitation Practice in Business and Industry," *Rehabilitation Education* 2 (8): 119–121.

Lewin, Kurt (1951) *Field Theory in Social Science.* New York: Harper & Row.

Mazaway, Jackie (January 1987) "Early Intervention in High Cost Care," *Business and Health* 4 (3): 12–16.

McDonald, M. (May 1990) "You Can Control Your Disability Costs," *Business and Health* 8 (5): 28.

Merrill, Jeffrey C. (July/August 1985) "Defining Case Management," *Business and Health* 2 (8): 5–9.

Meyer, Bruce D., W. Kip Viscusi, and David L. Durbin (1990) *Workers' Compensation and Injury Duration: Evidence from a Natural Experiment.* Working Paper No. 3494. Cambridge, Mass.: National Bureau of Economic Research.

Minnesota Department of Labor and Industry (1988) *"They'd Rather Be Working: Return to Work in Minnesota."* St. Paul.

Mitchell, Kenneth, and Steven Leclair (1988) *Work Disability, Disability Management and the Older Worker—The Politics of Negotiated Disability Final Report.* Worthington, Ohio: International Center for Industry, Labor and Rehabilitation.

MOW International Research Team (1987) *The Meaning of Work,* 79. London: Academic Press.

Moxley, David P. (1989) *The Practice of Case Management.* Newbury Park, Calif.: Sage Publications.

Nackley, J. V. (1989) *Primer on Workers' Compensation,* 2nd ed. Washington, D.C.: Bureau of National Affairs.

O'Connor, Stephen (Summer/Fall 1988) "Management of Individuals With Disabilities in the Workplace," *Journal of Job Placement* 18–21.

Olson, Edward, Jeanne E. Prochnow, and Mary L. Zelenko (May 1986) "Hospital-Based Case Management Coordination," *Coordinator* 20–22.

Peskin, Stephen R., and Karen M. Rolail (May 1988) "Case Management for AIDS Cuts Costs, Improves Care," *Contract Healthcare* 10–11.

Polakoff, Phillip L., and Paul F. O'Rourke (1990) "Healthy Worker-Healthy Workplace The Productivity Connection," *Benefits Quarterly* (2): 37–57.

Polakoff, Phillip L., and Paul F. O'Rourke (March 1987) "Managed Case Applications for Workers' Compensation," *Business and Health* 4 (5): 26–27.

Ray, Margaret P. (1986) *Summary Report of Work Related Injury: Workers' Assessment of Its Consequences for Work, Family Mental and Physical Health.* Pullman, Wash.: Washington State University Injured Workers Project.

Reynolds, Mildred M. (March 1976) "Threats to Confidentiality," *Social Work* 21 (2).

Sanborn, Charlotte J., ed. (1983) *Case Management in Mental Health Services.* New York: The Hayworth Press.

Schwartz, G. E., S. D. Watson, D. E. Galvin, and E. Lipoff (1989) *The Disability Management Sourcebook,* 1. Washington, D.C.: Washington Business Group on Health.

Schwartz, Gail (1986) *State of the Art: Corporate Behavior in Disability Management Survey Results*. Washington, D.C.: Institute for Rehabilitation and Disability Management, the Washington Business Group on Health, and the National Rehabilitation Hospital.

Schwartz, Gail, and Susan Heckard (November 1988) *Social Workers and the Case Management of Catastrophic Care*. Washington, D.C.: The National Center for Social Policy and Practice and The Washington Business Group on Health.

Schwartz, Ronald, M. Rollins, and Pierce Rollins (October 1985) "Measuring the Cost Benefit of Wellness Strategies," *Business and Health* 24–26.

Shrey, D. E. (1990) "Disability Management: An Employer-Based Rehabilitation Concept." In *Multidisciplinary Perspectives in Vocational Assessment of Impaired Workers,* ed. S. J. Scheer, 89. Rockville, Md.: Aspen Publishers.

Sonsel, George E., Frank Paradise, and Stephen Stroup (1988) "Case Management Practice in an AIDS Service Organization," *Social Casework: The Journal of Contemporary Social Work,* 388–392.

Sparrell, Charles F., and William F. McKeon (May 1985) "Preventing Low Back Pain in Industry," *Business and Health,* 16–19.

Stein, Jane (September 1987) "Planning a Health Care Strategy at Weyerhaeuser," *Business and Health* 4 (11): 44–46.

Sullivan, Sean, and Nancy Bagby (1989) "Employer Initiatives in Disability Management and Rehabilitation." Project on the Effectiveness of Health Care Cost Management Strategies, prepared for the National Chamber Foundation.

Tate, Denise G. (March 1988) "Managed Care in Rehabilitation," *Rehabilitation Report* 4 (3): 4–5.

Taylor, Humphrey, Michael R. Kagay, and Stuart Leichenko (1987) *The ICD Survey II: Employing Disabled Americans*. Conducted for International Center for the Disabled in cooperation with the National Council on the Handicapped and the President's Committee on Employment of the Handicapped. New York: Louis Harris and Associates, Inc.

U.S. Equal Employment Opportunities Commission (1991) "Equal Employment Opportunity for Individuals With Disabilities: Notice of Proposed Rulemaking for ADA." Reprinted from the *Federal Register,* February 28, 1991, 29 CFRIEND Part 1630: 1–129.

Victor, Richard B. (May 1985) "Work Place Safety: Present Costs, Future Trends," *Business and Health,* 7–10.

Weil, Marie, and James M. Karls (1989) *Case Management in Human Service Practice*. San Francisco: Jossey-Bass.

Wilson, Susanna J. (1978) *Confidentiality in Social Work.* New York: Free Press.

Wolfhagen, Carl (1989) *Comprehensive Intervention Project: Preliminary Findings*. Olympia, Wash.: Vocational Rehabilitation Section, Industrial Insurance Division, Department of Labor and Industries.

Yelin, Edward (1986) "The Myth of Malingering: Why Individuals Withdraw from Work in the Presence of Illness," *Milbank Quarterly* 64 (4): 622–649.

Index

[n. refers to a note; an italicized number refers to a figure.]

About the Authors

Sheila H. Akabas, Ph.D., is Director of the Center for Social Policy and Practice in the Workplace (The Workplace Center) at Columbia University and a professor at Columbia's School of Social Work. One of the country's foremost experts on disability management, she is now directing two federally supported research programs and has been a consultant to corporations, unions, and not-for-profit institutions. She has also been the principal investigator on five federally funded projects devoted to different aspects of disability management.

Dr. Akabas has examined comparative employment practices in Sweden, England, Israel, New Zealand, Australia, and Canada. Her work has been published in many professional journals, and she is the coauthor of *Mental Health Care in the World of Work* and coeditor of *Work, Workers and Work Organizations*. She is the recipient of the Research in Rehabilitation Award from Boston University, the Switzer Memorial Fellowship, and the World Rehabilitation Fund Fellowship. In 1991 Dr. Akabas was honored by the National Association of Social Work for her pioneering work in the workplace and by the Dole Foundation for her contribution to issues of disability management.

Dr. Akabas serves on numerous advisory boards, including the President's Committee on Employment of People with Disabilities, on which she is chair of the Medical and Insurance Subcommittee; the Technical Advisory Committee to the Dole Foundation; and the New York State School of Industrial and Labor Relations. A graduate of Cornell University, she also holds a doctorate in economics from New York University Graduate School of Business Administration. She is listed in both *Who's Who in the East* and *Who's Who of American Women*.

Lauren B. Gates, Ph.D., is Research Director at The Workplace Center at Columbia University. For the past five years she has been engaged in the investigation of the problems workers face in returning to work or maintaining their jobs after the onset of disability. Dr. Gates was previously

Manager of the Division of Research and Planning at the Urban Redevelopment Authority of Pittsburgh.

Dr. Gates is coauthor of *Planning With Neighborhoods* and has also written numerous articles about neighborhood planning, the effects of crime on neighborhood rehabilitation, and disability management. She received her doctorate in city and regional planning from the University of North Carolina at Chapel Hill, a master's in regional planning from the University of North Carolina at Chapel Hill, and a master's in environmental psychology from the University of Massachusetts at Amherst.

Donald E. Galvin, Ph.D., is Vice-President of the Washington Business Group on Health and Director of the Institute for Rehabilitation and Disability Management. He has served as a senior consultant and principal investigator for several large-scale projects sponsored by governmental agencies, foundations, and corporations. Dr. Galvin has written widely on disability issues and has organized and participated in national and international conferences on the employment and reemployment of people with disabilities.

Previously Dr. Galvin was a professor at Michigan State University and Director of the University Center for International Rehabilitation. Dr. Galvin also served as the Director of The Michigan Rehabilitation Service and was an Associate Superintendent in the Michigan Department of Education. He is a former Switzer Fellow and was one of the original presidential appointees to the National Council on Disability. He holds a bachelor's degree from Central Michigan University, a master's from Michigan State University, and a doctorate in counseling and guidance from the University of Michigan.